GOVERNMENT CONTROL OF NEWS
A CONSTITUTIONAL CHALLENGE

GOVERNMENT CONTROL OF NEWS

A CONSTITUTIONAL CHALLENGE

CORYDON B. DUNHAM

iUniverse, Inc.
Bloomington

Government Control of News
A Constitutional Challenge

Grateful acknowledgment is made for permission to reprint material from *Fighting for the First Amendment: Stanton of CBS vs. Congress and the Nixon White House*, Corydon B. Dunham, Foreword by Walter Cronkite. ©1997 by Corydon B. Dunham. Reproduced with permission of ABC-CLIO, LLC.

iUniverse books may be ordered through booksellers or by contacting:

iUniverse
1663 Liberty Drive
Bloomington, IN 47403
www.iuniverse.com
1-800-Authors (1-800-288-4677)

ISBN: 978-1-4502-6406-8 (sc)
ISBN: 978-1-4502-6408-2 (dj)
ISBN: 978-1-4502-6407-5 (e)

Printed in the United States of America

iUniverse rev. date: 12/06/2011

To Janet for her wisdom and warm support
and to Cory and Chris for their interest and enthusiasm.

To Reuven Frank, who helped create television news.
At heart a newsman,
he was—for many years—the respected president of NBC News.

ACKNOWLEDGMENTS

This study was initiated at the Woodrow Wilson International Center for Scholars, Smithsonian Institute, Washington, DC. I wish to thank the Center and Michael A. Splete, their excellent intern, for their valuable help. The study was expanded and developed for the Corydon B. Dunham Fellowship for the First Amendment at the Harvard Law School, Cambridge, Massachusetts, and the Dunham Open Forum for First Amendment Values at Bowdoin College, Brunswick, Maine. I am thankful for the skill and patience of my editor, Angela Foote, of Old Greenwich, Connecticut.

I am deeply grateful for the many suggestions from others
for clarity and cogency
and for their interest in a challenging subject.

CONTENTS

INTRODUCTION

The focus of this book is how the government seeks to control and regulate the content of television news and speech. This denied the American people access to free and independent news and information in the past. It threatens to do so again.

Government regulation of the content of television news started with television broadcasting in 1949. The theory was that government regulation of news content would provide contrasting views about controversial issues. It would also make sure there was a balance of views. The Federal Communications Commission called its regulation the Fairness Doctrine. It was applied to all broadcast stations and, in practice, to the broadcast networks.

In 1985, the FCC completed an exhaustive, official review of its almost forty years of regulating and editing the content of television news and speech under that doctrine. The commission found that contrary to the theory, government management of broadcast news and speech had in fact distorted and suppressed the news. It had chilled speech. It had enabled the use of government power to silence political views. The doctrine had, in practice, reduced the public's access to diverse sources of information and to political dissent.

Enforcement investigations into news decisions had deterred investigative news reporting and had disserved the public's ability to learn of public problems needing public solutions. The FCC also

1

found that unscrupulous government officials had used the doctrine to intimidate broadcasters who criticized governmental policy.

The facts in the FCC record are overwhelming. The results of its news and speech regulation were seen as so destructive to the flow of information to the public that the FCC itself revoked the Fairness Doctrine in a unanimous decision in 1987. The FCC decision was upheld and endorsed by the reviewing circuit court. The Supreme Court did not take up the decision for review.

Attempts to control broadcast news content by having the government act as editor and make editorial judgments have long persisted in broadcast history. Some believed they could provide better accuracy or balance than the thousands of broadcast journalists. Others, that they could use the news to editorialize for social or political goals they favored. The FCC tried many policies over the years and judged stations' performance of them, threatening nonrenewal of the license to broadcast if a station failed to comply. Commission experience with the Fairness Doctrine between 1949 and 1987 was not theoretical. It was reality. Much of it was recorded in FCC decisions. There is no doubt about the destructive results.

The government is now, once again, seeking to gain control over television news content. Even as the FCC eliminated all remnants of the old Fairness Doctrine, it proposes a new control doctrine. This time the titles are "localism," "balance," and "diversity." In addition to control regulations, an official local advisory board would be established for each station to enforce the new localism, balance, and diversity policy. Members of local boards would review station performance and recommend the station's license be shortened or denied if members of the board viewed station performance as unsatisfactory under FCC rules.

Enforcement would require government investigations, government proceedings, and revisions in news and other program content to meet government views on localism, balance, and diversity. The new doctrine would inevitably have much the same results as the old Fairness Doctrine: the coercion of stations, the FCC dictating how to cover the news, and FCC orders chilling speech.

Under the Fairness Doctrine, when someone involved did not like a news report and complained to the FCC, broadcasters were threatened with government investigations and even the loss of their broadcast license for how they reported the news on matters in controversy. No other news medium faces such a procedure.

The imposition of such a process again would again, in practice, suppress news reporting and chill speech. It could again, in practice, intimidate and deter station news coverage needed by the public.

As the FCC found in revoking the Fairness Doctrine, the record of FCC news control in the past demonstrated that such control is not in the public interest. The FCC opinion revoking the Fairness Doctrine after years of experience with government editing of news urged that the broadcast press be granted the same independence from government as the print press.

There are now other new and growing threats to broadcast news. Congress and the president have recently mandated an expansive development of the Internet to make it the dominant communications instrument in the United States. This will require the use of large amounts of electronic spectrum. To provide the spectrum necessary for the growing mobile and other new Internet technologies, the president, Congress, and the FCC adopted a ten-year plan to reallocate the spectrum currently used for broadcasting and assign it to the Internet for mobile and other uses. This would reportedly start in a few years. Some broadcast stations would have to close down.

For stations wanting to continue broadcasting, the FCC is exploring relocation, sharing of spectrum, and other engineering options. The FCC official in charge has indicated that a condition for the use of spectrum for broadcasting would be government control of news and public affairs programming as provided by the Localism, Balance, and Diversity Doctrine. There would also be an inevitable reduction in broadcast news, and the possible introduction of government-approved propaganda.

Print news revenue losses are now forcing many administrators of newspapers and magazines to reduce their news gathering and news reporting. The print press is currently searching for ways to continue to publish and inform the public, but long-term solutions for present publication levels appear problematic. The weakening of the print press could lead to even more reliance by the public upon broadcast news and political speech reporting.

Regulation of broadcast news and speech to achieve political and social goals through government-managed news has long been the announced objective of the president's Chief of the White House Office of Regulatory Affairs, some in the Congress and some new FCC officials. As the FCC relocates broadcasters or seeks to impose its new Localism, Balance, and Diversity Doctrine, the government must be prevented from gaining control of news content and reducing the freedom of broadcast news and speech, as happened when the Fairness Doctrine was adopted.

In a decision in December 2010 the FCC took control of some Internet content. According to that decision, the FCC could perhaps review news and speech content carried on the Internet. The FCC appears to claim the constitutional authority to do this under the views asserted in the past by the Chief of the White House Office of Regulatory Affairs.

Public opinion polls show that television hard news now delivered by broadcast networks, broadcast stations, satellite, retransmitted by cable, and added to the Internet is not only a crucially important source of news and information for the public. These polls also show that the public counts on a free press to be independent of government and a watchdog over government policies and actions. Proposed FCC regulations would prevent this. They threaten government control of speech and news and are direct challenges to the Constitution and to the First Amendment in the Bill of Rights.

On World Press Freedom Day, May 3, 2011, a U.S. State Department official spoke to journalists from around the world of the commitment needed. He said all citizens must take time to think about the role of a free press and what it means to society. Journalists should not be the only ones standing for press freedom. "Each one of us who recognize the value of an informed citizenry must also stand up for this fundamental right." (See Note 80, Chapter 7).

CHAPTER 1

ᴄᴍ

Television Journalism Begins

Television news came into its own in 1948, after World War II, when the FCC resumed licensing of broadcast television stations. Although the number of electronic signals and stations was still limited, television network and station programming soon became a major source of entertainment and information for the American public. When political coverage on television news programs was created by American broadcasters, it was free of government oversight and interference.

The first broadcasts showed the nominations of the candidates for president of the United States at the political conventions in Philadelphia. AT&T had inaugurated regular, commercial intercity transmission of television pictures by coaxial cable. At first, this linked nine cities on the East coast from Boston in the north to Richmond, Virginia in the south, and reached seventeen television stations. Four television networks were launched—NBC, CBS, ABC, and Dumont.[1]

Television News – An American Innovation

What turned out to be the beginning of a new nationwide, pervasive, and vital communications service with live, electronic images edited and delivered simultaneously to a mass audience was developed almost on the spot. The political conventions of 1948 were the first big political event for television news. The networks planned live television coverage of all the proceedings, both scripted and unscripted.

Engineers had to learn how to manage the new, large, and cumbersome television cameras to broadcast the news. The cameras of the time required intensely hot, bright lights and were installed in rooms and halls without air conditioning, in what was an especially hot summer in Philadelphia. Corporate network executives were uncertain whether the coverage would be successful or if the revenues from advertisers new to television would even begin to cover the costs.

Manufacturers of television sets were for it—television coverage of the conventions would sell TV sets. The political parties were all for it. They had selected Philadelphia because it was connected to the coaxial cable and it reach an audience served by television in nine cities. Advertisers had to decide whether to buy advertising time.

Some television stations would broadcast live. Those that could not would receive a kinescope, a film of a television picture, through the mail for broadcast the next day. There was a potential viewing public in the reception area with about three hundred and fifty thousand television sets in homes and public places. A third of America, 168 electoral votes' worth, would be "within reach" of a television set.[2]

Leaders of Congress and other political figures could see the advantages of attending the convention and being available to the cameras. Reuven Frank, who was there in charge of production for NBC News, recounts the events in his book, *Out of Thin Air: The Brief Wonderful Life of Network News*.[3] He concluded that the two conventions included every official, every legislator, every regulator "who could shape a radio or television company's right to exist. In network contacts with politicians in Philadelphia's restaurants and hotels, no one said a word about licensing—but no one forgot about it either."[4]

Radio stars who had been sought as anchors for the convention coverage had declined. They did not know how to conduct television broadcasts in which their every gesture would be transmitted live to the viewing public. They had little interest in this new, upstart operation. Television's future was dubious at best. No one knew if it would be successful.

Those prevailed upon to try it unexpectedly became public figures of note. The face of the network anchor at a political convention would become the network news's "standard bearer," and this sometimes lasted for decades. Those adventurous anchors included Douglas Edwards, John Cameron Swayze, Walter Cronkite, Chet Huntley, and David Brinkley.[5]

On Monday, June 21, 1948, the Republican convention was gaveled to order. Reuven Frank writes that for reporters, chasing down a story at the convention with a television camera was just not feasible given the camera's size and the need for big, hot lights. So cameras were positioned where the news director expected a significant event would take place. The first press conference carried on live television showed Governor Thomas E. Dewey, candidate for the Republican nomination for president, claiming the lead in promised delegates over Robert Taft of Ohio and Harold Stassen of Minnesota. There were many such firsts. Reporters learned the news by following the story themselves and then hurrying to a stationary camera to report it live, standing in the lights in front of the camera. Frank reports that *Life* made a substantial editorial contribution to NBC with help from their executives familiar with photo coverage and received some media promotion from that, but he could not find out why the "oldest, richest network agreed to share its moment with *Life*'s 'promotion scheme.' " He asks, "Above all, where were NBC's lawyers? Nothing happens in broadcasting without lawyers."[6]

"The intent was to cover news; whatever news there was … What politicians considered interruptions was journalism to the news people from NBC and the magazines. They filled otherwise dull or empty time with remote broadcasts of panels and discussions, man-in-the-street interviews, and a dizzying array of special features." Among these was a "four-foot lady elephant, hired to promote the Taft candidacy … [the elephant] made frequent appearances on all the networks when the Taft candidacy was being discussed. There were also serious, sometimes news making, sometimes substantive interviews, and there were times when no one could think of anything better to fill the passing minutes than to have reporters talk to each other."[7]

Frank writes in *Out of Thin Air* that the defeat of Senator Taft and Harold Stassen had seemed to come about inexorably. At 9:00 PM, the cameras showed Dewey riding to the convention hall in his limousine, "toward the rainbow, into a horizon of black clouds moving rapidly away." A violent thunderstorm struck Philadelphia that Thursday evening. On the roof of the convention hall, Clarence Thoman, chief engineer of NBC-affiliated television station WPTZ in Philadelphia, became famous for hanging onto the transmitting antennas on the roof into the night to hold them in place so the television signals would reach the viewing public.[8]

The Democrats gathered in the same place on July 12 to nominate Harry Truman. Frank reports, "It was a gloomy, sodden occasion. No one could believe Harry Truman could win except Harry Truman." In contrast to the Republican convention, things looked grim at the Democratic convention. "On television, everything changed, mood, pace, the story. Everyone was upset about something. They took their cases to the lights and the cameras."[9]

Reuven Frank writes that in the midst of all this, the television audience watched an event of historical importance take place, live, before its eyes. "Two days of conflict and resolution that changed the course of the country … to commit the Democratic Party to redress the disabilities that burdened black America." Frank reports that this issue, which would dominate American society for the rest of the century, never was "seen so clearly as by the people who saw it covered live on television." The television cameras showed an African-America delegate, George Vaughn of Missouri, unexpectedly approaching the podium. He moved that the convention refuse to seat the delegation from Mississippi because they had said they would walk out if a strong civil platform were adopted. The hall erupted with demonstrations. Big-city and big-state delegations supported Vaughn. Demonstrations continued. In spite of all this, his motion was rejected.[10]

The next day, the coverage ran for fifteen continuous hours of speeches and demonstrations for the pros and cons of a civil rights plank. Southern states' demonstrations continued in opposition to the liberal plank. Northern states demonstrated and voted unanimously for it. It finally carried.[11]

At 8:02 PM, the clerk called the roll to nominate the Democratic candidate for president. By 1:00 AM, Harry S. Truman had won the nomination. He spoke without notes. With his chopping gestures, he gave it to the Republicans. He called for support from the farmers and laborers he had helped. He kept after the Republicans. He was interrupted by a shout from the back, "Give 'em hell, Harry!" That would become his campaign slogan.[12]

The convention adjourned at 2:31 AM with a reinvigorated party led by what television had shown the viewing public was an indomitable figure. No longer so discouraged, his party would warmly support him when he toured the country, primarily by whistle-stop train. Since there were few television cameras at stations across the country[13] at that time, television could not cover that train campaign to any extent.

Truman's vigorous campaign led to a stunning upset victory over Dewey, catching the nation by surprise. The spirit of that Philadelphia Democratic convention prevailed. A large segment of the American public had seen what live television could do to inform them. It also reflected for the viewers the character of a presidential nominee and the vital impulse of a democracy.

Regulation of Television News

Television was and is a powerful communication medium and rapidly became the nation's foremost source of local, national, and international news, sports, and entertainment. The federal government immediately began to seek to control and regulate the content of broadcast television news and broadcast political speech.

CHAPTER 2

✑

Regulation of Television News Content Upheld by the Supreme Court

A congressional regulatory agency, the Federal Communications Commission, regulated radio news under the Communications Act of 1934, as amended. In 1949, the FCC then applied similar control regulations to the content of television news. Congress further passed a law in 1959 to approve and enforce that FCC control and management of television news content. When a complaint was made to the FCC about a view that had been broadcast on an important and controversial public issue, the Federal Communications Commission would investigate and review the issue and the other views broadcast. It could order a change in the news report "in the public interest," the vague but ultimate statutory standard of the Communications Act that the FCC enforced. The FCC called its regulation the Fairness Doctrine.

In effect, Congress endorsed this regulation that applied to all broadcast stations across the country. Stations and the suppliers of broadcast news, including the broadcast networks, had to comply with the Fairness Doctrine and the many investigations and decisions by the FCC to enforce it. The content of all news and public affairs programming by television stations across the country was subject to that government control and management and to the threat of that control and management.[1]

Investigating and Revising News Reports

To enforce the Fairness Doctrine, the FCC investigated broadcaster news judgment in selecting and deciding on the issue to be broadcast and how it would be presented. The FCC also examined the views that had been presented on the issue broadcast. If it concluded that a view should be changed, it ordered that. If it concluded still other views should be presented, it ordered those views to be broadcast. If the FCC determined that some other issue or view had been raised or implied by the broadcast, it ordered further contrasting views to be broadcast. It could also order the broadcast of some other relevant issue it thought had been raised in the process and should be addressed and then order the broadcast of contrasting views on that issue. The theory was that this would provide "robust debate" on controversial issues of public importance "in the public interest."[2]

The reasoning was that a national central government agency could best oversee and require fairness in news coverage by individual broadcast stations in their local markets and by the networks in their national market. Since there were limited broadcast frequencies, not everyone could own a broadcast station or broadcast a point of view. To see that all views on controversial issues were presented if *any* view was presented, the government ordered station licensees to present all contrasting views. A central government agency would thus be the ultimate news editor.

The regulation was carefully and deliberately drawn to place a government agency in a position to investigate and make final editorial news decisions necessary to make the news conform to what that agency found was appropriate. The FCC standard was not "truth," which few wanted a federal agency to decide, but "contrasting views." The Fairness Doctrine included harsh FCC penalties for licensee failure to comply.

They were a refusal to renew the broadcast station license, shortening the period of the license if the license was renewed, or creating a negative record applied at license renewal time.[3]

The Supreme Court and the *Red Lion* Philosophy

The First Amendment in the Bill of Rights provides that Congress shall "make no law … abridging the freedom of speech … or of the press." When Congress passed a law endorsing the Fairness Doctrine, its vague and subjective news and speech regulations, and its *in terrorem* penalties, the law was challenged as a violation of the First Amendment. After all, the First Amendment seemed to prohibit Congress from making such a law. The new law did not seem to accept our nation's free speech and free press traditions, or the historical understanding of the purpose and goals of the First Amendment, which essentially prevented government interference with news and speech content so the people could govern themselves in a democracy.[4]

But the Supreme Court took the view that the First Amendment permitted government control and management of broadcast news and speech for purposes of the Fairness Doctrine in light of the scarcity of broadcast frequencies. In a 1969 opinion by Justice Byron R. White, the Court ruled that the Fairness Doctrine was constitutional. This *Red Lion* decision was, remarkably on an issue of free speech and free press, unanimous. Of the eight justices then in office, the vote was seven to zero, Justice William O. Douglas not participating.[5]

The case involved two long-fighting religious figures. Reverend Hargis bought radio station broadcast time to say that Reverend Cook had written a book to smear and destroy conservative Senator Barry Goldwater (R–AZ), a candidate for president. Hargis said Cook had been fired from a newspaper for making false charges against city officials, had worked for a Communist-affiliated organization, had defended Alger Hiss (allegedly a Communist agent within the state department), and had attacked J. Edgar Hoover (head of the FBI) and the CIA.

The Fairness Doctrine included a right of reply to a personal, demeaning attack. Cook argued he was entitled to free broadcast time to answer the Hargis charges and asked the broadcast station for time to reply, free of charge. The station took the position that it would provide the time, but Cook would have to pay for it, just as Hargis had paid for his time. The FCC decided that Cook should be granted time to reply and the time should be free.

The Supreme Court agreed. The Communism charge was a serious charge at the time. To provide the injured party, Cook, a remedy for the injury, the Supreme Court upheld as constitutional the Fairness Doctrine right of reply and in the process upheld the constitutionality of the Fairness Doctrine as a whole. All of its provisions for control of broadcast news and speech content were held to be consitutional.[6] For the first time in history, the Supreme Court held that a federal government agency had the lawful and constitutional power to investigate and revise press coverage. This would haunt and distort television reporting on America's news and political speech for many years.[7]

There were at the time many radio stations. There were fewer television broadcast stations across the country, with only three stations in some markets. It was thought that this gave unusual power to the television station owners in a local market and the three network owners who might provide network programming to them. Those who did not own stations or could not gain access to them might not be able to broadcast on television their own views or the views they favored. Television was seen as limited by the electronic technology it used. It was also seen as having a new kind of power to influence society. Even though there were many markets where there might not be many newspapers, and in all events, individuals' access to their pages would be quite unlikely for the expression of differing points of view, this was almost irrelevant compared to the perception of the power of those television stations.

The argument was just repeated that broadcast frequencies were scarce and that television stations were licensed by the government, which allocated those scarce frequencies to stations for broadcasting in their local markets. Without a broadcast frequency, there could be no broadcast. If station management or a station owner in a local market excluded a particular view, that view might not get on the air at all. This seemed to give a television station or network owner far too much power in a new, exploding medium.

The print press, on the other hand, did not use scarce electronic frequencies. It was familiar, a known medium. Perhaps most important, print news content had not been regulated by the government. The print press had fought against its regulation. The values of the First Amendment for newspapers and magazines and the public had been recognized for many years.[8]

Broadcast station applicants were happy to get a license to broadcast. When granting that license, the FCC required that the station meet certain FCC regulatory requirements for station programming. This could and did at first include a specified amount of news and public affairs programming. That did not seem too difficult.[9] But when the Supreme Court held in *Red Lion* that it was constitutional for the FCC to regulate the content of news and public affairs speech, this went beyond quantitative requirements for a number of hours devoted to news. By then the industry was heavily regulated and that was accepted. The Court also ruled that the Fairness Doctrine regulation of content would provide robust debate and assumed with not much proof either way that broadcast stations and the broadcast press would not otherwise provide that debate.

The Supreme Court concluded that the government would best deal with television news and speech content on what was called the "public airways" and could ensure that all stations presented contrasting views on the important public issues of the day. Congress had passed a law to deal with this new medium and the Court upheld it.[10]

The Supreme Court also reasoned that empowering a government agency to investigate and require broadcast stations to provide news coverage of contrasting views on controversial issues, as determined by the government, would not abridge the freedom of the press. A newspaper editor would have been incredulous at such a proposition. But the Court concluded that while this might interfere with broadcasters' news judgments, it would further First Amendment goals. This was a breakthrough for regulation, since many news and speech controls might be described as furthering public goals.

Justice William O. Douglas wrote in 1974 his view of the *Red Lion* decision. He wrote that had he been present in that case, he would have rejected the Fairness Doctrine "out of hand." He criticized the Fairness Doctrine in the strongest terms:

> Censorship or editing or screening by government of what licensees may broadcast goes against the grain of the First Amendment.
>
> The Fairness Doctrine has no place in our First Amendment regime. It puts the head of the camel inside the tent and enables administration after administration to toy with TV or radio in order to serve its sordid or its benevolent ends. In 1973—as in other years—there is clamoring to make TV and radio emit the messages that console certain groups. There are charges that these mass media are too slanted, too partisan, too hostile in their approach to candidates and the issues.
>
> The prospect of putting Government in a position of control over publishers is to me, an appalling one, even to the extent of the Fairness Doctrine. The struggle for liberty has been a struggle against Government ... It is anathema to the First Amendment to allow Government any role of censorship over newspapers, magazines, books, art, music, TV, radio, or any other aspect of the press ... the regime of federal supervision under the Fairness Doctrine is contrary to our constitutional mandate ... and makes the broadcast licensee an easy victim of political pressures and reduces him to a timid or submissive

segment of the press whose measure of the public interest will now be echoes of the dominant political voice that emerges after every election.[11]

The Supreme Court, in *Red Lion*, subordinated free speech and press to what it determined was an implied First Amendment goal of fairness, even though the explicit goals of the First Amendment were stated to prevent abridgement of the freedom of speech and press by government and particularly by congressional legislation. If robust debate were added to the First Amendment as an objective and an exception to the amendment's prohibition against government interference with news and speech, then it could be concluded that government control of news and speech to serve the goal of robust debate was constitutional. In the process of reaching that result in *Red Lion*, however, the Court created a critical modification of First Amendment philosophy as the American public, journalists, and legal scholars had understood it for many years. It did so on the stated ground that there was a scarcity of television frequencies.

But the Court, in its *Red Lion* decision, went further. It seemed to suggest there should be a vast expansion of the First Amendment's language and scope to add still other goals and these should be considered a "right" of the public. The Court said, "It is the right of the public to receive suitable access to social, political, esthetic, moral, and other ideas and experiences which is crucial here."[12] This may be seen as an expression of judicial philosophy and not necessary to the legal decision reached by the Court. But this *Red Lion* formulation has not been limited to a medium where there is a scarcity of frequencies. It has been extrapolated by some commentators to read that the government should control and manage speech and news for the pursuit of social and political goals of the times.

In 1969, when the *Red Lion* case was before the Supreme Court, the results of government investigations for government review of television news to enforce the Fairness Doctrine had not yet been recognized by the FCC or the courts. This would prove to be, however, one of the most critical elements in news and speech regulations in practice. The Supreme Court did not foresee in 1969 that government investigations of licensee news judgments and news coverage, with orders to insert government supplements to that news coverage, would deter and suppress news reports or chill speech. In fact, there was little consideration of how FCC management of news for Fairness Doctrine objectives would work in practice.

There was no recognition of how the prospect of government inquiries into the content of news reports might deter the reports or the coverage of controversial issues. The Court dismissed as speculative the concerns about government interference and censorship that were voiced by journalists and broadcasters. In all events, the Court concluded that the FCC could readily correct any enforcement problem by ordering the licensee to broadcast whatever the FCC deemed necessary, with the threat of using its power to revoke a station's license to assure compliance.

A form of the FCC regulations had been in operation for radio for some years. The Fairness Doctrine sounded and was called "fair." Fairness was a desirable policy and human objective. The thought may have been that in all events, government review and revision would be better than the risks from an unknown, private-sector, free, and powerful television press. A holding that the Fairness Doctrine was unconstitutional and unenforceable against the broadcast press might have prevented some useful future control of possible broadcast press abuse.

The vigor of the belief in the need for protection of news and speech from government interference, which characterized the drafting of the First Amendment by those with knowledge of censorship by the British king and Church, had diminished over time. With freedom taken for granted, there was a surprising lack of judicial interest in the practice of journalism and how news is gathered and published. In the course of the Court's debate and discussion in *Red Lion*, the concern voiced by journalists about the Fairness Doctrine was largely ignored. It may have seemed that a little government control and management of television news would be a good thing, would prevent radical influence and even civil disorder, a reasonable compromise for the public good. Even after twenty years of television, some were still concerned in 1969 that television's influence was too powerful. It was hard to predict what freedom for this new medium might do to social values, morals, and political power. It was not unusual for a community or the government to fear the influence on public morals and society of a new medium of information or entertainment and try to manage, suppress, and censor it for as long as they could.[13]

It may have seemed overall best to impose oversight and government control over news. It is said that good judges do not seek to decide cases for some particular result, but rather follow the law, interpret it, and apply it to particular events in light of the existing conditions. Yet, perhaps the *Red Lion* decision should be understood as an attempt by the Court to manage what, at the time, was seen as something already too powerful and something of a danger. Television was overwhelming the country with attractive entertainment and information offered free to the public in their homes. Existing media like newspapers and movies feared television was marginalizing them. A federal agency could protect the public from what might be an irreversible injury to American society from this new, addictive, and even alarming mass-communication visual technology. Or, it may just have seemed that some control of news would be a good thing.

In 1969, a critical factor may also have been that television news was not only thought to be too powerful, it was "controlled by those three men in New York" who ran the television network companies ABC, CBS, and NBC. Members of Congress privately voiced the revealing question: "Who elected them?" Professor Archibald Cox of the Harvard Law School argued to the Court on behalf of the three broadcast networks in the Supreme Court's *Red Lion* case. He later confided that when one of the justices mentioned those "three men in New York" as setting the agenda for the nation, he knew he would lose the case. Their private power looked too great.[14]

Granting the government power over the broadcast press was regarded as protective of society and acceptable. The print press had always had First Amendment standing, but not the broadcast media. Proponents of government regulation of speech and press saw it as bipartisan and benign. The Supreme Court must have had this general view. Under the congressional statute, Congress had provided that the FCC would be made up of representatives of the two major political parties. Control of the commission would shift between them to follow the party of the elected, incumbent president.[15] At the time, the country had concerns that were more pressing than historical notions of freedom. The Vietnam War had ignited virulent public demonstrations and there was considerable civil unrest.[16] If some radical or undermining political direction was taken by some element of the public or its television press coverage, the basic governance as well as the basic morals of the country could be endangered. This could be handled by the FCC and society protected.

The Court accepted the FCC as the ultimate and official television news editor, rather than those three men in New York, despite the explicit language in the First Amendment protecting the press from the government. The principle of free speech and free press had been adopted in a simpler time, in the 1700s, for the then-familiar print press and pamphleteer, however outspoken and even radical they may have been. The Fairness Doctrine approach was to deal with a new and unpredictable electronic medium, and it had been approved by Congress as one way to deal with it.

The Court was familiar with the role of administrative agencies. The Court may also have believed in the ability of a central government agency set up by the president and Congress to be a wiser and better ultimate television news and speech overseer for the country than the many individual journalists and editors developing news stories in the television press, most of whom were unknown to the establishment but making critical editorial news judgments across the country for the powerful new television medium.

Oversight by a central state agency for control of the news is always the censor's most effective method. The Court assumed that a central government administrative agency could review news reports by stations across the country and improve them. It assumed that a government agency could appropriately shape, free of political control and without confusion about the facts and conflicts of views on controversial issues, a "fair" news report. Assumed, perhaps, that a government agency could best inform the public about national and international issues. It assumed that the agency could in practice require the addition of some other material which had not been broadcast and order it or other related material to be broadcast after the original broadcast to achieve balance. The supposition was that the public would relate that later material back to the original broadcast. That was the process the Congress and the Court endorsed in preference to the risks of free speech and a free press.

The announced purpose of the grant to the FCC of overriding authority over news and speech was to promote "robust debate" on controversial issues. That was the goal. However, as the FCC history shows, the result was not robust debate. The result of that grant of authority to a government agency was the suppression of news. It inhibited, even prevented, stations and journalists from providing accurate news coverage, which was their primary obligation and needed by the public.[17] The print press would certainly have seen this as censorship had an effort been made to apply the Fairness Doctrine to newspapers. But the Supreme Court did not see it that way. It accepted the argument that the doctrine would increase robust debate of public issues.

In the 1970s, the FCC was to say that the Fairness Doctrine was the "single most important requirement of operation in the public interest— the *sine qua non* for grant of a renewal of license."[18] This was a remarkable proposition. It appeared to condition the existence of the broadcast press in markets across the country on broadcast stations satisfying a central government agency's views on news coverage, including what the news should be and how it should be presented. With a majority vote by an appointed regulatory commission of seven (later five) people, the FCC would decide at license renewal time whether the news coverage of a renewal applicant had complied with the Fairness Doctrine. If so, this compliance, among other factors, would justify the renewal of a broadcast license "in the public interest." If not, then that broadcaster's license to broadcast could end.

While there is only one officially recorded case of the loss of license for a fairness violation, the threat was always present during the era of the Fairness Doctrine. The recurring threat of one FCC investigation of a news judgment where the penalty could be loss of the license to broadcast was enough to create for station licensees a "climate of fear and timidity" in covering controversial issues, as the FCC later found. For a licensee, there had to be concern that if its news coverage was considered by a majority of the politically appointed FCC commissioners at license renewal time to be unacceptable under the government's standard, the FCC could refuse to renew the license. Ironically, that final act of censorship would also officially be portrayed as taken in the public interest. A reviewing appellate court might therefore believe it had to accept the expert agency's finding under standard administrative law doctrine and uphold the non-renewal of the broadcast license.

At the same time, the Supreme Court had no difficulty continuing a sharp line on the merits between the familiar print press and the electronic press. It had long been the belief that the government could not constitutionally require a newspaper to provide space in its news coverage for government-ordered news. Nor could it be required to do so for a reply to a newspaper report. In 1976, the Supreme Court followed this traditional constitutional view and held that a Florida state statute providing a right of reply for political candidates in a newspaper was unconstitutional. [*Miami Herald Post Co. v. Tornillo*, 418 U.S. 241 (1976)].

The Court did not find in the *Tornillo* decision that there was some possibility of increasing debate by upholding the grant of a right of reply to material in a newspaper. It found that a right of reply as a practical matter would suppress debate. The requirement would suppress debate because, "faced with the penalties that would accrue to any newspaper that published news or commentary arguably within the reach of the right-of-access statute, editors might well conclude that the safe course is to avoid controversy. Therefore, under the operation of the Florida statute, political and electoral coverage would be blunted or reduced." Government-enforced right of access, the Court said, inescapably "dampens the vigor, and limits the variety of public debate."[19]

Yet, only seven years before, the Court had unanimously held that a right of reply and balancing of views under the Fairness Doctrine would increase robust debate and was constitutional. In terms directly applicable to the Fairness Doctrine, the Court in *Tornillo* addressed what government "mechanism" would have to be used to regulate the right of reply or access. The Supreme Court said, "At each point the implementation of a remedy such as an enforceable right of access necessarily calls for some mechanism, either governmental or consensual. If it is governmental coercion, this at once brings about a confrontation with the express provisions of the First Amendment and the judicial gloss on that Amendment developed over the years."[20]

Any mechanism for enforcing news and speech regulations imposed on broadcast media would necessarily include investigation, intrusion, examination, review, and possible adverse decisions under some government standard about speech and news coverage. It would, like the mechanism used by the Fairness Doctrine for its purposes, result in a regulatory agency process that would suppress news and chill speech, enable the silencing of opposition views, and intimidate and censor speech and news, as the FCC later found had resulted from the Fairness Doctrine.[21]

On the fundamental issue of whether a mechanism such as that used under the Fairness Doctrine could even be considered consistent with freedom of the press, the Supreme Court in the *Torillo* case ruled that it could not. In setting aside the right of reply legislated by the Florida legislature, the Court said that "[t]he choice of material to go into a newspaper, and the decisions made as to limitations on the size and content of the paper, and treatment of public issues and public officials—whether fair or unfair—constitute the exercise of editorial control and judgment. It has yet to be demonstrated how governmental regulation of this crucial process can be exercised consistent with First Amendment guarantees of a free press as they have evolved to this time."

This decision was reached not because the case involved a reply but because it involved interference with the freedom of press and the editorial control and news judgments necessary for the press to do its job. In a concurring opinion in another case involving such First Amendment protections, Justice Potter Stewart stressed the dangers to the public when the government regulated speech and news. "Those who wrote our First Amendment ... believed that 'fairness' was far too fragile to be left for a Government bureaucracy to accomplish. History has many times confirmed the wisdom of their choice."[22]

The state of Florida also argued that the law providing for a right to reply was constitutional because it had been passed to ensure journalistic responsibility. The Supreme Court, rejecting this argument, explained that the First Amendment mandates freedom from government review. A determination of responsibility is not its purpose. In the *Miami Herald* case, the Court held "Governmental restraint on publishing need not fall into familiar or traditional patterns to be subject to constitutional limitations on governmental powers . . . " The Court said, "We see that beginning with *Associated Press* . . . the Court has expressed sensitivity as to whether a restriction or requirement constituted the compulsion exerted by government on a newspaper to print that which it would not otherwise print. The clear implication has been that any such a compulsion to publish that which 'reason' tells them should not be published is unconstitutional. A responsible press is an undoubtedly desirable goal, but press responsibility is not mandated by the Constitution and like many other virtues it cannot be legislated."[23]

The Supreme Court explicitly held that a government requirement for a right of reply was effectively censorship. "The Florida statute operates as a command in the same sense as a statute or regulation forbidding appellant to publish specified matter. Governmental restraint on publishing need not fall into familiar or traditional patterns to be subject to constitutional limitations on governmental powers."[24] The mechanism used by the FCC's Fairness Doctrine to censor or control speech and news in broadcasting is virtually the same as that enacted by the state in the *Tornillo* case, where the Supreme Court condemned it on constitutional grounds.[25]

The different treatment by the Supreme Court of television news and print news was said to be justified because of the technological limitations of broadcasting with its scarcity of electronic frequencies (and the potentially monopolistic condition created by the government in the grant of broadcast licenses). But, even later, when there were many other sources of electronic news, government regulation of television news and speech content continued unabated. Removal of control regulations once established is exceedingly difficult. Regulators still found that the limited number of electronic frequencies for a market justified continuing the Fairness Doctrine; it lasted for decades despite the ever-increasing number of broadcasters and other electronic and cable publishers.

New Control Doctrines

A new Supreme Court will have regulatory decisions before it that would permit government's use of news and speech on television and the Internet to achieve certain government goals. It will be argued that it is worth compromising the historically established values of a free press and free speech with a new interpretation of the First Amendment to achieve these new goals and other social objectives.

One reason for concern is how easily the Supreme Court in *Red Lion* breached the First Amendment's explicit protection of speech and press freedoms to authorize government control and management of news for purposes of fairness and debate. The Court may give preference to other speech and news content for other government purposes. When the Court does so it reduces the freedom of speech and press. It also legitimizes the appointment of a government agency to act as the ultimate authority for the country in making that selection and enforcing preferences for that speech and news over other speech not so favored by the government.

Claims are already now being made that new speech and news content doctrines will provide balance and diversity and improve local community interests and relations, claims made before to support the Fairness Doctrine. But the FCC history and the record of the Fairness Doctrine of suppressing news, chilling speech, and silencing opposing views and political dissent are essentially being ignored by the government and not revealed to the public in the pending proceedings.

This study is directed to the impact of such government control and management on station news. It shows also how new doctrines and rules to govern news content will inevitably have the same destructive results as past rules that were tried and had unintended and regrettable consequences. It seeks to inform the public of these threats to their news and speech freedoms.

CHAPTER 3

⌒✺⌒

How FCC Regulations
Suppressed News and Speech

U nder the Fairness Doctrine, truth was theoretically irrelevant. The broadcast of "contrasting views"—not truth—was the agency's test for legal compliance. And whatever the journalistic news report, intent, or production, when the government agency took a view different from the journalist under regulations adopted to serve a general statutory principle, such as "contrasting views" or "the public interest," journalism had to give way to the regulator and the government's view of what the news should be.

FCC review of news content necessarily dealt closely with the ideas and information presented, and even how it was presented. The commission and staff brought with them their own personal and political knowledge of the issues, their own experience, and their own views, as in any judging process. But this was not the removed, impartial, and insulated world of an appeals court looking at a trial record. It was review of current and usually ongoing coverage—often daily—of contemporary controversial events, which were fresh in the public eye and often directly affected by the exercise of government power. The issues addressed were not only controversial, but usually they were the object of contemporary discussions in government and political circles as well.

Under the Communications Act of 1934, as amended, the position of commissioner of the FCC was a political appointment.[1] Most commissioners had extensive experience and connections with the political world, in addition to their substantive knowledge in the communications field, which had led to their appointment. FCC jurisdiction ranged over all electronic and electric communications and a host of related matters.

Spoken words and pictures strike people differently, particularly when they are viewing the coverage of controversy, different parts of a controversy, or changes in the controversy over time. The broadcast might show persuasive public or private authority figures, defensive and poorly spoken public or private figures, or pointed or discursive comments. A news report could show pictures of demonstrations or just background locations, interesting or dull interviews and sidebars and fillers. It could show comments of unequal force made by casual witnesses or the overriding, familiar, and authoritative appearance and voice of a news anchor or expert, to say nothing of a host of other differences in the manner or style of speech and presentation.

The FCC and staff did not usually look at the video of the news report, but relied on the text of the program and written descriptions. This practice was required because there was not sufficient time for the commissioners to view the videos, which were numerous and would have required many hours of viewing. Commissioners instead read written descriptions of what the videos showed about the news reported and the oral statements made.[2]

It is generally understood that much communication comes from physical appearance and gestures and expressions in addition to the words spoken. But FCC judgments were based on transcripts, not video. The commissioners did not see the faces. They saw only the verbal statements reduced to writing in a transcript. They had to make mental translations from written text to what impressions they imagined had been given to the viewers by speech and pictures in news accounts. They usually did not see the videos even though on the emotional level it is generally thought that the video can be dominant and the most moving, with a powerful influence on the viewing audience. Yet they passed on the nuance of arguments made and countered.[3]

When the FCC reviewed transcripts, they viewed them not for information or entertainment, but for judging. This required care and precision. The possibilities for different understandings, however, were almost endless. It is difficult, if not impossible, to convey a precise impression of ongoing events with still pictures and often even with video. There are too many variables for any reviewer to be certain of how a particular nuance of a point of view looked to viewers when it was seen on the video. But the FCC review required looking at transcripts of language and then trying to imagine the audience's impressions from the broadcast of video and audio and assess whether sufficient contrasting views had been presented on some controversial public issue. Glossed over in theory, the government depended upon this difficult process in practice.

This was done to determine, for example, whether there was balance, as the Fairness Doctrine required, in the views the commissioners found were presented. Government officials counted lines in written transcripts to determine balance. They measured physical lengths in the transcript. They timed sentences and segments with stopwatches for balance. They matched sentences and segments. Rough mathematical ratios were then applied to decide whether and how much more of a particular view should be broadcast when ordering counterviews or arguments and counterarguments. These ratios were determined by the FCC for purposes of the Fairness Doctrine as a matter of its own discretion and applied to the written language in a transcript made from the verbal sounds. The ratios of pro and con could vary but might be 3:1 or 5:1—that is, a response or contrast was sufficient and fairness was achieved if three or five of the times or the lines of the original point of view were met with one time or line in opposition or what was considered as contrast. This was certainly not the same as a journalistic judgment about news reporting.

As the public knows, some speculation or uncertainty is part of almost any judgment about the force of ideas, the effectiveness of written or oral presentation, pictures and arguments, and the impression created in the mind of the viewer. Television advertisers and broadcasters spend enormous sums of money measuring audience impressions of commercials and entertainment program material. They seek expert judgments on the appeal of such programming and commercials and the audience's impressions. They know from daily experience that precision on close questions could be disputed when financial payments were involved. Yet the FCC (and reviewing courts, for that matter) took firm judgmental positions on programs and segments, on their significance to viewers and, as well, on the public's overall impression when overruling broadcasters' and journalists' news judgments and substituting their own.

While the FCC sometimes stated it deferred to a broadcaster's discretion in deciding these questions, in practice the commission decided cases consistent with what it saw as its obligation to regulate news content in the public interest. It did not apply the experienced standards of journalism. This was particularly true when it saw what it thought was some other issue or some other view than what the news producer intended and reported or when it saw some error, imbalance, or unequal treatment. It would order change in the news report as a matter of its regulatory oversight duty.[4]

Current events are dynamic and changing. Views and arguments about them can multiply daily. In advance of a broadcast on an issue of community or national controversy and various contrasting points of view about that issue, it would not be apparent to even a compliant broadcaster precisely how its news reporting would later appear to a government regulator charged with furthering contrasting views on controversial issues and the public interest. Broadcasters and broadcast journalists learned that as a practical matter, FCC staff and commissioners would not necessarily accept broadcaster or journalist news judgment as to what the broadcast was about, what issues were presented, or what the views expressed.

The print press had no such problem, was freer, and was thought by many to be more vigorous. As for television news, Bill Monroe, former Washington editor of NBC's *Today Show* and an experienced news broadcaster explained, "We ... know there are stations that don't do investigative reporting. There are stations that confine their documentaries to safe subjects. There are stations that do outspoken editorials, but are scared to endorse candidates. My opinion is that much of this kind of caution, probably most of it, is due to a deep feeling that boldness equals trouble with government, blandness equals peace."[5]

Government News Inserts and Added Material

When the FCC found a violation of its doctrine, it could order the broadcast of different news or other material it determined necessary, not for public information as such, but to bring the offending report into compliance with the Fairness Doctrine standard. The commission and its staff could simply accept added material or approve proposals submitted by the licensee to add material. When the FCC required added material, it was necessary to make revisions or insert segments to expand or add a view or to add material to cover a new issue found by the FCC, in order to meet the commission's judgment of what should have been reported under the doctrine. Further work and time by the broadcaster and commission were then necessary. Theoretical judgments had to be made on what other material hypothetically should have been aired on this new issue or other views ordered by the government different from those already shown.

The commission might negotiate this with its licensees under an informal procedure that was conducted under administrative agency rules and was considered lawful.[6] An appeal could be taken from an adverse commission decision, but appellate court reversal of the agency was not easily obtained, and there would be significant legal costs.

The commission might conclude the doctrine had not been violated. It did so in a number of instances—perhaps most of them—although the public record may not be sufficient to estimate this accurately. The FCC inquiry would nonetheless have intruded into the station or network news gathering and editorial process. The news report had to be justified by reporters and documents. This necessarily involved a review of how the station or network news judgments and editorial decisions were made. That would likely involve decisions made by the news editors about what to broadcast, what not to broadcast, and why. When this government investigative compliance work was required, it not only took time but also could create the apprehension any second-guessing by government was likely to create for a possible target.

Penalties for doctrine violations were severe. The possible intimidation of news personnel from such government investigation and possible adverse decision had to be of management concern. This increased when the initiating complaint could be based on so little and filed by parties with their own private or parochial interests who attacked news coverage to defend or advance their own interests. The government was required to prosecute their claim. The ultimate dismissal of those complaints did not lessen the intrusion by the government into the regular news reporting process.

The cost burden imposed, including lawyers' fees, could be substantial. The fees could easily range from twenty thousand dollars at the time to an amount greater than what a broadcaster in a small market could make in a year, and even much more. The amount would depend on the issues, the litigation, the stakes for the broadcaster and the FCC, and the principle of news and speech freedom thought abridged. The licensee also carried the responsibility for defending the values of a free press and free speech when the FCC was regulating news. This too could be expensive. The drain required for the inquiry on the time of both management and news staff, who could not then be working on news coverage or other broadcast operations, was considerable.

The original audience might not even be watching when the subsequent government-added material appeared, so it would not clear up some issue or view for that audience, even assuming the FCC was right in its analysis that more or different views were desirable. When the subsequent audience viewed that new government material, members of that audience might not have seen the original broadcast. Standing alone, an added announcement could certainly create distortion of news coverage for viewers. The FCC did not see this as either a procedural or a substantive problem. The FCC commissioners and staff did not view their actions as misguided. They were correcting broadcasters who they had decided had failed to perform under the terms of an FCC doctrine.

Most important, FCC regulations providing for investigations and revisions of broadcast stations' news and speech created a general apprehension and concern beyond any individual investigation (discussed in Chapter 6, The FCC Revokes the Fairness Doctrine). This may happen in any system where significant penalties, such as the loss of a license, can be levied for error. FCC proceedings could also have quite unpredictable outcomes, which created further apprehension. FCC decisions were about vague and ambiguous subjects such as controversial issues, contrasting views, public issues, reasonableness and the many factors leading to news selection, and what the FCC might see as licensee failure to meet a standard of reasonableness required in the public interest. This kind of proceeding, investigation, and decision must be part of any government regulation of the news. The likely impact of such government investigations will result in the loss of information the public needs. This can be significant and contrary to the public interest (see discussion in Chapter 6, The FCC Revokes the Fairness Doctrine).

Nature of Complaints to the FCC

From the record available, it appears that complaints were typically made by those who were the subject of a news report, those who held commercial or ideological views at odds with what they believed was shown in the material presented, those who claimed journalistic error, and still others. Large corporations or organizations that could afford their own access to the public through media as part of their regular business sought FCC rulings under the doctrine for added broadcasts, typically to preserve their corporate image or interests. They argued that a broadcast had not adequately presented their views or that they had not had an opportunity to present their views in the way they wanted or that the issue really was different from what the news reported. Asking for a debate on the air was not a likely request. In fact, there was relatively little demand for presentation of views about social issues generally or for the purpose of robust debate as the FCC and the Supreme Court envisioned it. Complainants typically asked, in practice, for some correction or addition, not for a debate.[7]

As for personal appearances, diversity, and replies to personal attacks, there were not many instances where an individual succeeded in gaining access for his or her personal appearance for debate or otherwise through the commission process. The doctrine did not require that the licensee present the complainant or any particular person or organization the opportunity to present their view. It was enough if the view was covered.[8] Particular views had often already been covered in the regular process of reporting the news. Diversity was not a customary objective of complainants. The right to reply to a personal attack was created by the FCC and affirmed by the Supreme Court, which saw it as appropriate and, in effect, warranting Fairness Doctrine regulation of all broadcast reporting by broadcast stations. It seems, in practice, that relatively few claims were made under the right of reply to a personal attack.[9]

The commission had difficulty with complaints seeking to present unpopular or anti-establishment views. For example, when considering demands to present views favoring communism and atheism, the FCC no doubt considered public and congressional attitudes on such issues, which were very negative, to say nothing of its own views on these issues. The commission held that such issues were not controversial, so there was no requirement that favorable views be presented. Asked to broadcast the view that the Holocaust had not happened, the FCC held there was no controversial issue of public importance involved, so there was no requirement that such a view be aired. Proposals for provocative views were not welcomed. For example, in one case a viewer sought the broadcast of the view that the deity should be referred to as "she" since virtually all of broadcasting used "he." The FCC ruled six to one that this was not a controversial issue of public importance and dismissed the complaint. This sort of regulatory procedure adopted by the FCC did not appear to increase significantly the diversity of views. Diversity in employment and of ownership was addressed in other FCC proceedings. Intense complaints could come from politicians and candidates who had a great deal riding on any press coverage or any reporting that might affect an election or reelection. It soon appeared that one necessary consequence of press regulation like the Fairness Doctrine was the expansive use of state power to silence opposing views. If someone was motivated to use government power to silence some view, it took only a complaint to the FCC claiming a violation of the Fairness Doctrine. The record shows this could shut down the offending broadcast to avoid a government investigation of whatever the complaint might charge and the legal and administrative cost of defending against the FCC investigation.[10] Such filings could ultimately prevent the expression of opposing views and could silence the expression of opinions on important controversial issues. This was the pattern and the result of broadcast censorship, as the FCC itself would ultimately find.[11]

News programs, opinions, and editorials that could have alerted the public to innovations and new ideas as well as problems and needed solutions were hampered if not dissuaded by the inherent threat of FCC investigation. Some programs were not broadcast when, as the FCC ultimately found, it was thought they might trigger government investigation. Investigative journalism also had to suffer because it was bound to prompt complaints from those exposed or involved in the problems revealed.[12]

Under the government's approach, reports were often not broadcast because of possible complaints provoked by the broadcast, which would be followed by FCC investigations of the news reports and possible government hearings and penalties. The government might well take a different view than the journalist and the station, and decide against the station on some aspect of fairness or how the report was presented. In addition, the government standard of contrasting views could be a problem since it could require, in effect, a balance of the disclosure of the wrongs with statements by the broadcaster, or required of the broadcaster by the government, that there were no problems. This operated in practice to deny news and information to the public about conditions of public significance that required public attention and possible change.[13]

The persuasive premise, on which the doctrine was based and then embraced by the Supreme Court, was that the doctrine would promote the broadcast of controversial issues of public importance and encourage robust debate. It simply did not work in practice. Yet, this was the premise that led to the Court's approval of the Fairness Doctrine and it was an important part of the public interest rationale for overcoming the First Amendment and authorizing the government to regulate broadcast news and speech.

Many broadcasters operating under the more general obligations of their licenses did produce news and public affairs programming that presented controversial issues of public importance. While often referred to in the process of reviewing a broadcast, no FCC decision ordered an issue to be covered apart from the regular news flow except when the commission disagreed with the licensee as to an issue covered, defined some new issue, and then ordered new material broadcast on that different issue.

As the FCC's exhaustive record shows, and as the FCC found when ending the Fairness Doctrine, the doctrine inhibited the broadcast of controversial issues and contrasting views. In 1987, when the FCC reviewed its record, it found only one licensee who claimed the doctrine had not inhibited its news coverage. And the FCC had questions about that.[14]

Penalties

The penalties of the Fairness Doctrine did more than correct or punish. They could be fatal to any broadcast station. There may have been some difference of opinion about the likelihood of what the FCC would really do in a particular case to penalize a non-complying broadcaster for Fairness Doctrine violations, but a finding of violation was not something any broadcaster wanted seriously to risk, much less an FCC sanction for non-compliance with its regulations.

The FCC found this intimidating prospect created a climate of timidity and fear for those covering controversial issues who did not have the resources and ability to resist the government or its charges of Fairness Doctrine violations.

Under the congressional scheme, fines were not authorized for Fairness Doctrine violations. License revocation, the denial of a license renewal, or the grant of a short-term renewal were the only punishments.[15] These were threatening and intimidating sanctions. Whether the FCC would revoke or not renew a broadcast license for fairness violations was an unknown. If there was only one violation and the broadcaster was compliant, then these punishments seemed unlikely. If four violations, or if the commission saw a pattern of non-compliance, who knew? Upon a licensee showing of good past performance, a renewal of its license was usually granted for a fixed, three-year term. It was generally expected that if a licensee had shown many years of service and performance satisfactory to the commission, it would have a substantial likelihood of renewal. However, the FCC could renew for a much shorter time, say, one year, and sometimes did. This put the station management even more under the gun during that period.

The FCC investigated a *Pot Party at a University* news report broadcast by the CBS Chicago station in 1964, which was directed toward informing the public of the relatively new and extensive use of marijuana by youngsters in college. The FCC accepted the CBS position taken by its president, Frank Stanton, that CBS News should not turn over the outtakes, that is, material collected and filmed but not broadcast. Stanton argued that CBS News should be judged by what it broadcast, not by what was "left on the cutting room floor." If the outtakes were part of the trial, then the only purpose could be to investigate and judge the editorial decisions made by the news editors and reporters. This could be seen as violating the First Amendment protection of the press from government interference with the news. The FCC did find staging—that the party was arranged for the report by CBS News—and granted the station only a short-term license renewal.[16]

The House of Representatives Special Subcommittee on Investigations of the Committee on Interstate and Foreign Commerce conducted its own investigation. It believed that edits of a program could reflect editorial decisions about the primary point or purpose of the program and how to present the program. These edits, therefore, should be made available to Congress for its oversight. The subcommittee ruled that limiting government review to only what was broadcast was "contrary to the public interest." It deprived public authorities of the "most important evidence for ascertaining if a news program has or has not been slanted by a licensee."[17]

If such television outtakes had to be kept by stations for congressional or other official government inspection, Congress could at any time subpoena television records for a review of editorial decisions and second-guessing. Even if no action were taken, this would be an easy way to maintain the threat of more hearings. This could help discourage television news from reports criticizing Congress or exposing problems that could embarrass congressional members. No bill was ultimately passed.

The mere announcement of a short-term renewal was enough, at the time, to put the license up for a competitive contest. This was changed in later years. A short-term license was a problem for the incumbent, since challengers would be attracted and file with the FCC to acquire the license. In the ensuing comparative hearing between the challenger and the incumbent to decide which should be granted the broadcast license, the commission would be presented with what it had already determined was a poor broadcast record or some offensive misconduct by the incumbent. That would be compared to what the challenger with no bad record was promising. Challenges typically included promises of extensive public affairs programming or other undertakings preferred by the commission. How could the FCC refuse to transfer the license away from a convicted incumbent?

If an appeal was made to the judiciary, how could a court reverse the expert FCC when it had held that a licensee was no longer broadcasting in the public interest and the challenger held out such promises for the better use of the public airways? This regulation was then changed to provide that the FCC would first decide if the incumbent's license would be renewed. Only if the FCC decided it would not renew the license would the station license then be up for grabs among contenders, which could file with promises of outstanding service but often no record of performance.

Intimidation

It was sometimes suggested that the threat of the loss of license should not intimidate broadcast journalists. But no broadcast management or owner could rationally hope to win all its disputes with the FCC in cases about essentially vague and partly subjective judgments of fairness, public importance, issues, controversial or contrasting views, selection, or whether or not the point and counterpoint had fallen within the acceptable ratio of views. This was not made easier when the ultimate standard was what the FCC would see as licensee "reasonableness" or whether the licensee decisions had been made in the "public interest." Certainly, no broadcaster wanted to be a test case.

If the licensee ignored the commission findings or did not follow its orders, violations could pile up until renewal time, when there might then be a number of violations outstanding, and it would be too late to correct them.[18] The FCC might consider these violations as a group, going to an issue of licensee character, which could then result in final termination of the license if a majority of the FCC commissioners thought loss of license was appropriate. Or, at least, that was always the threat. As a result, substantial efforts were made by broadcasters to be in full compliance with the FCC's regulations. Few were willing to risk seriously antagonizing their licensor. At one panel discussion, a commissioner who believed strongly in regulation expressed outrage and, visibly irate, publicly condemned a broadcast lawyer who questioned the constitutionality of the Fairness Doctrine. Raising such a question was evidence of a non-compliant attitude and sufficiently unusual that it prompted press inquiries to confirm that such a question had even been voiced.

Journalists in print press organizations could emphasize their independence, pointing out they could hang up on the mayor. No broadcaster dared hang up on an FCC commissioner. Intimidation was often present. The possible penalties for a broadcast station error or government-perceived misconduct were so draconian and sometimes unpredictable that under the resulting regulatory atmosphere, the commission was described as able to regulate by "a raised eyebrow."

Some network executives did speak out against the damage to the public from this government intrusion into news decisions and resulting news suppression. Julian Goodman, president of NBC and a former reporter, warned about the threats to public information from government oversight of television news decisions. Frank Stanton, president of CBS, at first did not object but then came to see problems in what the FCC was doing. Some station managers and broadcast industry leaders and organizations came to express their own reservations about the doctrine. A forthright and experienced broadcaster, once appointed as a commissioner, told of his own station experience with an FCC fairness inquiry. He said that after it was over, station management instructed that no more controversial issues be presented.[19] Others reportedly came to have much the same attitude.

Investigations were also practical problems. The loss of executive and personnel time was substantial, as were the legal costs. And there would be a pall on the operations while the inquiry was in progress or a possible violation considered.

Newspapers protected by the First Amendment through court decisions and general and public recognition of the need for a free press have had no experience at all with this kind of government intimidation or coercion. The public is familiar with what a newspaper or magazine can freely report. Broadcasters do provide contrasting views on important public issues and controversy and have continued to do so. However, during the period of the Fairness Doctrine, a broadcast station's news could easily become a target of some commercial or personal complaint and then investigation by Congress or its agency, the FCC.

Complaints from private organizations of staging or bias or unfairness could easily be couched in terms sufficient to require FCC action under the Fairness Doctrine, in an effort to punish or to deter and keep views and news reports about a controversial issue off the air. When a complaint was made, the FCC usually had to act, if only to investigate. This was one vice of the Fairness Doctrine. It would be a vice of any similar regulation that required purposeful government interference with the free flow of information to the public to achieve some FCC investigation and possible revision of news or speech for social goals or otherwise.

For example, as the FCC itself later found, special-interest groups opposing nuclear power plants threatened to file fairness complaints against television stations that ran pro-nuclear views. The FCC found that two-thirds of the threatened stations refused to provide time for pro-nuclear views because of concerns about FCC proceedings, which could follow anti-nuclear complaints. Explanations of the contribution nuclear power could make to the country's energy could inform the public, could show the benefits and risks, and prompt discussions. Television could have helped provide this through network and local broadcast station news programming, but the Fairness Doctrine and the threat of government interference with television news effectively suppressed that, as the FCC concluded when it ended the Fairness Doctrine.[20]

This pattern can be seen throughout the enforcement of the Fairness Doctrine. Suppression and censorship took the form, not of some direct order of silence, but as the predictable result of possible government regulatory agency investigation of news reports, where commissioners could find that something else should have been broadcast or presented in a different way than the journalists decided, with all that could follow. The result was the deterrence and silencing of views. As a result, the broadcast of points of view on controversial issues was often avoided, as were controversies.

FCC investigations of editorial decisions for hard news, news discussions, debates, editorials, and other news led to a broad pattern of broadcast self-censorship. The FCC itself did finally recognize this, but only after many years of government interference with news coverage. Reporters and managers who sought to protect their journalists from FCC investigations knew their editorial judgments and work might attract a fairness complaint and a hearing at the FCC. Fairness complaints were not routine, but they were particularly likely where new or controversial subjects needed to be explored and identified for the public. The more controversial the issue, the more important it was that the public should hear about it, and the more likely there would be criticism or opposition and a government inquiry, litigation costs, and the possibility of an adverse ruling, as can always occur in litigation of subjective issues.

Self-censorship by broadcasters resulted not from objections by complainants, but as the result of broadcaster concerns about what the FCC might be prompted or forced to do. The vice of the government investigations and suppression of news and points of view was inherent in the regulatory scheme itself.

The public was largely unaware of commission orders or the exercise of its influence to change the news. A commission order to change the news was exercised under the Fairness Doctrine, and had the standing and authority of a federal regulation order and was seen therefore as appropriate and proper. Announcements were not usually made to the public about government revision of a news report. Nor were they made about revisions to avoid a government investigation, review, or regulatory order. The public may have thought it was getting news from a news program independent of government, but this was not always exactly the case.

Intimidation by the government was also caused by the vague articulation of the Fairness Doctrine tests. Broadcasters could guess wrongly about compliance, and almost any private complaint that satisfied the pleading requirements could prompt a government inquiry. In the *Red Lion* decision, Justice White wrote, "The litigants embellish their First Amendment arguments with the contention that the regulations are so vague that their duties are impossible to discern. Of this point it is enough to say that, judging the validity of the regulations on their face as they are presented here, we cannot conclude that the FCC has been left a free hand to vindicate its own idiosyncratic conception of the public interest or of the requirements of free speech. Past adjudications by the FCC give added precision to the regulations; there was nothing vague about the FCC's specific ruling in *Red Lion* and that Fred Cook should be provided an opportunity to reply ..."

This was a surprising misunderstanding by the Court. The vagueness claimed was not in the terms of the order of the commission to put Fred Cook on the air. It was in the language of the doctrine for a possible violation that used such vague terms as "issues," "contrasting views," "controversial," "public importance" and "in the public interest." The Court's reassurance to licensees that warnings would be given was also surprising: "Moreover, the FCC itself has recognized that the applicability of its regulations to situations beyond the scope of past cases may be questionable ... and will not impose sanctions in such cases without warning."[21] It should be added that FCC warnings rather than orders to comply were not the custom.

The Fairness Doctrine tests were sufficiently vague in meaning that often no reliable, precise prediction could be made in practice when controversy was involved. Justice William O. Douglas made the point that regulating speech could not hope to be entirely predictable: "Free speech is not to be regulated like diseased cattle and impure butter. The audience that hissed yesterday may applaud today, even for the same performance."[22] The language of the Fairness Doctrine had to be deconstructed in order to make a prediction before the news was broadcast about what a commission majority might later find was not countered by another view, or was missing from the report on a controversy. Individual differences among commissioners had to be examined. Review by an appellate court was quite limited. Under accepted legal procedure, an appellate court could not reach a different result on the facts of record if there was a reasonable basis for the FCC decision. Moreover, the court had to recognize that the FCC was the expert agency for broadcast matters. As a practical matter and for a small market broadcaster, fighting the FCC was something far beyond its capacity and financial resources and certainly would make little sense.

When broadcast reporters and correspondents were planning news reports, they could not know or predict quite what would result at the FCC when their news reports dealt with controversial issues or when public emotions were inflamed. Even comments expressed by others after the broadcast could influence the commission's view of a news report. What could be described as a brooding licensor in the background ready to enforce the vague terms of the doctrine as well as its lack of transparency could only increase a sense of intimidation. The president of a major network news organization who served during this period of the Fairness Doctrine said the doctrine created "a brooding omnipresence which limits robust journalism."[23]

Government orders to put on news to provide government "fairness" would be directed ultimately at the license holders, the owners of television networks and stations, their boards of directors, and their stockholders. Depending on the issue and the license risk, this could be a significant corporate and financial matter and would easily lead to self-censorship. Operations under broadcast licenses and relations with the local community had been developed with investment in talent, programming, and management reliability over a number of years. It was important that the station have the public's trust. If the FCC refused to renew a broadcast license, the loss of assets and goodwill developed over years of broadcasting, often worth millions of dollars, would have been devastating for almost all broadcasters.[24]

Not every reporter or news organization was intimidated and many displayed courage in reporting on controversy despite the Fairness Doctrine. The judgment of the FCC ultimately was that the broadcast industry as a whole was required to report the news in a climate of fear caused by the Doctrine and this was not in the public interest. It certainly does not provide for a free and independent press to serve the public as the First Amendment seeks to do.

Political Speech and Political Influence

The Fairness Doctrine was used to silence political views, the most protected speech in a democracy. The impetus for the Fairness Doctrine started with political speech in the 1930s. President Franklin D. Roosevelt was upset at some Republican newspaper owners who also owned broadcast stations and were editorializing against him. "In the public interest," the FCC issued a report banning station editorializing. When that immediate problem passed, the FCC withdrew that report and in the 1940s substituted the Fairness Doctrine.[25]

The use of supposedly benign government regulations to suppress and censor political speech was clearly demonstrated some years later. Political candidates found that the Fairness Doctrine could be used to shut down opponents by the repeated filing of fairness complaints against them. For example, the John F. Kennedy campaign for president filed Fairness Doctrine complaints against stations broadcasting his opponent's views. A former Kennedy administration official, Bill Ruder, has written, "We had a massive strategy to use the Fairness Doctrine to challenge and harass the right-wing broadcasters, and hoped the challenge would be so costly to them that they would be inhibited and decide it was too expensive to continue."[26] Whether justified or not, a regulation of the government adopted to further debate was used, in fact, to suppress or silence news, opposing views, and the most constitutionally protected speech, political speech. The commission applied the Fairness Doctrine to political news programs and appearances by political figures speaking about the major national issues of the day. This was often the case for speeches and reports when great public controversy was at hand. The public often did not know why some figures were selected to speak and some were not or on what subjects and for how long.

The Supreme Court decided that cable news and talk shows should be protected from news regulation because they do not use the airways or scarce broadcast frequencies, and FCC jurisdiction under the Communications Act of 1934, as amended, does not reach cable programs. There is no technological scarcity as with broadcasting. The Supreme Court at first decided that speech and news on the Internet, which is so open and far-reaching with an enormous number of users and sources, should be protected pretty much as the print press is protected. Part of this may be the impracticality of closely regulating Internet content from so many sources and international sources. But this may change as the FCC is now entering upon a full-court press to regulate the Internet.[27]

When the Fairness Doctrine was in force, the commission played an important political role in deciding who would be on television and who would be permitted to speak on political subjects. Congress created a commission of seven commissioners, the majority appointed by the incumbent president from the president's party, and three commissioners appointed from the opposition party. The appointments by the incumbent president came from political positions, regulatory agencies, or regulated industry backgrounds. The commissioners interpreted and applied the terms of the Fairness Doctrine to politics and political communications.

The FCC could determine for the political parties and the country some of the scope of political speech. It approved time for some speakers and denied time to other speakers. It was a political government agency, given the make-up of the commission under the statute, and in that sense, an arm of the government. On the one hand, it enabled political speech that otherwise might not have gained access under market conditions. On the other hand, when a fairness question was raised, the FCC could limit speech in practice to those and to the time and subject that a majority of the commissioners approved. For example, it was accepted that an FCC majority vote along party lines could decide whether the president should have more time on some subjects than others.[28]

The public knew little of the political decisions made by the FCC under the Fairness Doctrine, although the FCC made important structural decisions about how and when political speech and broadcasters' live reports could inform the public. For example, an appellate court upheld the commission's refusal to provide regular or automatic reply time for the opposition party to speak to presidential broadcasts:

> Addresses of the President are subject to the Fairness Doctrine when they concern controversial issues of public importance. [But] the President is obliged to keep the American people informed and as this obligation exists for the good of the nation the court can find no reason to abridge the right of the people to be informed by creating an automatic right to respond reposed in the opposition party.[29]

The circuit court said that adding a right of reply was an abridgement of the right to be informed and the Supreme Court declined to review the decision. What was unacceptable under this court's reasoning was pretty much the basis for the policy of the Fairness Doctrine in requiring broadcast speech on controversial issues to carry replies. When the president was making his informing reports, there should be no FCC required reply or seeming debate since that would be considered by the FCC and the reviewing courts as an abridgment of the right of the public to be informed. This decision illustrates some of the difficulty of regulating speech.

There was considerable jockeying in conducting FCC proceedings on political appearances. After the Democratic National Committee had been granted time to reply to a presidential speech, the Republican National Committee, at the instruction of the White House, demanded time to reply to the DNC reply. The RNC argued that the DNC was not replying to the president in its broadcast but was making a case of its own. Therefore, the RNC said, the RNC should be provided time to reply to the DNC about the DNC's program. The FCC granted the request. (See discussion of this proceeding in Chapter 5, Executive Branch Censorship. The circuit court of appeals ultimately reversed this FCC decision and criticized its reasoning.)

Again, the point is not necessarily the result but the process for deciding on appropriate political speech for the country, how that inevitably spread to reach more and more political speech, the incumbent government's involvement in that process through its ultimate control of the FCC along with Congress, and how that could be used for political advantage. For example, on November 17, 1970, Charles Colson wrote H. R. Haldeman, both members of the Nixon White House staff: "Through Dean Burch [Republican chairman of the FCC] we should keep heavy regulation pressures building. The networks are fully aware that we can influence the FCC in policy matters and this is a cause of great concern to them."[30]

Government as Chief News Editor

The FCC revision of news to conform to the government's preferred selection of fairness was based on a review of the program and issues, sub-issues, and contrasting points of view in a news broadcast or public affairs program. It could lead to serious government journalism error. The following brief description of two cases provides an illustration. As already noted, truth was not the test, nor was it a defense to a complaint.

Considerable dispute could arise when an FCC investigation expanded to reach FCC-discerned inferred issues or sub-issues, which then required additional program material about those issues and the contrasting views on them. An issue not explicitly addressed in a program could readily be found from some facts that were part of the report, and this new issue, or the FCC view of it, could be held to require the broadcast of contrasting points of view about it. A regulator looking at any news report could see a need for more information about some part of it (or some related issue) or a need for more information about the same general subject, which would serve the public interest. This is where the theory of government review of issues and points of view could enter a space without boundaries.[31]

Airport Congestion Case

Station WNBC-TV, New York, New York, broadcast a news report in 1969 about the fact of congested airspace over New York's LaGuardia Airport and other urban airports. A large number of commercial and private aircraft were flying into that airspace. At that time, there were no holds on aircraft takeoffs from departure airports until it was clear that there would be openings for their landings at destination airports, as later became the practice. Aircraft could arrive in the airspace over a city without a plan for their immediate turn at landing or a gate for the discharge of passengers. Flights arriving at destination airports would stack up over the airport or at nearby locations and could circle for long periods waiting for landing and terminal slots. In bad weather, the situation became much worse, as the circling could take longer and longer with little visibility. The danger of collision, however unlikely, would be on the minds of some passengers. This already significant congestion was growing.

To describe the fact of this congestion, a station news crew interviewed pilots suggested by fellow pilots. The "flying grandmother" was an interesting story at the time—an older woman with grandchildren and still flying—but she was not interviewed on air since she was not considered a typical private pilot, and this could raise issues other than the subject of congestion. One private pilot identified on the broadcast told of flying across New York's LaGuardia Airport when his radio failed. That was broadcast.

The private pilots' association claimed the broadcast unfair, not because of what he had said, or because the association denied the congestion depicted, but because private pilots were shown wearing their regular flying clothes, which were pretty much street clothes. The commercial pilots wore their flying clothes, which were impressive uniforms. This created the appearance, the private pilots said, that commercial pilots were better trained.

Private pilots were worried at the time about pending FAA changes, which would restrict their use of commercial airports. A private pilots' association sought the broadcast of contrasting views, that is, that material should be added to show that private pilots were as well trained as commercial pilots. NBC News thought it was reporting on airport traffic congestion. Once started on issues of the causes of congestion, however, the inquiry and the remedy shifted. When a regulator considered the "public interest" of the news report, the possible issues to be explored became almost endless. In theory, to suggest a hypothetical example, pilot dress could reflect pilot competence and training. This could then become relevant to an issue of safety, and the danger from congestion, and ultimately, perhaps, to the issue which concerned the private pilots, whether private pilots should be permitted to fly into LaGuardia airport or any congested air space. This was not a predictable sequence but is typical of how news regulation can work in practice.

The FCC chairman was a private pilot so he recused himself. The remaining commissioners split three to three on whether to order a broadcast segment on private pilots' flight training. A journalist would not likely have predicted coverage of such training would be held to be an essential requirement for a news report on the fact of airport congestion. This illustrates how FCC regulations could deter news coverage. Theoretically, the station news crew would have had to anticipate this kind of FCC review—a possible requirement for covering the significance of private pilot outfits and the training of pilots as related to airspace congestion—when planning a report in a local news program about local airport airspace congestion. If these requirements could be anticipated, the station would have to include them or plan to revisit the subject in other news programs. If not anticipated, a violation of the Fairness Doctrine would occur and discourage other reports alerting viewers to problems.

The local news program had to cover a number of subjects of interest to the viewing public on any given day and, as well, the breaking news of that day, and might not have had the time available for these elements in that local news report. To include something on private pilot uniforms and pilot training would use time. A counterpoint of commercial pilot uniforms and training would require more time. A program on airport congestion would require too much discussion and too many portrayals and too much research for station personnel who were working on a local nightly news report covering a number of pressing subjects of that day. If the fact of airport congestion ran under journalism standards and did validly inform the public of a problem, the regulatory system would require the finding of a Fairness Doctrine violation under the views of half the commissioners in this case.

This also illustrates the problem of the FCC as the ultimate editor. The FCC was supposed to react to complaints. However, once involved, it would find it appropriate or necessary to expand or shape the news as reported by the journalist to cover the FCC commissioners' views of what should be included in the broadcast. There was no majority of four votes for either position in the Airport Congestion case, and therefore no full commission decision. In the absence of a decision by the commissioners, the staff of the FCC ruled that the training sub-issue was too remote.[32]

On the face of it, a contrasting view would have been seen as "There is no congestion." But the issue instead was changed to a created sub-issue, pilot training. Would the station have been required to show that the training for private and commercial pilots was the same? Or would NBC have to compare them if a decision went against NBC? If there was an issue of danger, would that have to be covered with contrasting points of view about danger over airport airspace from congestion, and all the contributing components? Did private pilots flying into that airspace cause danger? Would the local news have had to report that private pilot training or equipment was equal to that of commercial pilots, so there was no danger from congestion? Or that flight training on light aircraft was as thorough as that for heavy aircraft? Or that material on some other airport, pilot, aircraft and air traffic control, or bad weather conditions, and other factors that might affect the congestion, alternative transport, and related issues, had to be covered? If this did not fit in the local station time period, did this mean that the local station should not report on the fact of local airport congestion? A commission decision of a Fairness Doctrine violation could be unpredictable, as can be seen by the happenstance of a split vote of the commission in this one instance.

Failed Pension Plans Case

NBC News reported in 1973 about a pressing social and employment issue, that under some corporate pension plans, when workers retired they discovered the money they had been promised and earned for their pensions was not there.

The NBC News program, *Pensions, the Broken Promise*, explored the plight of those pensioners who had worked for many years and relied on the pensions promised them, only to find when they retired that the pension funds were gone and there was little they could do about it. It was important that the public learn of this. Legislative proposals were even then pending with hearings in Congress to grant retirees much needed and greater protection from failed pensions at some companies. This was certainly something to be considered by America's workers and the public, as well as something to be addressed by Congress.

Accuracy in Media, a private complainant interested in how news is covered, charged that the program portrayed all pension plans and the pension system as defective and asked that contrasting views be broadcast, essentially to the effect that the pension system was working. NBC submitted affidavits of how the program was developed, its purpose, and the value to the public of journalists' historical role of reporting on society's problems so the public could correct them. NBC News affidavits set out instruction from news management to the news team "to write and produce a documentary with respect to the problem caused by the failure of many private pension plans to pay the money promised them." Against the AIM claim that the program was directed at the entire pension system and should have included substantial material on pension plans that worked and that the pension system was working, NBC journalists explained at length the purpose of the program and what it showed and the need for such investigative journalism.[33]

Under journalism standards, a report on some tragic cases of failed pensions to inform the public about the problem would not require that each time the problem was shown, a report of "good" pension plans or individual "success" stories be included for "fairness." To report to the public that the private pension system was working in order to satisfy some FCC-ordered regulatory "balance" or "fairness" test would mean there would be little or no exposure by the broadcast press of this problem in our society, or any other, which was not then offset or denied by a contrasting view. Moreover, the requested parts of that government "balance," (i.e., that "the pension system is working") would mislead the public on something of vital importance.

Reuven Frank, president of NBC News, had many years' experience as a print reporter, and many years' experience in reporting, producing, and managing television news and news documentaries. The commission's decision that NBC News had violated the Fairness Doctrine made no sense to him. The doctrine was not part of journalism. It did not reflect the purpose of journalism. It served a regulator's needs instead of the needs of the public.[34]

His affidavit stressed the amount of work, the number of people, and the kinds of people required to produce the documentary. Investigative reporting requires persistence and care, and it seemed to him "inconceivable that this program has been ruled in contravention of the commission's Fairness Doctrine, and must be 'balanced' by putting on a spokesman to present the other side." He did not see how NBC News "by concentrating its entire program on the problems of the system and the people whose pensions had for whatever reason not been forthcoming, had thereby been 'unfair' in that not enough time had been spent on those who had received their pensions."[35]

He pointed out that if this were a rule of reporting, then "we in television news must never examine a problem in American life without first ascertaining that we had piled up enough points on the other side, a little bank account of happiness to squander on an area of public concern. Otherwise, we should be overdrawn and would have to schedule a program in payment of the debt."[36]

CBS had similar concerns and joined in the proceedings. The distinguished CBS journalist Edward R. Murrow had been a pioneer in investigative journalism. He explained in an affidavit to the commission that such journalism reported on a problem and focused the public's attention to it "so the public could decide whether it should be remedied." This did, in fact, characterize investigative journalism as found in television news like the famous *Hunger in America* investigative report and reports on problems in health care, crime in the streets, urban housing conditions, corruption in government, and corruption in the criminal justice system, among others. Seeing the problem, the public could then require reform, if it chose to do so.[37]

CBS News President Richard Salant noted that the contribution that investigative journalism made was generally in "direct proportion to the courage, vigor, and initiative of the journalists involved." He also said that the FCC's news content regulations "create a brooding omnipresence, which limits robust journalism … [regulatory laws and the Fairness Doctrine] constrict, not expand the flow of information."

CBS broadcast journalists said there was "a genuine concern with the prospect of working in an atmosphere where the Government's critical eye is a ubiquitously felt presence, which subtly dictates editorial decisions and investigative paths."[38]

The *New York Times*, an unregulated print medium newspaper, said, "Investigative news, by the limitations of time and space, deals with the negative part of the subject matter. To require the media to 'balance' by presenting the 'positive' part would be to create a production problem which would make investigative reporting impossible … One of the purposes of journalism is to provide the public with facts with which it can solve its problems."

The *Times* did not believe the government's interpretation of the program should prevail, as that would clearly constitute censorship. Moreover, the *Times*'s reading of the transcript of the program led it to conclude, as did NBC, "that the program focused on the [pension] problem areas. It was similar in vein to the scores of articles printed in the *New York Times* during 1972 and 1973, which told of the criticism and defects in pension plans."[39]

NBC's *Pensions, the Broken Promise*, received considerable critical acclaim. It received the Christopher Award, National Headliner Award, American Bar Association Award, and the George Fisher Peabody Award, which described the program as a "shining example of constructive and superlative investigative reporting."

NBC was supported in the FCC proceedings by a number of professional print press organizations. None of them was regulated by the FCC, but they saw how outrageous the proposal was for any news organization. These included the Society of Professional Journalists and Sigma Delta Chi, as well as those who were regulated, such as the Radio and Television News Directors Association and the National Association of Broadcasters.

The FCC rejected all of this. It found that the program should have been balanced, failed to report on the plans that were working, and violated the Fairness Doctrine. It ordered NBC to provide in its "overall programming" contrasting views, in effect, that the pension system was working. It ordered further, "The Commission expects prompt compliance with its ruling." AIM advised stations affiliated with NBC that had carried the report that they were also in violation unless they did something promptly. Stations had to be concerned about FCC pressure on them. Apart from the falsity of what the FCC was ordering NBC to broadcast, the commission's version of the report would have created a misunderstanding and an unjustified complacency on the part of retirees. It was a clear interference with news coverage and misinforming the American public of an important problem.

Reuven Frank declined to comply with the FCC orders. He sought an appeal to the Circuit Court of Appeals of Washington, DC. For the first time in many years, a reviewing court looked closely at what the doctrine was doing to this kind of news content. A three-judge panel of that court unanimously reversed the FCC decision. It saw that the FCC was redefining the issue covered and then ordering material to be broadcast that was false. The panel of that court issued an extraordinarily thorough opinion with a careful analysis of all the factors of the Fairness Doctrine.

Judge Leventhal's opinion was extensive. He noted that this was the first case to address an investigative news report under the Fairness Doctrine and recounted judicial history from the reasoning in the *Red Lion* case and in subsequent cases. He carefully analyzed the facts of the program and the complaint against it. His description of the program began:

> The *Pensions* program studied the condition under which a person who had worked in an employment situation that was covered by a private pension plan did not in fact realize on any pension rights. Its particular focus was the tragic cases of aging workers who were left, at the end of a life of labor, without pensions, without time to develop new pension rights, and on occasion without viable income.

The program had no set format, but its most prominent feature was a presentation of tragic case histories, often through personal interviews with the persons affected.

One group of workers lost pension eligibility when their company decided to close the division in which they had worked. The first of these was Steven Duane, who after 17 years with a large supermarket chain, lost his job as foreman of a warehouse when the company closed the warehouse and discharged all its employees, leaving them with no job and no pension rights. Now in his fifties, starting again with another company, he felt ill-used and frightened of the future.

There were a number of other specific examples of employees terminated by closing of plants or divisions. The program also focused on the problems of vesting, the years of service with the company required for a worker to become eligible under its pension plan. NBC interviewed employees with many years of service who were suddenly discharged just prior to the date on which their pension rights were to have become vested. Thus Alan Soresen asserted that he was the victim of a practice—a "very definite pattern"—under which his employer, a large department store chain, fired men just prior to vesting, assigning "shallow" reasons to men who had served with records beyond reproach.

A similar account was given by Earl Schroeder, an executive fired by Kelly Nut Company, after he more than met his twenty years of service requirement but was six months shy of the age-sixty condition ...

The documentary gave instances of pensions lost for lack of portability, citing plans that required the employee be a member of the same local for the requisite period. NBC interviewed a number of teamsters who had worked for the same employer for over twenty years, but who later found that certain changes in work assignment entailed changes in union local representation and ultimately loss of pension.

Much of the program was a recount of human suffering, interviews in which aging workers described their plight without comment on cause or remedy. They told of long years of working in the expectation of comfortable retirements, finding out that no pension would come, having to work into old age, of having to survive on pittance incomes. Interspersed with these presentations by workers were comments by persons active in the pension field, public officials, and Mr. Newman ...

None of those interviewed—and these included two United States senators, a state official, a labor leader, a representative of the National Association of Manufacturers, a consumer advocate, a bank president, and a social worker—disputed that serious problems, those covered by the documentary, do indeed exist ... (See Appendix 2, Excerpts from the Failed Pension Plans Case).

The court emphasized the concluding remarks of narrator Edwin Newman of NBC News:

It may be appropriate to quote the concluding remarks of narrator Edwin Newman of NBC News, since the FCC considered them "indicative of the actual scope and substance of the viewpoints broadcast in the *Pensions* program."

[Newman] This has been a depressing program to work on but we don't want to give the impression that there are no good private pension plans. There are many good ones, and there are many people for whom the promise has become reality. That should be said ...

There are certain technical questions that we've dealt with only glancingly[:] portability, which means, being able to take your pension rights with you when you go from one job to another, vesting, the point at which your rights in the pension plan become established and irrevocable.

Then there's funding, the way the plan is financed so that it can meet its obligations. And insurance, making sure that if plans go under, their obligations can still be met.

Finally, there's what is called the fiduciary relationship, meaning, who can be a pension plan trustee? And requiring that those who run pension funds adhere to a code of conduct so that they cannot enrich themselves or make improper loans or engage in funny business with the company management or the union leadership.

These are matters for Congress to consider and, indeed, the Senate Labor Committee is considering them now. They are also matters for those who are in pension plans. If you're in one, you might find it useful to take a close look at it.

Our own conclusion about all of this, is that it is almost inconceivable that this enormous thing has been allowed to grow up with so little understanding of it and with so little protection and such uneven results for those involved. The situation, as we've seen it, is deplorable.

The circuit reviewing court reversed the FCC because it had not given sufficient recognition to the discretion granted a broadcast news organization under the statute and the Fairness Doctrine to make editorial decisions without FCC interference. The circuit court panel could not go so far as to take on the Supreme Court and address the basic issue—the validity of the doctrine itself. It ruled only that under the doctrine, the FCC had to give deference to the licensee's reasonable discretion in identifying the issue presented. Under this ruling, NBC's understanding of its program and its editorial judgment was upheld.[40]

The FCC asked for a rehearing before the full circuit court *en banc* (as contrasted with the three-judge panel that had rendered the decision) to reexamine the panel's decision. The rehearing was granted by the full court and under procedural law, that judgment to revisit the decision automatically vacated the panel decision, which thereupon became a nullity. The FCC then asked that the case be dismissed as moot, withdrawing its order of violation on the ground that Congress had passed corrective pension legislation. Technically, the public controversy had ended, so that the Fairness Doctrine was no longer applicable. The full court sent the case back to the original panel, which sent it back to the FCC, and nothing further was done about it. The FCC had saved its interpretation of the doctrine and continued to enforce it, perhaps more cautiously.[41]

The FCC and courts were on a track that was difficult for a journalist to follow. As Reuven Frank would say, "a lawyer is someone who thinks a news documentary is a transcript." There is an important and powerful point in that expression for lawyers, the commission, and reviewing courts. It is the overall and particular impression of the program on the audience that should count, but regulatory and fact-finding commissions have no objective way to assess that. The public interest in learning of circumstances such as the failure of some pension plans was subordinated to upholding the FCC Fairness Doctrine and limiting the exposure of such circumstances for the public's benefit. What the FCC was ordering was, in effect, a retraction.

Subordinating Truth to Government Doctrine

Under the Fairness Doctrine, attempts were not made to replace journalism standards with truth, but to impose a matched set of opposing views on a news report about an issue or an event. Matching was the important undertaking for the agency. The primary government objective became weighing the expression of views and issues along with inferred issues and views, and descriptions of visual presentations against their opposing expressions to satisfy contrasting tests or "balance" as the decisive dialectic for finding compliance with government news regulations. This could approach, if an analogy is appropriate, the angels dancing on the head of a pin arguments conducted at length in the Middle Ages. Even the public interest could become irrelevant when the FCC found that not truth but some different balance of transcript or pictorial views had to be presented, including even counterpoint false ones. When achieved to the agency's satisfaction, this balance would then be the final words.

Political figures who deliberately used the doctrine to suppress opposing political views and those in government who used state power to censor were often doing what the regulations permitted them to do. This was despite the fact that the participants knew and the FCC knew their actions were being used to suppress opposing points of view and dissent. All involved became caught in a government doctrine adopted to bring about an objective that sounded good, but whose actual and heavy consequences could include suppression and silencing of news and information, as well as distortion of truth. The unavoidable result was that the broadcast press, unlike the print press, was not entitled to rely on the First Amendment since management had to take the FCC's views into account.

It is sometimes said that the Fairness Doctrine was desirable because it kept the threat of FCC proceedings ever present to discourage wrongdoing or injurious or libelous behavior. But the libel laws apply to broadcasts just as to other media and provide a remedy that the courts enforce. Rarely has a general government threat against the press been used in this country to censor news except in national security matters. A general threat to keep the press in line has never been accepted as good policy or permitted by the First Amendment. For those who would urge that the doctrine must have done some good, the best judge of that is the FCC itself, which found in its many years of enforcement that it was harmful to the public.

The Supreme Court's approval of the Fairness Doctrine in the 1960s and the FCC's determined enforcement of it show how easy it can be for government to gain significant control of news and political speech and manage them under the cloak of desirable goals. Under the Fairness Doctrine, First Amendment protection of the press and its reporting of news to inform the public were deliberately subordinated by the FCC and the Congress to a regulatory fairness mission as seen by a government agency, the FCC.

This is a record of government control and management. The FCC staff and commissioners ruled and required revisions in television news reports, news coverage, speech, and expressions of political opinions and political speeches for four decades, from 1947 to 1987, when the Fairness Doctrine was finally revoked.

What Now?

In 2010, new government officials of the FCC and the White House Office of Information and Regulatory Affairs urge that news and speech content be regulated for localism, diversity, and balance, terms that are vague and concepts that are amorphous. They will be defined by those in government and local advisory boards as they enforce them.

Like the Fairness Doctrine, the new Localism, Balance and Diversity Doctrine would be, at the same time, a broad avenue for government informal censorship, suppression of news and information, and a continuing threat to broadcast journalism and the public's right to know. Lucas A. Powe, Jr. asked the fundamental question in *American Broadcasting and the First Amendment* (1987), "How do we explain severing from the First Amendment protection the very source of news for most Americans?"[42]

Moreover, the threat to speech and press is directly focused on preventing criticism of government policy, as is found in any number of foreign countries where dictators announce the news and the intimidated accept and agree. It is hard to imagine a more important freedom for the press and public than the ability to criticize and change government policy.

Cable program content has not been regulated. It does not use electronic frequencies for its transmissions as broadcasting does, so the FCC jurisdiction, which extends to electronic frequencies, does not apply to cable. Congress has so far been unsuccessful in imposing regulation on cable except for obscenity and pornography, although it may be regulated by local towns and cities when the cable license is granted, usually to carry local information and local government hearings and events. The Supreme Court has upheld cable freedom under the First Amendment with those exceptions.

The Internet and its content were not regulated for many years. The Supreme Court upheld its news and speech freedoms under the First Amendment, holding that the Internet is more like the print press than the broadcast press because of its openness and great diversity. The FCC asserted regulatory control over the Internet on December 21, 2010. (This is discussed in Chapter 7, New Government Threats.)

Regulation of the press and news content, however benignly it may be described, will easily become an instrument of suppression and censorship. When government has power over the press, a government agency can quietly reach out to prevent news coverage or just suggest some press inaction and the publisher will know the safest course to follow. Suppression of news and opinion is not likely to be difficult when official regulation is in place and accepted. The fact is that those who control the government can already informally control a great deal of what is reported about the government. Official government regulation and official management of news and speech content expand that control beyond likely protection for free speech and news and hope for correction of government abuse.

The commission's Fairness Doctrine was one of many reactive pressures on broadcasters. It put the FCC in place to intervene in the editorial process. It gave those covered by news reports an appeal to a law enforcement body to delve into the news process and pursue a complainant's private interest. Some journalists could not help concluding, "Who needs this?" The doctrine deterred journalists because they knew they would have a fight with the government prompted by those being reported about if those involved did not like the broadcast. No other news medium has such a process.

Since the FCC has been considering imposing localism, balance, and diversity requirements on television news and now managing Internet news and speech, its past experience with this kind of content regulation should be part of that consideration. This is especially so because its news management regulations and experience were studied and found conclusively to be against the public interest. The newly formed FCC cannot institutionally deny the 1985 and 1987 FCC findings that content regulation and enforcement were destructive of news and speech freedoms. Yet the commission is not addressing this experience of over 40 years of controlling and managing television news, the climate of fear and timidity it created, or the distortion and suppression it inflicted. Only strong public opposition and attentive government prudence will prevent a repeat of that public misfortune.

CHAPTER 4

⌒⁀⌒

Congressional Investigations and Censorship

C ongress sets much of the regulatory environment for its agencies. It has oversight authority and sets the budgets. It can pass legislation it concludes is required. In the case of the television industry, it passed a law in 1969 approving FCC control over news and speech content "in the public interest." The record shows how Congress used the Fairness Doctrine as well as its own powers to investigate, intimidate, and discourage news coverage and the expression of views and opinions its members did not like.

Congress and News Coverage

Congressional investigations of television news broadcasts were often conducted in public hearings where the public could learn of error. This could reflect congressional oversight leading to better results. It could also reflect other purposes. News executives and reporters were chastised publicly for what Congress viewed as improper conduct warranting its investigation of news reports that undermined an official's public standing. News executives could publicly assure Congress that errors would not be repeated. These hearings were particularly intense when political issues were at the forefront. One example of this is the congressional investigation of the television news coverage of the Democratic political convention held in Chicago in 1968.[1]

When the Democratic Party met to nominate a presidential candidate, the convention turned out to be the occasion for great controversy among party delegates, political figures, city officials, young hippies, and others who had come to Chicago to demonstrate against the Vietnam War. There were many scenes of police charges, beatings, and provocations of the police with increasing violence by the people and the police. When this was covered on television, including the brutality of some of the actions, the Democratic Party and the Congress it controlled charged that the network news organizations were biased, staged events they reported, slanted news coverage, exaggerated Chicago police beating of the demonstrators, and failed to show or had deliberately omitted showing the provocation for police action. A congressional special subcommittee investigated and announced the networks were guilty.[2]

At the outset, when plans for the convention were being made, Mayor Richard Daley wanted to showcase Chicago. However, he did expect trouble. He was concerned particularly about the young people and others who would demonstrate against the Vietnam War, which then–President Lyndon Johnson was prosecuting. The mood in the country was one of turmoil, following the assassinations of Martin Luther King, Jr. and Robert F. Kennedy. In addition, the Yippie movement (the Youth International Party) had announced that a "festival of life" would be held to coincide with the political convention in Chicago. The Chicago Seven, an activist group seeking major social change and led by Abbie Hoffman and Tom Hayden, as well as Students for a Democratic Society and the National Mobilization Committee to End the Vietnam War, planned to attend and demonstrate. It was also a gathering for many of the counterculture opposed to the established social structures. They expected to create confrontations.[3]

At the mayor's suggestion, the Illinois governor called up 5,649 members of the U.S. National Guard. The U.S. Army provided 6,000 riot-trained soldiers. All 12,000 Chicago police were put on twelve-hour shifts. About 1,000 FBI and Secret Service agents were also mustered for duty. Then more were called. It has been estimated there were ultimately 10,000 demonstrators and 23,000 police and members of the National Guard in Chicago that week.[4]

These numbers alone point to the difference from the Philadelphia presidential nomination convention in 1948. Twenty years had elapsed and television was no longer just a magic carpet to a major event. As American society changed, television news not only reported that change, but it showed it, live, and often to the discomfiture of many. Union telephone installers had been on strike since May, and if they did not install the network cables and connections, there would be no live television coverage. Reuven Frank, in charge of NBC television news coverage in Chicago, wrote that the terms of a strike settlement apparently arranged by Mayor Daley prevented live television coverage by the three networks except from the International Amphitheatre and from each network's offices and studios.[5]

Bill Small, a CBS news executive, recalls that the city's antagonism toward the demonstrators was evident from the very start. Mayor Daley's Chicago was not going to let them interrupt the proceedings. The telephone company refused to empty the coin boxes of public pay phones. They were soon filled and could not be used by the press, the demonstrators, or anyone else. This, of course, was before cell phones. Small says, "But neither the city nor anyone else could stop television coverage. One, we had walkie-talkies and two, the geography was not spread out so far that footage could not quickly get to the studio for editing."[6]

Mayor Daley tried to limit the demonstrations by limiting the number of permits to hold lawful demonstrations at selected locations, but that did not succeed in stopping the students and others from organizing ongoing demonstrations and riots during the convention. While Mayor Daley successfully prevented the use of television cameras other than at the Chicago International Ampitheatre and each network's offices, the students demonstrating against the war learned where the cameras were located and went to them. And so did the police.[7]

The intense feelings about the Vietnam War resulted in clashing confrontations on the streets of Chicago. Students and others demonstrated ferociously against the war, those conducting it, the Democratic administration generally, and other things. Young demonstrators called the police "pigs" and "whores." The Yippies planned to nominate a pig for president to ridicule the whole nominating process. Provocative chants, still familiar to many, included, "Hey, hey, LBJ, how many kids did you kill today?" and "Hell, no, we won't go!" Most of the demonstrators dressed to be different and to show they were against the Vietnam War. The city refused to let them sleep in the parks or parade in the streets. But things happen in such circumstances. At one legally approved demonstration in Grant Park, a young boy took down the American flag. Police charged the demonstrators. The crowd threw food, bags of urine, rocks, and chunks of concrete at the police. Pictures were broadcast into the homes of viewers, both of the provocation of the police and of the police assaults on the demonstrators with police batons.[8]

The Democratic Party was concerned this coverage would hurt their presidential election chances. It may have.[9] At the time, some Republicans were also critical of the television coverage.[10] When the Democratic Congress accused television network news of exaggerating the police beatings of demonstrators, distorting the news, and showing police violence but not the provocation that caused it, a special subcommittee on investigations of the House Commerce Committee of the Democratic Congress was activated under its chair, Harley O. Staggers. It subpoenaed all films, thousands of documents, dozens of witnesses, and many news reporters for investigation of the network news reporting on the convention. This investigation and the hearings continued for months.[11]

The networks had to gather material, witnesses, and witness statements to comply with the subpoenas. In the end, the subcommittee staff concluded that the networks had deliberately sought out for interview those with known biased feelings against holding the convention in Chicago. The evidence officially identified was slim and pretty much in the minds of the subcommittee investigators. They thought the networks would rather have kept their locations set up in Florida, where the Republicans had held their convention, to save costs. Therefore, they concluded, the networks held a grudge against the Democrats when they had to move to Chicago. The investigators did not accept that network news was accustomed to travel around the country and appear in different locations to cover news events. The staff did note that a finding of bias was "of course, of necessity, extremely subjective."[12]

The staff examined outtakes to determine whether the networks had "deliberately withheld" materials from broadcast that would have been derogatory to demonstrators and that were not broadcast. The investigators reached the conclusion that some material not shown on the air could have presented a different picture than what was shown. They said outtakes included such material as "Crowds . . . shown in violent and ugly moods. Police were shown being stoned and pelted with rocks and bottles. Obscene signs and language were discernible, both of which might have diminished any sympathy felt for the demonstrators by the average viewer." They reported they found some such materials in the outtakes, but also found material that was critical of police conduct, which also was not broadcast. This is the inconclusiveness that often results when trying to determine from outtakes whether bias was driving news selection.[13] It was the staff's impression, as they reported, that material in the outtakes would have been generally unfavorable to the demonstrators. But this did not mean that material unfavorable to the demonstrators was not shown. In fact, it was, and to a substantial extent. Both sides made charges of exaggeration about both the provocation shown and the police response shown.

Congressional investigations can cost real money, both taxpayer money and news organizations' money. The inquiries from Congress and the FCC cost the networks hundreds of thousands of dollars worth of lawyers' and clerks' time to find, organize, and copy documents and files as well as taped material that had not been broadcast. News people had to spend hours answering questions and trying to recall what was done and why and reading and rereading transcripts of the hours of their Chicago convention coverage.[14]

The staff finally concluded that it saw bias in the news and animosity toward Chicago. On this precise point, however, it still only cited the move from Florida to Chicago as the cause.[15] It did no good to explain, as David Brinkley did, on the air, that "We showed what we could, that our locations were circumscribed and what we showed was unedited."

In the background, of course, was disapproval of the network news by a Democratic congress. This included the threat of adverse action against the networks. The staff did not accept the reporters' testimony that given the restrictions they had to work under, what they showed was the essence of what had happened. The staff at the outset had also said, "No attempt has been made to investigate the very substantial and significant charges that the Chicago police or Democratic Party officials … attempted to intimidate and obstruct the work of the newsmen." Journalists from all media had been injured and many were harassed by the police. The Associated Press did a story on that and reported that the total reached twenty-one. For example,

"I'm from Newsweek."

"Fuck Newsweek!" And his glasses were smashed.[16]

Reuven Frank wrote that what took place away from the news cameras, which were limited to the locations the city permitted, was worse than what was shown on television. "Bystanders and some demonstrators fled police and tear gas to seek refuge in a restaurant; police pushed some through a plate glass window; other police ran into the restaurant randomly clubbing those inside. We saw none of that; we read about it in the next morning's newspapers … Most of the horrors later testified to … were in fact not seen on television, police shouting, 'Kill 'em! Kill 'em!' or clubbing kneeling young women and well-dressed middle-aged bystanders." Several NBC News reporters explicitly reported that the demonstrators had "set out to goad the police." Of the thirty-five hours of NBC news coverage, a total of one hour and five minutes had been devoted to the demonstrations.[17] Reports of police entering a restaurant (chasing demonstrators or otherwise), randomly clubbing those inside, and violent street clashes with bloody results were reported by the print press, with pictures. The tied-down television cameras did not have that same access. The print press reports did not prompt the same investigation by Congress and others that television reports did.

The turmoil in the streets was reflected in the convention itself. Chicago police with billy clubs removed demonstrating delegates and others. Some objected to outsiders brought into the convention hall by Mayor Daley to demonstrate for Senator Hubert Humphrey. The mood grew worse as echoes and rumors of what was going on outside worked their way inside. Reporters inside the convention reported on the concentrated use of tear gas by the police on demonstrators outside and thus on reporters as well. An NBC news reporter, John Chancellor, was restrained by force and even carried from the convention floor. The police roughed up CBS reporters Mike Wallace and Dan Rather, and Chicago strong-arm squads were moved into the convention to try to keep order.[18]

The long-simmering antagonism between President Johnson and his opponents broke out in demonstrations with chants and uproar. Mayor Daley tried with little success to manage things from the floor. There were difficulties at the podium as well. Senator Abraham Ribicoff's endorsement of George McGovern veered aside to say that with George McGovern, there would not be "Gestapo tactics on the streets of Chicago." Mayor Daley was shown shouting back from the floor. Television showed these events on the floor live.[19]

The Democratic nominee was finally chosen—Senator Hubert Humphrey. President Johnson was eligible for reelection but had said he would not run. The turmoil in and out of the convention was enough to persuade Johnson to not even go to Chicago for the convention. As the coverage was discussed, public opinion was set and network reputations suffered. The public could not believe what it saw and Congress helped with that. The Democrats continued to call the coverage "biased and irresponsible" and cited its Congressional committee report. Many people thought the pictures of Chicago police clubbing the country's young people must have been distorted. Even network-affiliated stations thought the network news had exaggerated the problems in Chicago. Few had seen it, but they were relying on what they had read about the network news reports and what people were saying. Network news had shown a darker side of the political community and of some youngsters in America, disillusioned by the Vietnam War and striking out at authority. The scenes of demonstrations outside and the hostility inside the convention hall were shocking to many viewers who were their elders and, as well, to the community at large. As *Broadcasting* [now *Broadcasting & Cable*] magazine reported, "If Chicago was a garrison city last week—most would agree that it was—it was a garrison city in a fishbowl." As Reuven Frank put it, "Network television did that. We had not led the protests or clubbed demonstrators, we had not goaded police or fired tear gas. Our sin was being there—with cameras."

What they showed was a scene many believed was false, an exaggeration, or should not have been inflicted on the public.[20] The hostility was not confined to Democrats. Republican Whip Leslie Arends proposed that the House investigate the role of "the networks in our national affairs and just how these federally licensed activities ought to be allowed to get into the business of influencing the public." This was one of the threats of congressional investigations; those federal licenses could be ended or amended. Senator John O. Pastore (D–RI) extended his hearing on network sex and violence to look at the coverage. Senator Russell Long (D–LA) called for a "full scale" investigation. He said, "The [c]ity of Chicago was convicted by the television media without its side ever being heard."

The National Commission on the Causes and Preventions of Violence also issued a report on the investigation it conducted. This led to the

Walker Report entitled "Rights in Conflict." This blue-ribbon, independent commission reviewed 3,437 statements of eyewitnesses and participants, 180 hours of motion picture film, and 12,000 still photographs. This exhaustive study, which continued for months, concluded there was neither news distortion nor bias.[21] In fact, the Walker Report found a "police riot." From the interviews the staff conducted, it concluded the police had lost control of the demonstrators and then themselves. It also found that what happened at the convention was largely "what the networks had reported at the time." The Walker Report stated,

> The vast majority of the demonstrators were intent on expressing by peaceful means their dissent either from society generally or from the administration's policies in Vietnam ...

> Most of those intending to join the major protest demonstrations scheduled during convention week did not plan to enter the Amphitheatre and disrupt the proceedings of the Democratic convention, did not plan aggressive acts of physical provocation against the authorities, and did not plan to use rallies of demonstrators to stage an assault against any person, institution, or place of business. But while it is clear that most of the protesters in Chicago had no intention of initiating violence, this is not to say that they did not expect it to develop.

> It was the clearing of the demonstrators from Lincoln Park that led directly to the violence: symbolically, it expressed the city's opposition to the protesters; literally, it forced the protesters into confrontation with police in Old Town and the adjacent residential neighborhoods. The Old Town area near Lincoln Park was a scene of police ferocity exceeding that shown on television on Wednesday night. From Sunday night through Tuesday night, incidents of intense and indiscriminate violence occurred in the streets after police had swept the park clear of demonstrators.

Demonstrators attacked too. And they posed difficult problems for police as they persisted in marching through the streets, blocking traffic and intersections. But it was the police who forced them out of the park and into the neighborhood. And on the part of the police there was enough wild club swinging, enough cries of hatred, enough gratuitous beating to make the conclusion inescapable that individual policemen, and lots of them, committed violent acts far in excess of the requisite force for crowd dispersal or arrest. To read dispassionately the hundreds of statements describing at firsthand the events of Sunday and Monday nights is to become convinced of the presence of what can only be called a police riot.[22]

Even without video, the descriptions of the clubbing by police as set forth in this independent report of the Walker Commission are disturbing. The public is generally supportive of the press role as a watchdog over government, but the Yippie demonstrators' behavior and that of others prompted public support for the police. This was one time when the networks had become part of the story because they had covered it. They felt then that the public no longer trusted them as they had before.[23] Viewers did not want to see what had happened or have to believe it. Although the cameras had been restricted and there were not as many television pictures of the gratuitous and frequent brutal beatings as reported by the print press, which the Walker Report describes, damage to the network press reputation had been done. It was easier, in a way, to say the networks must have staged it or exaggerated it than accept it as true. The Walker Report, when it was later published, came too late to show the public that what network news had shown was what had happened.

Television news did not have the public standing that the print press held at that time for unflinchingly reporting the news. The print press also had recognized First Amendment standing and protection. Without recognition of that standing by the government and the public, the government can easily portray the press as abusive, unworthy of credibility, and a maker of false charges. That can be the time to propose censorship laws with the expectation they will garner substantial support. That is why the press and news must be protected by the Bill of Rights and the First Amendment, since freedom of the broadcast press is essential to the open and free flow of information to the public.

Congressional investigations and hearings of this kind, as in the Chicago coverage, are perhaps part of what the press must expect when political power is so directly the subject of its reporting. And, such hearings will be claimed to be serving a purpose declared by Congress to be in the public interest and necessary for legislation. If the purpose of a Congressional committee investigation is to examine or revise news editorial judgment, however, then it does not serve a valid legislative purpose. History shows that although during this period House committees said they were conducting hearings into news coverage under their oversight powers, they did not call government agency officials. "The only apparent purpose of many of the hearings was to provide a forum for exposure and criticism of broadcast editorial practices that were already the subject of FCC or other regulations that were beyond the power of Congress to reach."[24] When used to deter or sanction the press, however, such investigations and hearings are clearly a part of abusive state censorship. The subcommittee staff did propose a bill for legislation which would have required broadcasters to maintain all records of editing so that a public authority could examine the material to find bias or distortion—in effect a record of outtakes for official review and restrictive action. No legislation was adopted.

Claims that broadcast coverage of the 1968 Democratic Chicago convention was biased against the Democratic party and that there had been network staging of events were filed with the FCC by the Congress itself. All three networks opposed such an FCC review and took the position that there was broad coverage of all views. NBC, for example, said, "Few spectres can be more frightening to a person concerned with the vitality of a free press than the vision of a television cameraman turning his camera to one aspect of a public event rather than another because of concern that a government agency might want him to do so, or fear of government sanction if he did not."[25]

The FCC decision was that the networks had presented contrasting views during the Chicago convention. Under the Fairness Doctrine, the question was not, as a technical and legal matter, if the broadcast was fair but had the broadcast presented contrasting views. Obviously, all kinds of views had been presented. The commission said, "There is no substantial basis for concluding that the networks failed to afford 'reasonable opportunity for contrasting viewpoints' on the issues at the Chicago Democratic Convention, such as the Vietnam War and the civil disorders."[26]

The networks also opposed the FCC investigations of their broadcasts for staging incidents. The FCC did not review tapes of material broadcast or material not broadcast. It said this was being done elsewhere by the National Commission on Causes and Prevention of Violence. The FCC said it was "not now finding that there were 'staged' incidents on the part of some television news personnel, or, if such incidents did occur, that network news personnel were responsible."[27] It said it would rule based on representations the networks had submitted to the FCC that there had not been staging. It quoted representations that staging was against network policy, such as NBC's submission: "We do not reenact, simulate, dramatize, state, or aid a demonstration of any kind. If it happens, we try to cover it; if we miss it, we don't fake it. We don't try to make it happen. This simple injunction must not be forgotten. If it is forgotten, we will attempt as severe a punishment as possible."[28]

Editorial decisions were the area of considerable interest to Congress since it was believed those decisions were where the investigators could find proof of bias and slanting, i.e., news deliberately covered or not, in order to injure or embarrass or slant the news. If Congress could at any time subpoena television press records for a review of editorial decisions in public hearings, this would be a way to maintain the threat of investigations and more hearings and possible punishment for slanting editorial decisions with second-guessing and continuing intimidation of the television press.

Congress investigated news programs and documentaries during this period far more to condemn than to enact legislation. Congressional hearings charged unfair treatment and criticized news documentaries' reports on hunger, migrant workers, highway construction, Pentagon propaganda, corruption, and the like. After the CBS documentary *Hunger in America* revealed that the U.S. Department of Agriculture was scuttling its own food-for-the-poor program with the encouragement of congressional farm committees, the FBI was sent after anyone who had worked with the producer of the program. That producer had to spend a year doing nothing but answering inquiries and meeting with lawyers and going to Washington, DC to defend the program. Peter Davis, the producer of the CBS News program *The Selling of the Pentagon,* was required to prepare more than seventy pages of rebuttal following that program. He said, "The Pentagon, now that we've told the truth about it, is telling lies about us, and they are telling them at a very rapid pace … We have to answer each of these things." The cost of that was expected to exceed what the program cost to produce. The producer noted that no one after that seemed to do news documentaries on how Congress operated.[29]

This investigation and others required television news reporters, producers, news editors, news managers, and corporate executives to appear at congressional hearings for cross-examination and headline-making charges against them and their work. As Walter Cronkite observed, Congress did not call journalists down for its hearings to commend them.

Congressional Investigation of *The Selling of the Pentagon*

CBS broadcast *The Selling of the Pentagon* on February 23, 1971. The program exposed substantial Pentagon funding of what could be described as propaganda supporting the Vietnam War. It was reported that the Pentagon spent more than $30 million that year on public relations, up ten times more than what it had spent twelve years before.

It was later reported to have spent $190 million. The program described a number of Pentagon propaganda activities.[30]

Congress has virtually unfettered power to investigate matters it oversees or to find out if legislation is needed and to enact legislation. Harley O. Staggers (D–WV), chair of the House Energy and Commerce Committee and of its Special Subcommittee on Investigations, pressed by F. Edward Hebert (D–LA), chair of the House Armed Services Committee, decided to conduct an investigation into claimed deception in the CBS News program. It did so and issued a committee report in 1971.[31]

The documentary news report was hosted by CBS correspondent Roger Mudd and showed the large propaganda machine used by the Pentagon to urge greater military power for American foreign policy and the Vietnam War. Military officers in uniform appeared at public meetings supporting the Vietnam War. The domino theory required fighting in Vietnam because if Vietnam fell to the Communists, other nearby countries would also fall. But the military was not supposed to make foreign policy. Army regulations provided: "Personnel should not speak on the foreign policy implications of U.S. involvement in Vietnam."

The program showed one of the many military demonstrations held at military bases every year on Armed Forces Day. The cost of ammunition for this demonstration alone was $2 million in 1971. In the "mad minute" at the end, weapons from tanks to rockets "blazed away in a thundering display of firepower. In the bleachers, the audience cheer[ed]." Young children turned away from the sight and held their ears against the noise. They were then shown running down and playing on the guns.[32]

One army exhibit unit went to 239 cities in 46 states and was seen by more than 20 million people at a cost to taxpayers of almost one million dollars. Thunderbirds flew over in dramatic formation. They had flown over 208 such exhibitions that year with a total audience of six million people. The program reported that each year thousands of VIP officials and citizens got a tour and demonstrations illustrating America's military power. Military officials were interviewed. General Lewis Walt, a leading

Marine representative, was shown explaining that the "Communists in Vietnam and China were … trying to keep the war going—why? Because they think we're going to give up and pull out before the job is done. That's what they've been told and that's what they read in our newspapers and our magazines. [He added,] This is what's kept the war going on. If we could have had the entire American nation in back of us, all of our Americans in back of our armed forces in South Vietnam, this war would have been over a year and a half ago. [Applause.]"

Mudd reported that the Pentagon circulated propaganda films for the war with lead actors from Hollywood, and "52 million Americans saw Pentagon motion pictures, 45,000 public gatherings viewed them, and at least 356 commercial and educational television stations have presented them as part of their public service broadcast time." One popular film, *Red Nightmare*, starring Jack Webb, showed a communist scheme to take over the United States and pictured Soviet troops occupying a U.S. community. Nine hundred prints of that film were in circulation.

The films had been distributed during the three prior presidential administrations. President Nixon had ordered this propaganda to stop and ordered the curtailment of "broadcasting, advertising, exhibits, and films."[33] But it had not stopped. It was said that the Pentagon had turned into a runaway bureaucracy that frustrated attempts to control it.

One former public information officer, Jack Tolbert, said the Pentagon military information arm was so vast and pervasive with ready access to all the country's national and local newspapers and electronic news that it could present its view to the American people overwhelmingly. Tolbert said that this was what allowed the Vietnam War to happen. He warned that "if we allow this pervasiveness to continue, frankly it could lead us to another Vietnam."[34]

The primary charge that the Staggers Special Investigation Subcommittee was investigating was "deceitful editing" by CBS News. It was accepted that the CBS News producer had combined two separate questions with two answers given by a Pentagon public relations representative in an interview into what appeared to be one question and one answer.[35] This had been done for brevity and relevance and was not that unusual in television reporting. But, in this instance, it made it appear that an answer had been offered to one question when it had actually been provided for another question.[36] The statements had been made by an experienced Pentagon public relations official, the Honorable Daniel Z. Henkin, Assistant Secretary of Defense (Public Affairs).

This combination of two questions and the answers was to become the center of the government's investigation of a television news documentary on improper Pentagon spending and propaganda. It was the basis for a contempt of Congress proceeding against Frank Stanton and CBS.

Henkin was answering questions about the Pentagon public relations campaigns and demonstrations of military equipment. Mudd reported that going into and out of the 30,000 Pentagon offices each day were 200,000 phone calls and 129,000 pieces of mail. He turned to the man in charge of all Pentagon public relations for answers:

Mudd: What about your public displays of military equipment at state fairs and shopping centers—what purpose does that serve?

Henkin: Well, I think it serves the purpose of informing the public about their armed forces. I believe that the American public has a right to request information about the armed forces, to have speakers come before them, to ask questions, and to understand the need for our armed forces, why we ask for the funds that we do ask for, how we spend these funds, what are we doing about such problems as drugs—and we do have a drug problem in the armed forces. What are we doing about the racial problems? I think the public has a valid right to ask us these questions.

Mudd: Well, is that sort of information about the drug problem you have and the racial problem you have and the budget problems you have, is that the sort of information that gets passed out at state fairs, by sergeants who are standing next to rockets?

Henkin: No, I wouldn't limit that to sergeants standing next to any kind of exhibit. Now there are those who contend that this is propaganda. I don't—do not agree with this.[37]

The producer of the program, Peter Davis, insisted that there was condensation but not distortion. "No charge was ever made, much less sustained, that editing changed anyone's true meaning." He said the charges did succeed in causing people to argue about editing techniques instead of the Pentagon's political agenda, an agenda set mostly by civilians, not the military. But the editing could be seen as incorrectly claiming Henkin said that the demonstrations were used to explain the military's request for funds to help deal with drug and social problems in the military. It could be said that the editing made Henkin look dishonest. The producer explained that his purpose was to present Henkin's answers as relating to the theme of the program, which dealt with public information.[38] He said he had no intent to mislead, and Henkin had a copy of the interview to use as he wanted.[39] Stanton viewed this as unacceptable and ordered CBS News to change its editing practices. They did.

After additional material illustrating the runaway bureaucracy point, Mudd said they had reported on only a fraction of the total public relations apparatus belonging to the Pentagon and supported by taxpayers.

Following the broadcast, the public response was "predominantly favorable." That of the Nixon administration and other public officials was "sharply critical."[40] Vice President Spiro Agnew, House Armed Services Chairman F. Edward Hebert, Secretary of Defense Melvin Laird, and many others thought it a disservice and, because it was critical of the American military during a war, it was un-American. *Barron's* magazine called it un-American and criticized the editing.

The *Washington Post* and others criticized the editing.[41] Congress did not investigate the Pentagon, which later said it had continued the activities shown, with some minor changes.[42] Harley Staggers officially called for a public hearing as chair of the House Commerce and Energy Committee Special Subcommittee on Investigations.[43]

Because of the criticism, Frank Stanton decided to rebroadcast the program and add a postscript to carry the critical views.[44] Hebert maintained his view that it was un-American and asked, "Do you want these Pentagon people to go over there and tell you that Hanoi's right?" and Defense Secretary Laird said of a Pentagon official, "words were put in his mouth."[45] Agnew leveled five attacks against the program, calling it a "vicious broadside against the nation's defense establishment" and accused CBS of "deliberately publishing untruths."[46] Dick Salant, the president of CBS News, replied, "No one has refuted the essential accuracy of the program or that the Pentagon's manipulation of news, the staging of events and the selling to the public of the Pentagon's point of view" were not done.[47] Vice President Agnew continued his attacks against CBS at televised press conferences, and said he was "totally dissatisfied" with what CBS called an opportunity for a rebuttal.[48] Chairman Hebert reiterated his charge that he was misled into supplying film to Davis who, he said, was guilty of a "vicious fabrication."[49] Hebert spoke on the floor of the House on March 3 to say he had answered the false innuendos concerning him in the program. On March 24, he spoke about the rebroadcast of the program with its critics: "Obviously, CBS believes in the Goebbels method of propaganda—if a lie is told enough times, people will eventually begin to believe it ... CBS, in the Goebbels style, replies to the charges of inaccuracies with more inaccuracies replying to the charges of misrepresentation with additional misrepresentation."[50]

The House Energy and Commerce Committee was one of the most powerful in Congress. As the chair, Staggers controlled the committee, which had oversight of the television industry. Staggers was an experienced legislator and had many friends in Congress. The Democratic majority would support his lead and the views of Hebert. The reputation of the military, patriotism, prosecution of the war, and the essential powers of Congress to investigate for legislative purposes were more than enough reasons to proceed.

Frank Stanton was prepared to rely on the protection of the First Amendment for the free press. As for the editing, there had been a change in CBS News policy and Congress had been given a copy of the new policy. Congress already had the Henkin interview it was subpoenaing.

The substance of the CBS News program—that the Pentagon was deliberately and officially engaged in improper propaganda activities—was not addressed by the critics. But an activist role by the military in determining U.S. foreign policy violates the rule for civilian control of the military. Only elected civilian leadership is accountable to the people.[51]

In the months that followed, there was little public or government criticism of the Pentagon's expenditures of millions of dollars on propaganda and no investigation of the Pentagon's advocacy of foreign policy. Public attention shifted from *what* was said in the program to *how* it was said. This is often the result of criticism by high officials covered in the news when they do not like the portrayal of them or their views.

At this same time, President Nixon was still carrying on a major campaign against the press for criticizing him and his conduct of the Vietnam War. He was particularly incensed at television network news. He had support for this from members of both political parties who did not like television news for any number of reasons. He saw in the Staggers hearing a golden opportunity to hurt the reputation of CBS. More important, investigating and punishing CBS in this very public way would intimidate not only CBS but also other broadcasters, who would then not dare to criticize Nixon. Since the Democratic Party controlled Congress, he believed, at first, that the Democrats would get any blame for punishing CBS News for the program.

He instructed Republican members of Congress to vote in favor of the subpoena for outtakes and confidential reporters' information. Other members of the administration joined in. For one, Attorney General John Mitchell, who had been conducting a program of subpoenaing network news notes and interviews for some time, criticized the press as having contempt for the truth.[52]

Staggers convened his subcommittee investigative hearing and charged the issue was deception. Staggers was not expert in the news communications field but was briefed for the hearing by the knowledgeable and experienced subcommittee staff. If the audience thought it was seeing an actual interview—when in fact it was watching a scene created by a program editor, an arrangement and combination of questions and answers that could give a misleading impression of the substance or the manner of the interview—the public would have no way of knowing it was watching a fabrication. The hearing could be used to stop the potential for such deception and require disclosure of edits in the future. For that, the program outtakes were needed to see if and how the program had been edited. Staggers insisted that "[t]he First Amendment has nothing to do with it." He was seeking legislation to stop fraudulent editing practices. If broadcasters' freedom to edit as they choose went "unchecked," then "Big Brother has arrived."[53]

Stanton had said at the outset that the investigation was an abridgment of the freedom of the press.[54] "If newsmen are told that their notes, films, and tapes will be subject to compulsory process so that the Government can determine whether the news has been satisfactorily edited, the scope, nature and vigor of their news gathering and reporting will inevitably be curtailed ... to control editing practices in broadcast news reports and thereby engage in official surveillance of journalistic judgment has no constitutional warrant."[55] He held to his position and refused to produce outtakes, news reporters' notes, and confidential sources of information subpoenaed by the congressional subcommittee for its assessment of the CBS editorial news decisions as to what to include in the program as broadcast. He invoked the First Amendment's protection for the press. Staggers then announced, "It is my duty to advise you that we are going to take under serious consideration your willful refusal today to honor our subpoena. And in my opinion you are now in contempt."[56] This was a major confrontation. It was to become what *Broadcasting* magazine called "a huge and bitter fight over the First Amendment."[57]

The chairs of the Senate and House committees pretty much ran Congress at the time. If convicted of contempt of Congress, Stanton could go to jail, and CBS could lose its broadcast licenses. CBS had to consider that a licensee would not likely retain its broadcast license granted "in the public interest" if it was defying a congressional investigation into misleading news and improper editing. One of the FCC's most important requirements was that its licensees disclose all pertinent information to the FCC. Keeping a license could be unlikely if the licensee had been held in contempt for dishonesty or withholding information sought by the Congress of the United States.[58] The FCC was conducting its own investigation at the time. Moreover, as the power of Congress to conduct investigations and subpoena material had been placed in issue when Stanton refused to obey its subpoena, there was little doubt how Congress would vote on a contempt of Congress motion for such defiance of its power.[59]

Many chairpersons and other legislators had committed their votes to Staggers and against CBS. This was usually conclusive since the House conducted its business by such chairperson commitments. At the initial subcommittee hearing, the members of the subcommittee were mostly condemnatory. The Republican ranking minority member of the subcommittee, Representative William Springer (R–IL) took the position that the First Amendment did not apply to television news. He relied on his dictionary, which predated television, for a definition of news. It did not mention television news. James J. Pickle (D–TX) had said at the hearing, "You are saying that we are trying to set up … Government control, that we are using government standards of truth. Now who else is going to pass judgment on these matters if it is not the government … ?" It was also argued that even if the First Amendment applied, that would not protect deliberate falsehood.[60]

The chair called for the vote. The subcommittee voted for contempt, and to send the motion to the full House by a unanimous vote of five to zero. The staff report concluded that CBS News had engaged in "highly deceptive practices."[61] The full committee then voted for contempt, twenty-five to thirteen, with thirteen Democrats and twelve Republicans voting in favor.[62]

Stanton wrote to Carl Albert (D–OK), the House Speaker, and described the new CBS News guidelines for editing, which went beyond those used in the industry generally. He informed Albert that a copy had been supplied to the Congress, and explained that he believed it was his duty to assert the First Amendment privilege for broadcast journalism.[63]

On July 8, 1971, Staggers sent an unusual "Dear Colleague" letter to all the members of the House asking for their votes. "Deception in broadcast news is like a cancer in today's society … We have clear evidence of deceit—man's words electronically altered to change their very meaning … The spread of calculated deception, paraded as truth, can devastate the earnest efforts of anyone of us seeking to represent our constituents."[64] A number of Democratic and Republican colleagues dissented from Staggers's views and sent around their own "Dear Colleague" letter in reply, pointing out that the Staggers motion would be seen negatively by the public as "an effort by government to crack down on a critique of government."[65]

Congressman James T. Broyhill (R–NC) sent his own "Dear Colleague" letter as well. The issue was not the Fairness Doctrine, he said, but was "news content." Protection of the First Amendment "must be extended to the electronic media if they are to provide the same essential, and sometimes painful, function of keeping the public involved in and aware of the working of its society." At the same time, he urged the networks to put their own house in order.[66]

Congressman Lionel Van Deerlin (D–CA), long a supporter of freedom for the broadcast press in thick and thin, saw little chance of killing the Staggers motion on the floor. But he spoke often and emphasized, "The committee action is an absolutely outrageous intrusion into the freedom of the press."[67]

One of the problems the press can run into is the belief of a legislator that he or she has been improperly treated. That belief can provide a negative attitude about the press of long duration. Ed Murrow invited a legislator to appear on a program and did not make clear the opposition would appear after him, and the legislator never forgave Murrow or CBS. Stanton remembered, "I don't think he ever took his foot off CBS's neck from that time forward. He felt he had been done in by CBS. And there were scores of stories like that. Congressmen would vote against CBS on this issue ... not because of the issue but because of some personal grudge ... there were people on the Hill who privately were saying, 'You know, the son of a bitch deserves it.' "[68]

Broadcast television anchors, reporters, commentators, and television and newspaper organizations submitted affidavits setting out the deterrent to news coverage from such congressional investigations and their subpoenas for confidential news sources and material. One of the many was submitted by Walter Cronkite, managing editor of *CBS Evening News*, who said that "if reporters and editors must be constantly looking over their shoulder for those who would have the product reflect the standards of those elected to public office on partisan platforms, and who represent, properly, the special interests of their region, who by their nature hold strong views on the issues of the day, then the coverage of the news cannot be done without 'fear' or 'favor,' and that means it cannot be done at all. News coverage would cease to be an energetic seeker of the truth and [become] a pallid conduit for that propaganda which is palatable to the majority of Congress or the administration of the moment."[69]

Cronkite also warned, "If reporters, editors, and producers must consider in their decision-making the possibility of being summoned before an investigative arm of the government to justify these [reporting and editing] decisions, I believe that independence and vigor in broadcast journalism will be inevitably sacrificed." He pointed out that a hearing into television news coverage would only be called if the purpose were to criticize or condemn—not just investigate what happened.[70]

Bob Schieffer, CBS News Pentagon correspondent, said that those interviewed made mistakes and to produce those for public consumption would serve no purpose and dry up interviews. So editing was useful for that reason. Bill Small, CBS News director and Washington bureau manager, said even the current investigation made some unwilling to come to CBS News with reports, because CBS was in hot water with Congress, and who knew where their investigation would lead. Marvin Kalb, diplomatic correspondent for CBS News, said reporters had to have discretion to edit. Daniel Schorr, CBS News correspondent, said a person interviewed would be inhibited, as he would be, if the government could investigate all a reporter's notes. Mike Wallace said there would necessarily be the imposition of a government standard of truth. Burton Benjamin, senior executive producer for CBS News, said condensation was essential in press reports. He knew of no country where government supervision and control had improved the vigor and integrity of the news.[71]

For CBS News, the issue was not only the program outtakes but also the confidential standing of news sources. Journalists see confidentiality of news sources as essential to finding out what really is going on for their news reports. To get the news, journalists often have to pledge they will not disclose the identity of their informants. Salant kept some of the news records of *The Selling of the Pentagon* program locked in the trunk of his own car.[72] The journalists' affidavits about the impact of government investigations of the press were dismissed by congressional staff as "the usual First Amendment press rhetoric."[73] They said they were looking at "rearrangements," not what it takes to cover the news.[74]

The television networks and their leaders and others of the television and print press lobbied Congress partly out of concern about the threat of possible contempt of Congress motions against the press in the future. The American Society of Newspaper Editors and the Committee for Education in Journalism called it an unwarranted interference with the press. The chair of the Freedom of Information Committee of Sigma Delta Chi, the professional journalist fraternity, said the subpoena was "repugnant." The Association for Education in Journalism called it "unwarranted." The president of the Associated Press and the president of the National Association of Broadcasters criticized the subpoena. The National Academy of Television Arts and Sciences said every medium of mass communication was threatened by this attempt to have government sit in judgment on news coverage. The *Washington Post*, which had criticized CBS for improper editing, said the subpoena was a substantial threat to the news media in this country and the program had provided a public service. It said the risk Staggers was threatening was "governmental control" of the content of television news and public affairs programming.[75]

There was considerable apprehension on the part of the CBS affiliates about the CBS refusal to comply with the congressional subpoena and what that could lead to for CBS and the affiliates of the network. Only five of those stations complimented CBS on the program at first. All were alert to the power of Congress and the FCC. Jack Gould, the *New York Times* broadcast reporter, observed that it was common knowledge in Washington, DC that many politicians wanted "to get" CBS.[76] He pointed out that for the networks and the stations, station income was "the core of the dilemma of electronic journalism." The threat of the loss of a federal license to individual stations meant possible jeopardy running into the millions.[77]

John J. O'Connor, television critic for the *New York Times*, explained that the program would not have gotten such a response from the government had it been in a newspaper. However, as many as forty million people might watch an investigative, provocative television news documentary. Because it was television, the program might stir strong emotions.[78] The government was not likely to go easy in the face of a broadcaster's charge that it was engaged in war propaganda. Clifton Daniels, associate editor of the *Times*, pointed out the basic danger. Any government control over the press leads to the "temptation" to determine who may broadcast and what may be broadcast. "If we are to preserve freedom of speech and of the press, that temptation must be resisted." [79]

A special Peabody Prize, one of the highest in all journalism, was awarded earlier than usual so that the CBS News documentary would have that recognition before the congressional vote on contempt. The program was hailed as "electronic journalism at its finest." [80]

Stanton traveled across the country repeatedly, and to the point of exhaustion, meeting with journalists, broadcasting stations, community and press organizations, and many others to enlist their support for the cause of television press freedom. His refusal to obey the congressional committee was risking CBS's licenses and more. But he had had years of experience with government attempts to influence and suppress news coverage. He believed in press freedom. He believed television news was one of broadcasting's most significant contributions to the public.

Stanton was strict about the standards for news coverage and its special standing in the eyes of the viewers: "We were scrupulous in applying the standards to news because of the juxtaposition of the news to entertainment. You could slide off an entertainment program where you had entirely different standards and in fact, where you could have fiction as well as reality. But when you came to news, there had to be a firewall there, or a break, a different set of standards went into effect. If you're going to have a continuing relationship with your audience, it seems to me you have to have certain fundamental concepts. And one of them is they look to you as being a responsible purveyor of information." [81]

Gordon Manning, vice president and director of news at CBS News and head of CBS hard news at the time, believed strongly in news integrity and defended his correspondents against government and private pressures. "The editor's chief allegiance must be to the viewer ... the editor is the 'Horatio at the bridge' of any news operation, an essential middleman to ensure the end product is in keeping with company policy and in the best traditions of American journalism. But the chief obligation is to the public."[82] Chairperson Staggers maintained throughout the entire proceeding the pervasive government view that the "broadcast media did not have the same rights as printed media because they are licensed by the government. But Staggers also believed in the supremacy of Congress and would fight for that."[83]

Congressional Debate

Carl Albert, the House Speaker and leader, was told that Stanton had changed CBS News's operating standards and had gone beyond customary practice to meet the subcommittee's objectives. Albert sought a compromise to avoid a House vote on a very difficult issue.[84] All the concern about the unrestrained power of the television networks surfaced. Patriotism, support for a war, and allegiance to America's military establishment mobilized. Two days before the vote in the House on the contempt of Congress motion, Staggers was confident.[85] He believed that what was at stake was "deception" and was going to prevent it.[86] *Broadcasting* reported that to Staggers "there is a moral question" posed by these activities of broadcasting's giants he believed had nothing to do with the Constitution. He thought the act was evil, and he would have none of it.

" 'We just want to be sure,' says the chairman of the House Commerce Committee, 'that people don't do the wrong thing.' "[87]

On *Face the Nation*, Representative John Dingell (D–MI) pointed out that the issue was whether the House was going to get the information useful for legislative action to prevent "deceitful practices" in broadcasting. In addition, the House needed to find out "whether our creature, the FCC, is properly carrying out its function in regulating the broadcast industry." It might be necessary for Congress to see that the FCC does a "more vigorous job," Dingell threatened, "perhaps even network licensing." He concluded, "The subpoena should be complied with."[88] The issue was seen as one of substantial public importance, as Dingell had pointed out earlier. If Stanton could refuse to produce the material subpoenaed by the subcommittee, the networks could deceive the public at will and Congress "will have completely lost control over how and by whom the airways are used."[89] *Broadcasting* magazine reported on July 5, "Straws in the wind all point to a House vote solidly in favor of contempt citation."[90] In the news accounts of the problem, with relatively few exceptions, there was not much said about the use of taxpayer funds for forbidden Pentagon propaganda or the need for Congress to stop it.

The chair of the House Judiciary Committee, Emanuel Celler (D–NY), for the first time in his tenure went to the office of another chairperson. He warned Stanton that he would lose the vote and had arranged a meeting for Stanton with Staggers to find some compromise.[91] When Stanton arrived, Staggers proposed one. If Stanton would just show him some of the outtakes, he would review them and tell his colleagues he had done so and that would end the proceeding. Stanton refused. Journalists could not get the news if their sources were subject to government subpoena. But Stanton's refusal to compromise or produce the material was a most unusual position for a network executive. Defying Congress was not financially, legally, or career prudent. Losing such a fight could be disastrous. Any corporate, business, or bottom-line assessment would see this. But Stanton believed Congress had no right to examine outtakes and confidential press material for reviewing editorial news judgment under the First Amendment. He also knew if this was not stopped, it would continue and become even more of a practice. There would be no freedom for broadcast news.[92] His stand further antagonized Staggers and others in Congress, who saw the CBS president as spurning a compromise mediated by the House leaders.

The CBS Board of Directors stood by Stanton in a determination not likely to be seen very often from a board of directors representing corporate stockholders in this kind of situation. The assets placed at risk were enormously valuable and depended upon station broadcast licenses. But the CBS board, which included outside directors, saw the great issue before the press and the country—the freedom of television news—and identified CBS News with that.

The debate was postponed and then held on the floor of the House on July 13, 1971. Extraordinary steps had taken place behind the scenes. Lobbying intensified at the White House, as it did in Congress. The Nixon administration had been counting on the Democrats in Congress to convict Stanton and CBS and bear the brunt of any public and other objections about punishing the news media. Then, on the receipt of legal advice at the last minute, Nixon realized that it would be his department of justice and his attorney general, John Mitchell, who would have to bring the contempt proceeding in court to convict Stanton and send him to jail. So Nixon would get the blame for that. Worse, this would be right before the presidential election. From a political point of view, this was not an attractive prospect. And to make matters even worse, the Republicans would be bringing this on themselves in aid of a Democratic subpoena against the press.[93]

Herb Klein, the White House chief press advisor, warned Nixon against supporting the contempt of Congress motion and said that the public would not like holding a man of Stanton's standing in jail. Nixon and his staff reversed course. Republican House members were released to vote their conscience.[94] Charles Colson also reported at the time that he had talked with Stanton and Paley of CBS. He said he thought the White House could do better coming to the aid of CBS rather than prosecuting them and have a better long-term relationship.[95] He also reported in a conversation with H. R. Haldeman that a new CBS lobbyist had said Stanton would cut a deal. This would be in return for help on the contempt motion. Haldeman had earlier told him "to get something" for any help.[96]

Professional lobbyists were retained by CBS. They not only argued the free press issue, they also pointed out to Republicans that the subpoena was invading the right of management to make substantive decisions, which should not be an area for government fishing and attack. The CBS-affiliated stations then joined in and actively defended Stanton. Many affiliates had not liked the program or thought it was broadcast at the wrong time in light of what was going on in the

Vietnam War. A long-standing member of the CBS affiliate board, Charles Crutchfield of Charlotte, North Carolina, an experienced radio and television broadcaster since 1993, called his own meeting of the affiliates and talked to them about news coverage and the standing of Frank Stanton. He pointed out that if Congress were going to review broadcast news programs, this would "kill radio and television news." The affiliates set out to save broadcast news freedom and Stanton.

No small station and very few other broadcasters, if anyone, could hope to mount such a major effort on behalf of the First Amendment as CBS was doing. And, they could not take the risk of such a fight with the federal government. But they could and did organize to help save Stanton from jail and save the existence of their free broadcast press. They knew their local congressional representatives well and were very effective—perhaps the most effective in the Congress. Vice President Gerald Ford was minority leader in the House. He saw a number of Republican representatives the afternoon and night before the vote. A number of legislators decided to oppose the contempt of Congress motion, something Ford had favored on the merits of the issues raised for the press. He saw the affiliates lobbying Congressional members and said this is after all "how democracy works."[97]

A startling development took place on July 12, the day before the full House debate, when the chair of the all-powerful House Ways and Means Committee, Wilbur D. Mills (D–AK), went down to the floor of the House and said he had "serious questions" about the contempt citation. He then entered into the record of the House a series of statements from the CBS journalists who described the chilling effect of a subpoena of outtakes and government review would have on press coverage. Mills had talked with journalists, the print press, the Association of American Publishers, the editor of the *Arkansas Gazette* in Mills's home state, and a number of others speaking for the press. This was a remarkable break with his fellow chairpersons and sent the signal that he would not support Staggers. It was unprecedented. It represented a major and perhaps fatal blow to the Staggers motion.[98]

On the floor of the House on July 13, the full debate brought many to the floor to speak. It was a unique moment in the history of the First Amendment. Observers said they could see how great debates could turn great issues. There was a genuine debate about extending the First Amendment to the television broadcast press to protect it from a congressional subpoena issued during a congressional committee investigation of alleged deception in broadcast news coverage.

First, invoking a privilege for the chair of the committee's motion and report, Staggers submitted the committee report and said, "The whole Congress of the United States was being defied" when Stanton and CBS refused to produce the material subpoenaed. He continued that he did not believe the First Amendment was involved.[99]

Emanuel Celler, as chair of the House Judiciary Committee, responded, "The First Amendment towers over these proceedings like a colossus and no tenderness of one Member for another should force us to topple over this monument to our liberties, that is, the First Amendment." Celler stressed that James Madison addressed himself to the evils of the press and found error in the debates they reported. But Madison had pointed out that "the media, even if guilty of misrepresentation, must be protected if freedom of expression are to have the breathing space that they need to survive."[100]

Congressman Clarence (Bud) Brown (R–OH) was opposed to the government overseeing the news. He explicitly took the position that even if CBS had edited to misrepresent the positions of public officials (and CBS vigorously denied this is what happened), since the electronic media had become the means by which most people received their news, this argued for the greater exercise of First Amendment freedoms by this medium rather than less. Since untrammeled freedom could be tolerated in newspapers, certainly Americans could "risk the same freedom" in the electronic medium.[101]

James O'Hara (D–MI) said, "I do not believe (CBS) can deny the U.S. Congress its right to inquire into the techniques employed ..." and Hebert said, "I was shown in the *Selling of the Pentagon*. The film that was shown was obtained from my office under false pretenses." He added that the public has the right to know and how will it know "if we do not make them show what they have under the table and up their sleeves?"[102] Chet Holifield (D–CA) said a CBS documentary, *The Dangers of Radiation*, took an hour of his time, but used only two-and-a-half minutes of the filmed answers and the balance of the program hour were used for arguments against his position.[103] Robert Sikes (D–FL), quoting Staggers, said, "The spread of calculated deception can devastate the earnest efforts of any one of us seeking to represent our constituents."[104] James Wright, Jr. (D–TX), said, "By their selection and treatment of news, the three networks are in a historically unrivaled position to mold the minds and control the impressions of many millions of Americans."[105]

A large number spoke eloquently on both sides of the issue. Staggers ended the debate. He said that the issues had produced the greatest lobbying effort ever made on Congress and concluded, "If this Congress is going to be intimidated by one of the giant corporations of America, and give up to them, then our Nation will never be able to exist as a free nation … They must not be permitted to intimidate this Congress on this issue …"[106]

The minority has the right under House rules to move that a motion return to the originating committee, that is, to "recommit" the motion and send it back and not approve it. The trial vote to recommit and send it back carried, 151 to 147.[107] Many who had supported Staggers went up to him and said that since he was going to lose, they wished to switch their vote or not vote. When the final vote was taken, the House of Representatives denied the motion to hold Stanton and CBS in contempt of Congress and sent the motion back to the committee, 226 to 181 with 26 not voting.[108]

Staggers was a senior figure in the House. *Broadcasting* magazine reported that Wilbur Mills's statement had persuaded the House leadership to "dump Harley Staggers."[109] William Springer, the Republican ranking member on Staggers's investigation subcommittee who had helped Staggers from the outset at Staggers's request and with what was then a "green light" from the other end of Pennsylvania Avenue, said, "A lobbying campaign such as they had never seen before … reached the peak of its intensity on the eve of the vote. I must have talked to between 60 and 80 Republicans who ran to me and asked what the hell was going on. They all had been contacted, most of them several times, by TV and radio people. I haven't seen anything like this in my 21 years."[110]

There were some hard feelings. Staggers never forgave Judiciary Chairman Celler, Speaker Carl Albert, Wilbur Mills, or others of the House leadership who he thought had not stood by him to uphold the institutional powers of Congress, and kept a list of the people who voted against him. Staggers was no longer available to meet with Stanton.[111] Since the House traditionally did business through commitments, those made to Staggers and then dropped by any number of members meant that his own leadership and his fellow chairs had deserted him. Congressman Lionel Van Deerlin says with the switch of that many votes, Staggers was entitled to be bitter.[112]

Congressional interest in summoning broadcast reporters and network news executives to investigate news content diminished. A majority of the House of Representatives had dealt with the issue. Congressional subpoenas were no longer issued for the purpose of hearings to review broadcast editorial judgments. Looking back at it, the acting chief counsel of the committee, Daniel Manelli, said that had it not been for the change in the Henkin interview, there would not have been a hearing. The committee thought it ought to address what it saw as irresponsibility. As one congressman said, "They still haven't got the message." While Counsel Manelli said that stopping distortion in news programs might not be susceptible to legislation, if what CBS was doing was disclosed so the public could see for itself what the "magic trick" was, this would be such an embarrassment to CBS that it would "discourage that sort of thing in the future." This could also mean if this kind of investigation was upheld that the role of Congress could be resumed to oversee editorial news judgments and practices. The view of the CBS News producer, Peter Davis, was that after that experience, broadcast organizations did few reports critical of congressional oversight of important government departments.[113]

The First Amendment protection for television news was thoroughly debated. While the vote was split, it could be said that Congress determined that the television press deserved constitutional protection from government review of its editorial decisions, as granted by the First Amendment. The effort and circumstances needed to defeat the Staggers subpoena, however, did show how enormously difficult such an undertaking might be on press issues. There is some doubt about whether such a campaign, however necessary for the protection of the broadcast press, could be mounted in the future, because of its cost or if commitment to a free press was lacking.

Stanton predicted, "The desire for government regulation will affect the next media generations. No matter how much a broadcaster talks about his freedom, there's still plenty of room to be harassed by government leaders, whether it's on the local or the national level. You won't have a free press that embraces broadcasting with the same freedoms as print until the Supreme Court comes down and says so."[114] Legal analysts would say the Court has not done so. Under new and pending proposals for government management of speech and news, a new Court could move toward approving greater regulation of the television press with a substantial reinterpretation of the First Amendment. The threat is once again a regulation that sounds good but in practice would abridge and curtail news and speech.

CHAPTER 5

c/∕

Executive Branch Censorship

The executive branch of government can suppress news by withholding information. It also can use government agencies, law enforcement, and the president's general power to prevent reporting of the news. It can indirectly censor the news by creating a dangerous regulatory environment in which government retaliation follows criticism of the president or publication of information the government doesn't want made public. As history shows, it also can directly threaten, intimidate, or order some of those in a licensed news media to change their news reporting to gain administration objectives.

The risk to the public is that news about what a president's administration is doing may not be reported or will be only cautiously reported.

One striking example of presidential intimidation of the press was the Nixon administration's searing and public campaign against print and broadcast news. The press reported some of this at the time. The intimidation efforts behind the scenes were not usually reported. The president's threats did not stop until the president was forced to resign by an impeachment proceeding.

Political Impact

Use of the Fairness Doctrine deliberately and intentionally to suppress news and opposing political views was kept secret by officials. For example, starting in 1963, the Kennedy administration used FCC power to harass conservative commentators critical of the administration. Under the Fairness Doctrine the administration's calculated campaign demanded reply time to conservative broadcasts. This was initially directed against conservative criticism of Kennedy's support of a nuclear test ban treaty with the Soviet Union. The administration figure active in this effort, Bill Ruder, Democratic campaign consultant and Kennedy's Assistant Secretary of Commerce, later described it as a "massive strategy … to challenge and harass right-wing broadcasters and hope that the challenges would be so costly to them that they would be inhibited, and decide it was too expensive to continue."[1]

This operation was expanded, funded, and established as the National Council for Civic Responsibility to run print ads against conservative broadcasters and provide training to assist in the filing of Fairness Doctrine complaints. The Johnson administration continued the strategy with increased funding.[2]

While one of Nixon's staff recommended they use FCC power under the Fairness Doctrine to harass stations as the Kennedy administration had done, this method was not duplicated. But nonetheless, "license harassment of stations considered unfriendly to the administration became a regular item on the agenda at the Nixon White House policy meetings."[3]

Richard Nixon had initially believed when running for state office in California that he could use television to go over the heads of the print press who he thought opposed him.[4] He then came to believe that members of the press, most particularly the television press, were out to get him. That view was reflected in a famous California press conference when he said, following his defeat in his campaign for governor of California in 1960, "Just think about how much you're going to be missing. You won't have Nixon to kick around any more, because, gentlemen, this is my last press conference."[5]

After his election as president, he wrote in his memoirs, "I considered the influential majority of the news media to be part of my political opposition ... I was prepared to do combat with the media in order to get my views and my programs to the people."[6] He viewed coverage by the television press as the most important. He told H. R. Haldeman, his chief of staff, "The only thing that matters is the TV."[7]

Television News as the Enemy

Nixon had taken office with the objective of disengaging from the Vietnam War with honor. As the Vietnam War continued, criticism of Nixon and the war by the press became more frequent. Henry Kissinger wrote of the president's underlying emotion at the time of his Vietnam withdrawal efforts. He said Nixon believed that "what he really faced was not a policy difference [about how best to withdraw] but the same liberal conspiracy that had sought to destroy him ever since the Alger Hiss case ..." [Kissinger explained, that for Nixon ...] "Here were all the old enemies in the press and in the Establishment, uniting once again; they would even accept if not urge the military defeat of their country to carry out the vendetta of a generation."[8] Alger Hiss had been a high-level official at the State Department. Congressman Nixon had accused him of acting for the Soviet Union. Hiss was tried and convicted of perjury for lying about some of his activities and jailed. Documents only later obtained from the Soviet Union's records were thought by some historians to show he was guilty of treason. At the time, the case polarized the political community and from some quarters led to constant criticism of Nixon for attacking Hiss.[9]

Nixon told his staff, "Just do what we want for the news on TV" and "We must realize the importance of TV."[10] He also had to deal with television coverage of the Vietnam War. Reporting the military losses, the lack of progress in the war, and domestic unrest discouraged

Americans and encouraged the North Vietnamese. There was a need, in the view of the White House, to stop or reduce the critical press coverage in addition to the desire for favorable political news coverage.[11]

But opposition to the Vietnam War was real and vigorous. A number of senators were calling for a unilateral cease-fire or a hastened withdrawal from Vietnam. Eleven anti-war resolutions were introduced in the Congress in less than a month after September 24, 1969. Students and others demonstrated relentlessly against participation in the war. Mainstream publications like *Time* and *Newsweek* reported a "crisis in leadership." Columnist David Broder wrote in the *Washington Post* that the same movement that broke Lyndon Johnson's authority in 1968 would break Richard Nixon's in 1969.[12] In response to press criticism, President Nixon and Vice President Agnew spoke publicly about their disdain for the press and the need to correct its "misinformation" and "distortions."[13] George Reedy, press secretary to President Johnson, explained that generally, "The only place a president gets real reactions from is the press." Since the staff supports his views and actions, when contrary views are reported, "A president can always blame the press. It's either the damn liberal press or the damn conservative press or the damn northern press." William Safire, Nixon's speechwriter and press advisor, later wrote, "I must have heard Richard Nixon say 'The Press is the enemy' a dozen times."[14] Nixon regarded reporters as his personal adversaries and saw press conferences as threatening.[15] He repeatedly lashed out at the media, calling their reporting about him "outrageous, vicious, distorted."[16] At first, he thought NBC was the worst television network, but then he came to believe CBS was the most aggressive in criticizing him. He created an "enemies list," which included the names of a number of journalists.

One staff member, Jeb Magruder, listed twenty-one requests from President Nixon in thirty days in October 1969 for action against unfair news coverage. He estimated there were many more made through others to improve the news coverage. President Nixon and Haldeman tried to develop a more focused assault on the press to get better coverage. Magruder proposed the plan "The Rifle vs. the Shotgun" to be more effective. The plan included creating an official monitoring system through the FCC to set up official action by it if the necessary proof could be found.[17] The new FCC chair, Dean Burch, would ask the networks for transcripts of their coverage. This would provide greater impact since the request would not be in the regular course for an FCC inquiry and would send a message. This was tried on one occasion with an immediate objection from the networks. But the message had been sent. Magruder also proposed to use the Antitrust Division of the Department of Justice to threaten the networks about their news coverage. For a while Nixon held this up, trying to use threats of antitrust litigation to stop adverse news coverage. Antitrust complaints against the networks were ultimately filed.[18]

Nixon's aides paid close attention to daily coverage. In the summer of 1970, for example, the White House conducted weekly surveys of network news, calculating to the second how much airtime was devoted to pro-Nixon and anti-Nixon stories.[19] Presidents do watch for press bias but Nixon can be seen as having a particularly intense hostility to television news and a willingness to act against it.

President Nixon decided he had to set a deadline for stopping the war, increasing the pressure and issuing in effect an ultimatum to Hanoi. To make this deadline effective, President Nixon believed there had to be a credible threat of military action, and it had to appear there was a minimum he could give in negotiating a solution. It also had to appear that the country was behind him. This made television coverage of this Nixon position a priority for the White House and Nixon made several prime-time speeches to support it.

There was no existing mechanism for any response by the opposition to the president's speeches. CBS inaugurated a series of prime-time programs, the *Loyal Opposition*, so the political party not in power could air its views. The head of the Democratic National Committee appeared in the first program to respond to a number of the president's speeches on the Vietnam War, the economy, civil rights, and other issues. Charles

Colson, Nixon's White House deputy counsel, wrote, "The president and I believed that Frank Stanton's *Loyal Opposition* program was totally politically motivated, in poor taste, and biased in its presentations. I talked with Dean Burch about it. Dean's response was very professional. We did have a legitimate complaint." Colson ordered the Republican National Committee to file with the FCC to claim network time to reply to that DNC appearance under the Fairness Doctrine. He argued the DNC presentation was an independent presentation on Democratic issues and not just a reply to the president's speeches. Colson wrote to Haldeman that the *Loyal Opposition* program and "other similar programs talked about by the other two networks would defeat the primary objective of the Nixon news domination campaign."[20] The FCC ruled in Nixon's favor and granted the RNC that reply time. When the DNC appealed, some time later the reviewing circuit court reversed and the RNC did not get the reply time.[21] Colson's effort to use the FCC in this way was unsuccessful. But the White House saw Colson's complaint as useful nonetheless. One press official, Herbert Klein, said that perhaps it "slowed down CBS in moving to grant other equal opportunities to the Democrats."[22] This may not be a legal offense but it demonstrates how easily a government agency regulation, despite its intent, can be used to distort the news.

Much later, in September 1970, Nixon sent Colson to each of the network heads—Paley at CBS, Goodman at NBC, and Goldenson at ABC—to stop the grant of any further prime time to the Democrats to reduce their political appearances on television. Colson reported that the networks were unusually accommodating "with their economic fortunes held on a tight tether by the Federal Communications Commission ... the significance of my visit was not lost on them." He said they were "scared and we should continue to take a very tough line, face to face, and in other ways." When this memo became public during the Watergate break-in congressional hearings, the networks disagreed vigorously with its style and substance. Participants and commentators have pointed out that Colson was obviously writing his memos to impress his boss, Nixon, and Haldeman, Nixon's chief of staff. But threats from government officials can have a serious impact in a regulated industry.[23]

The White House announced President Nixon would address the nation on Vietnam on November 3, 1969. Speculation grew as some thought Nixon would announce a pullout while others expected an increase in troop force or some other step. President Nixon wanted to solidify national support for the war to reach a negotiated settlement and decided he would reach the public over the heads of what he considered the opposition press. To prepare for any adverse response in the news coverage of his speech, he ordered Haldeman to hit the networks "hard on the positive side and taking them on if they take a negative view." On November 1 he met with Haldeman, who made notes of the meeting and of the instructions, one of which was "Concentrate only on the three nets." Haldeman noted the next day, "Nov. 2 ... wants us to buy a full page ad in the *New York Times* to run an editorial blasting them for what he expects their coverage and editorial to be. Also wants us ready to hit all the TV networks for commentators' knocking the speech ..."[24]

Nixon had to reach the "silent majority," as he described it, and gain some support for continuing the war about which the nation was undecided, wanting to leave but not in defeat. President Nixon noted in his memoirs that the message was, "We were going to keep our commitment in Vietnam. We were going to continue fighting until the Communists agreed to negotiate a fair honorable peace or until the South Vietnamese were able to defend themselves on their own—whichever came first."[25]

Immediately following the speech, CBS provided "instant analysis." NBC correspondent Edwin Newman reported there was nothing new in the speech. Marvin Kalb of CBS, however, went farther and said that for those who were not so willing to trust the president to get an honorable end to the war, there was no announcement on troop withdrawals or a timetable for one. He added that a letter from the North Vietnam leader, Ho Chi Minh, was not a flat rejection as Nixon claimed, but contained some of the "softest, most accommodating language found in a Communist document on the war in recent years."[26] The appearance of a leading Democratic figure, Averell Harriman, who had negotiated with the North Vietnamese before, to comment on the air immediately after Nixon's speech that he would do it differently and to say he had doubts about the Nixon approach, was greeted at the White House with outrage.[27] In addition, the president complained that the viewing public had no chance to reflect on what the president had said before being told by purported impartial reporters that Nixon was wrong and even not to be believed.[28]

As it turned out, the Nixon speech was a triumph with a majority of the public. Nixon wrote, "There were signs that the critics and the commentators were unrepresentative of public opinion …" The Congress became less critical of the Nixon stance on the war and more evenly split after the strong, favorable public reaction to the speech. Nixon had enough support. "Now for a time at least the enemy could no longer count on dissent in America … I had the public support I needed to continue a policy of waging war in Vietnam and negotiating for peace in Paris until we could bring the war to an honorable and successful conclusion."[29]

The FCC took up the CBS instant analysis question, noting there had been complaints about news bias and distortion, and complaints of possible government intimidation of the press. It found no extrinsic evidence of bias outside the report itself, which was its test for action, and decided not to act. It did not speak to the question of intimidation.[30]

Nixon then decided to go after the networks directly and had Agnew go on the attack. Agnew did so in his speeches and now included some of the print press. Hubert Humphrey charged that the vice president's attacks were part of the Nixon administration's "media guerilla warfare" and that "Nixon is condoning it."[31] After a criticism of Nixon by Chet Huntley from NBC News was publicly reported and the White House responded, Huntley called the White House and denied making the criticism. Magruder wrote, "The point about this whole thing is that we don't care about Huntley ... What we are trying to do here is to tear down the institution."[32] Riding herd on the networks, Colson noted that President Goodman of NBC had made three speeches "warning of the danger of government interference and political pressure on the networks."[33]

On November 17, 1970, after Burch's demand of stations for copies of the transcripts of their Nixon speech coverage became public, Colson wrote Haldeman, "Through Dean Burch [Republican chairman of the FCC] we should keep heavy regulation pressures building. The networks are fully aware that we can influence the FCC in policy matters and this is of course a great concern to them."[34]

The prospect of government intimidating the press for political (or personal) reasons is much more likely to be quietly successful when the government has avenues readily available to it to harass and manipulate the press with threats of government action against it under the cover of some government regulation. William Safire, who was part of the White House group, wrote, as noted earlier, "... Was this so-called 'anti-media' campaign encouraged, directed, and urged on by the president himself? Did this alleged campaign to defame and intimidate Nixon-hating newsmen succeed in isolating and weakening them politically? ... The answer to all these questions is, sadly, yes ... I must have heard Richard Nixon say, 'The Press is the enemy' a dozen times."[35] Nixon told Haldeman in February 1971, "Be sure to hit the networks. Top level. Use our biggest guns."[36]

Nixon held his own personal meetings with each of the network heads in early 1971. Colson wrote a memo of Nixon's March 9 meeting with CBS, at which their "Fairness Doctrine problems" were discussed. Nixon also referred to the CBS-proposed opposition party series and warned CBS against giving broadcasters time to reply to presidential speeches. He said the pattern of programming had been set before he became president and he had lived under it. Now that he was in office, there should be no changes in policies for prime-time coverage for him, but only for the next president.[37]

When Nixon considered using the Department of Justice and the antitrust laws against the television networks if they didn't change their news coverage, Colson called that use an economic club. Nixon responded, "As far as screwing them is concerned, I'm very glad to do it."[38]

When Colson heard that a congressional committee would take up the investigation of *The Selling of the Pentagon*, he urged the White House to support it and wrote the president that this was an "opportunity to raise serious doubts in the public mind about network reporting." Nixon told Haldeman to circulate copies of the *Washington Post* editorial critical of the editing in the program to newspapers and members of Congress, told Colson to call Stanton, and told Haldeman to "get someone to work on it." On March 31, Nixon ordered Haldeman to get from J. Edgar Hoover, head of the FBI, a "rundown on top CBS people," including Kalb (a reporter) and Salant, president of CBS News.[39] Colson talked with Paley and Stanton and concluded that the White House might do better by helping CBS with the Staggers motion and establishing a better relationship with CBS.[40]

Then, when it later appeared that Nixon could get the blame if Republicans supported the Staggers contempt of Congress motion, and Nixon's attorney general would have to bring the court proceeding to carry it out and try to put Stanton in jail, Nixon changed his view on supporting Staggers. Herb Klein explained that Nixon changed course when he talked with him in San Clemente just before the vote on July 12. Klein warned the president that Nixon would be seen as trying to jail a person of great stature and trying to destroy CBS by taking away its licenses, and that this would be covered all over the press right before the presidential election, and would be a terrible political mistake.[41] Gerald Ford, the leading Republican in the House, had earlier discussed this problem with the Republican House members and the White House staff. Ford thought a case could legitimately be made for opposing the committee subpoena and that "television and radio were covered by the First Amendment."[42]

Another issue was political. Would a Republican White House be in an awkward position if it carried out a decision of a Democratic committee on this press issue? Ford was against supporting the subpoena. When Colson had told Haldeman his thought of improving relations with CBS by helping them, Haldeman replied, "Get something for it."[43] Colson said he conveyed to Nixon the recommendations against supporting the contempt vote. The president released the Republicans in the House to vote their conscience shortly before the vote.[44] Gerald Ford reportedly worked all night to turn the Republican House members around.[45] After the congressional vote against the contempt on July 13, Colson reported to Haldeman that they did get votes for Stanton, but he confided to Haldeman, "I don't think Stanton needed our help," but he was going to try to get what he could from him, as Haldeman had suggested. He wrote Haldeman on July 14 that Paley called with "profuse" thanks.[46]

A 1997 *Washington Post* story reported that a Maryland Republican official, Sandy Lankler, had called Colson to discuss the situation. According to the *Post*, Colson wrote on a legal pad he used for the call that if there was a report Colson thought wrong, he could call Lankler for changes and CBS News headquarters would do it.[47] The *Post* story reported that after the Staggers vote, Lankler took Stanton to see Colson about the arrangement. In his written memo reporting on this July 15 meeting that Colson sent Haldeman on July 20, Colson wrote that using material he had prepared for the meeting, he compared the CBS coverage with that of the other two networks. He argued Nixon had been treated badly by CBS in its coverage of the economy, Nixon's popularity in the polls, and a list of other subjects, all of which he wished corrected. He reported to Haldeman in his July 20 memo that he had told Stanton "all the administration wanted was 'occasional fairness' and pressed hard on what he called 'dishonest journalism.' "[48] Colson concluded in his report to Haldeman, "I don't expect great things. Anything we gain will be a plus." He added that he thought CBS had given them a little better treatment the last few nights but noted that this was a typical pattern. "We get a rash of very good coverage for a few weeks, then they fall back into their old ways." The report notes that the president was "verbally briefed."[49]

In his report to Haldeman about the July 15 meeting with Stanton, Colson did not claim that he thought he already had a deal or that he had cut a deal with Stanton for favorable news coverage. His report to Haldeman and presumably the verbal briefing of Nixon reflected rather that he was trying to "get something" for it, in return for helping Stanton with the Staggers contempt motion, but had made no progress on that. Stanton later said in an interview that he was "apprehensive about the meeting with Colson because it might be misconstrued." He said he "listened to Colson's complaints about CBS coverage, noted them, and told Colson he would listen to any pitches they wanted to make in the future." Stanton said that what he heard from Colson were generally the same complaints as before, and he made no commitments about news coverage. He said he did not need any help from Colson.[50]

Criticism of the press is customary. But using state power to suppress the news or censor the press is not only an abuse of executive power, it is also an injury to the public. Public relations plans for favorable news coverage are a dime a dozen. But White House threats of punishment to gain favorable news coverage is something else. It is sometimes not recognized, when official government management of the press is promoted for what is described as a good social purpose, that government threats against the press can be much more effective when the press is regulated and already subject to some government interference, as was the case for the broadcast press. If news content is already subject to government revision, abuse of power over the press can be even more easily carried out. It also can be harder to detect.

Government Threats and News Suppression

The CBS news program, *The Selling of the Pentagon*, was produced when Richard Salant, who had served in the military, concluded the American public should be informed about what the Pentagon was doing with its massive distribution of propaganda for the Vietnam War. As president of CBS News, he had originated the idea for the program and had followed the program closely. When the program was attacked, he repeatedly argued that no one had shown that the conclusions of *The Selling of the Pentagon* documentary were wrong or that they should be kept from the public. In the program *Postscript*, Agnew voiced his criticisms of the program. The transcript reads:

CBS Correspondent Mudd: The most highly placed critic has been the Vice President. He has leveled five different attacks on the broadcast, the most widely reported in Boston last Thursday night.

[A video clip showed Vice President Agnew making a speech in Boston to a cheering audience.]

Agnew: The news organization that makes such charges should itself be free of any taint of misinformation, distortion, and propaganda in its own operations. [Sustained applause.] In this regard, it is the CBS television network, not the Department of Defense, that leaves much to be desired in terms of "the free flow of information." [Sustained applause.]

Mudd: In his speech last Thursday, the Vice President did not specify any "misinformation, distortion, and propaganda" he had found in *The Selling of the Pentagon*. He did, however, call it, quote, "a subtle but vicious broadside against the nation's defense establishment …"[51]

Richard Salant appeared on the *Postscript* program and responded to the criticism. He said, "No one has refuted the essential accuracy of *The Selling of the Pentagon*. You have seen and you have heard Pentagon activities for yourselves: the manipulation of news, the staging of events, and the selling to the public of the Pentagon's points of view. None of our critics has said that these things didn't happen or weren't done—and so the validity of the broadcast stands unscathed ..."[52]

On March 24, Agnew went after the CBS rebroadcast and the *Postscript*. He accused CBS of deliberately publishing untruths and said he was totally dissatisfied with what CBS called a rebuttal by administration officials.[53] He said he was not allowed to decide what he could say and that his remarks had been edited. The substance of the program—that the Pentagon was engaged officially and deliberately in improper propaganda activities—was not addressed.

The power of the executive branch to censor by making public allegations is not readily defended against. There is no reliable way to measure the impact on the public of such executive branch condemnations of the press. So public belief in constitutional protection of the news media is of great importance, as newspapers and magazines have learned over many years. Appeals and litigation may not provide enough protection soon enough even when successful. It is public acceptance and endorsement of that First Amendment protection that is crucial. But when censorship is carried out under cover of broadcast regulations, the public will not know of it and cannot question it.

In December 1971, Herb Klein visited each of the network heads with, as he said, a friendly warning that if their news coverage did not change, antitrust suits would be brought against them. The networks did not change their news coverage to satisfy the Nixon administration about the Vietnam War or to support the president as Klein suggested.[54] In 1972, the Justice Department did bring antitrust suits against the three networks and they moved to dismiss them as improperly brought. Herb Klein later confided that he could see how the timing and the outdated facts in the antitrust complaints would have made the networks suspicious.[55] The cases had been held up by Nixon himself, who wanted to use the threat of the lawsuits to gain more favorable news coverage from the television networks, but when this did not work, John Ehrlichman, Counsel and Assistant to the President for Domestic Affairs, in a note to the president in September 1971, urged that the antitrust case against the networks go forward. President Nixon's handwritten note said, "Vitally important to plan the PR aspects. Get Coulson [*sic*] in on this phase of it."[56]

The antitrust cases sought to make more binding FCC regulations already adopted to enjoin the three networks from broadcasting any programming in the early evening time periods, six to eight PM, and from owning any financial interests in programs bought from others. A district court at first dismissed the suit without prejudice because of the allegations and the evidence that it had been brought improperly. Stanton filed an affidavit with the court that Colson had called him to say, in substance, "We'll bring you to your knees in Wall Street and on Madison Avenue." On a later *60 Minutes* program, Colson denied saying this.[57]

Colson was an eager participant and understood he was to ride herd on the networks. He has written he was excited at working for "the single most important man in the world." More seasoned hands may have had a more balanced view. Some learned not to pay that much attention to Nixon's outbursts and saw confusion in his trying to deal with domestic issues raised by young demonstrators, as opposed to his skill in international diplomacy, including with China and Russia, as Henry Kissinger has reported.[58] Leonard Garment, White House counsel to the president, has said Nixon was able to achieve international diplomatic successes, such as the breakthrough to China and Russia and important domestic advances, but he would get very emotional and bitter on the subject of the networks. He said those familiar with Nixon often overlooked his emotional statements. For all his accomplishments, Garment said, Nixon "saw enemies." Press coverage may have been unforgiving, but he could not deal skillfully with it and responded with distrust and outrage.[59]

The *Washington Post* reported on the April 1972 break-in at the home of CBS television reporter, Dan Rather. The acting FBI director, William D. Ruckelshaus, made a statement later confirmed by a White House spokesman that telephones of thirteen government officials and four reporters had been tapped between May 1969 and February 1971. It also said the taps had been authorized personally by President Nixon. Nixon used the FBI to investigate CBS correspondents Marvin Kalb and Daniel Schorr and used the IRS to audit Kalb's tax returns.[60]

The break-in by Nixon operatives at the Watergate complex to see what the DNC might have and use against Nixon during the election campaign was first reported by the *Washington Post* and the press treated it as a local story, "inside the Beltway." In June 1972, the three networks reported this, accepting the White House characterization of it as a third-rate burglary and its statement that Nixon was not involved.

At an Oval Office meeting on September 15, 1972, White House transcripts reflect a conversation between Nixon and John Dean, his counsel, in which Dean brought up the *Washington Post* investigation of the break-in at the DNC. Nixon mentioned his plans to have the broadcast station licenses of the *Washington Post* taken away at their license renewal time. The transcript reads:

President: The main thing is the *Post* is going to have damnable, damnable problems out of this one. They have a television station ... and they're going to have to get [their license] renewed.

Haldeman: They've got a radio station too.

President: Does that come up too? The point is, when does it come up?

Dean: I don't know. But the practice of non-licensees filing on top of licensees has certainly gotten more ... active in ... this area.

President: And it's going to be goddamn active here.[61]

There were discussions at the FCC about forcing the networks to sell their five owned broadcast stations. Colson described to Stanton an administration plan that would bring about the loss of the CBS broadcast licenses and impose direct licensing of the networks.[62]

The White House was on full alert to prevent what was at that point still a local Washington, DC story about the Watergate break-in from expanding nationally until after the upcoming November presidential election.

CBS decided to devote two long segments to the Watergate event. On Walter Cronkite's *CBS Evening News*, broadcast on October 27, 1972, shortly before the presidential election, CBS reported on charges of a "high-level campaign of political sabotage and espionage apparently unparalleled in American history." Colson had earlier called Stanton to say the report would be unfair. Stanton had seen it at an early feed at 6:30 PM and did not agree. Colson then said the question was not fairness; the program should not be broadcast at all. Stanton said CBS News would broadcast the report. On October 27, 1972, Colson asked for the license renewal dates of stations owned by the *Washington Post*. Subsequently, the *Washington Post* station in Florida was challenged.

Stanton called William Paley, chair of CBS and its chief executive officer, to warn him about the call from Colson about the Cronkite broadcast and suggested Paley watch it when broadcast at 7:00 PM. When CBS did broadcast the story, the break-in became a national story. This CBS report on the scandal less than a week before the date of the presidential election provoked outrage at the White House and an Oval Office discussion on the morning of October 28. The *Post* transcript of the Nixon conversation reads in part, "Nixon said [to Colson] with apparent sarcasm, 'I was telling Bob [Haldeman] how beautifully you're controlling CBS.' " After the White House conveyed its anger to CBS, William S. Paley called Colson on November 3. "Paley was pleading," Colson exulted in a memo he wrote to Haldeman. "My voice was steely cold … Chalk up one for our new task of destroying the old establishment."

Daniel Schorr wrote that Walter Cronkite originally planned "to devote roughly half of two *Evening News* programs to extensive recapitulations of all that was known about Watergate … But after the hard-hitting first segment, White House counsel Charles Colson made a furious telephone call to CBS chairman William S. Paley, threatening retaliation against CBS through the regulatory powers of the Federal Communication Commission. Paley promised to kill the second segment."[63]

In her biography of Paley, Sally Bedell Smith writes, "Colson was more exercised than usual in his call to Paley on October 28 [about the report] … The previous April, Nixon's Justice Department had filed an antitrust suit against the networks and the FCC was debating whether to force each of the networks to sell its complement of five local television stations. 'Colson talked to me for a long time,' Paley recalled. 'He was pretty vicious.' "[64] However, other news reporters picked up the first segment. *Washington Post* publisher Katharine Graham would later say that it was Cronkite's CBS News report that made Watergate a national story.

After the first segment, Paley convened a meeting with Stanton, Richard Salant, and other top CBS executives. "Paley never mentioned the Colson call, but he was extremely agitated. He insisted that the first segment had been too long and had violated CBS standards by mingling fact and opinion." Salant went back to the news offices and worked to revise the second segment. Smith writes, "The second segment ran seven minutes instead of the planned fourteen and in the view of some had become a superficial summary …"[65]

This is an obvious example of pressure and threats of harm made by government to silence a news report by a broadcaster licensed to serve the public interest. It succeeded in restraining part of what otherwise would have been reported about a criminal break-in by the president's political party or others aligned with it, news that was relevant to the presidential election, and right before the election itself. The broadcast press would have reported this information about other regulated industries.[66] The importance to the public of presenting a report on such an abuse of power is brought home by the fact that there is no remedy after the event that can be effective.

The Nixon reelection campaign turned out to be highly successful. Nixon had written that modern presidents must try to master the art of manipulating the media. Some thought Nixon's success was partly because of his intimidation of the press. Some political observers concluded, "The press generally gave the president a free ride." The press did not dare embarrass or anger the White House and the conclusion was that this "coupled with the shrewd manipulation of the media by Nixon officials, has moved the American news system closer to becoming a propaganda arm of the administration in power."[67] Congressman Van Deerlin, who was a staunch defender of press freedoms, decried what he saw as a "surrender" to the Nixon administration. William Safire, a speechwriter for the president who was in a position to know, wrote that it was obvious to White House insiders that their anti-press activities forced the networks to tone down criticism of presidential speeches.[68]

Network executives spoke little publicly about the private threats Nixon made against them. One reason was "the fear of escalating the cold war into the open against an enemy who seemed to control the weapons of massive retaliation."[69] In addition, disclosure could affect the reporters and their credibility. NBC News President Reuven Frank supported the decision by NBC's President Julian Goodman not to speak publicly about Nixon's private threats so the reporters could do their job of reporting on the White House and remain impartial. CBS President Frank Stanton made that decision also. He believed it was necessary so CBS News in its reporting would not be defending its own interests, but rather fulfilling its professional obligations to cover the news. Some network-affiliated stations sided with the administration's criticisms of network news. Some did not. The print press did report at the time that broadcast network managements were confronted with serious threats of government retaliatory responses seeking to suppress network news.

After Nixon won the election by a large margin, he tried to bring broadcast news into line. The administration released a report showing that possibly sixty-seven major new stations could be added to the television spectrum in one hundred larger urban markets. This would be sufficient for the creation of a fourth and competing television network. This action and a number of other punishing steps could be taken if the three networks—ABC, CBS, and NBC—did not shape up their coverage of Nixon to meet the views of the incumbent administration. In addition, Dr. Clay Whitehead, director of the White House office of telecommunications policy, announced that licensed stations that failed "to correct imbalance or consistent bias from the networks" in their news reports or that even acquiesced by silence could only be considered willing participants "to be held fully accountable … at license renewal time."[70]

This was an extraordinary threat even for those times and reveals the overriding confidence the administration had gained from its intimidation of the broadcasting industry. *Variety* magazine reported that the network-affiliated stations were nervous about attacks on TV journalism and had to be concerned about the government's apparent attempt to split the networks and stations with the news issue.

Calling for "balance" or objecting to "imbalance" looks on its face to be an appeal for evenhandedness. But often when advanced by the government as something the press should do—achieve balance—it is often rhetorical pressure from the government to suppress or change opposing or unfavorable news reports in the name of balance. That continues to this day as an often-used government tactic.

Robert Sherrill, Washington correspondent for *The Nation*, wrote about the Nixon efforts. He reported, "Julian Goodman, President of NBC, and Frank Stanton, President of CBS, agree that the 'heavy-handed' government attempts to 'influence' network news is something new to their experience. They have pointed out that never before has there been an administration that publicly attempted to humiliate and whip the networks into line."[71]

The continuing oversight by government of television news together with the Nixon attacks was difficult for the networks to manage. Any rational broadcaster could not ignore the regulations and government threats. Salant said that the decision "not to do the story" was the problem. Salant said, "It takes an awful lot of guts for management to ignore these attacks, because they literally mean their economic life." When asked why the networks didn't just shrug it off, David Adams, NBC's experienced and brilliant staff chief, went directly to the heart of the matter. He could say it in four words: "We're a licensed press."[72]

Sherrill concluded, "There is also a limit, some believe, to how much of a drubbing television newsmen and their bosses can take from the government before they begin to give a little, to hold back the tough shots, to give even less depth to their coverage than is customary." He reported that "without exception," the network and news division heads insisted that this "is not what has happened." But he adds, "There are those who feel this could be a consequence."[73] Sherrill obtained unusual access to the views of the network chiefs. He concluded his report with this:

NBC News President Reuven Frank: Every time you undertake something that is just not quite as bland as all the other things you do, you worry about, will I be cited by the FCC?

NBC senior staff executive David Adams: If you are operating in the newsroom of a local broadcast station, and you are doing your job, and one day three lawyers from your company walk in with an FCC inquiry about something you have treated, and you spend 18 hours going through your files, maybe next time you have an issue you want to treat you'll think, "Jesus Christ, do I have to go through all that?" and you may not do it the same way.

CBS News President Richard Salant: I have to worry about guys out in the field getting unhappy about being taken off the job to answer these things, and saying "Oh, to hell with it, I'll do stuff on ecology from here on out."

CBS President Frank Stanton: These things are bound to have an effect on your organization, no matter how much you try to protect your staff. After several experiences where they are pulled up short, where they have to testify, it's bound to have an erosive effect.[74]

White House threats and actions against the television networks were frequent, serious, and cumulative. Threats and divisive arguments were also made against the network-affiliated stations. There were threats made in private that the administration would damage the network economies, subject the networks to direct regulation and its burdens, revoke station licenses, change spectrum use to reduce network broadcasting, and punish any network that provided broadcast time to the political opposition. The regulatory scheme of managing news content of the broadcast press, enforced by the FCC with investigations and the threat of possible license denials or short-term licenses, made the administration attacks far more effective than otherwise would have been the case.

What has been summarized represents only some of what was known at the time by the targets of the government's abuse of power. Nixon told John Dean, his White House legal counsel, in 1973, "One hell of a lot of people don't give one damn about this issue of the suppression of the press."[75] Herbert Klein, chief White House press official, confided years later in an interview that in addition to what was known at the time, Nixon's campaign against the press was for real and "would have gotten ugly."[76]

CHAPTER 6

⌒ℳ⌒

The FCC Revokes the Fairness Doctrine

I n 1987, the FCC found that its own Fairness Doctrine did not promote news coverage of controversial issues and contrasting views as had been claimed. It did not stimulate debate. The FCC, after an extensive review, found that in practice, the doctrine "suppressed" news coverage in practice. The FCC found that broadcasters avoided controversial issues because of the threat and the burden—financial and operational—of a government investigation into news reports and broadcast news judgment. This threat was made far more powerful by the threat of possible adverse license renewal rulings. The FCC concluded the doctrine had departed from the traditions of freedom in the United States and was of the view that, in practice, it was not in the public interest. Based on an extensive record of testimony and fact, it vacated the doctrine. This review was an unusual action by a government agency, examining whether its own regulations had served the public interest, and finding they did not, ending those regulations.

It was argued in the early years of the broadcast industry that regulation was useful because it prevented broadcasters who held licenses in markets where there were only a few stations from abusing their power to select programming and views for broadcast. If some views were excluded from the air, they might not be heard in reply or otherwise. When the industry matured, there were many television stations—well over thirteen hundred and over twelve television networks. These numbers would increase over time and deliver many points of view, more than any viewer could readily comprehend. Nevertheless, the government continued the Fairness Doctrine until 1987. Congress favored FCC control. Congress had oversight responsibility and authority. Congress provided the FCC's budget, and the FCC listened to Congress.

What started out as a rule for robust debate about controversial issues became a critical focus and general standard for license renewal judgments. The FCC called the doctrine the "single most important requirement of operation in the public interest—the *sine qua non* for grant of a renewal of license."[1] This made the reporting of news to the satisfaction of a majority of FCC commissioners acting under the Fairness Doctrine a priority of state regulatory control.

The FCC decision to end its enforcement of the Fairness Doctrine set out considerable factual and historical information. What can be learned from this actual, not laboratory, demonstration and its description of the experience of broadcast news with government regulation is really quite extraordinary. The FCC set out the facts it found on the evidence in considerable detail in its 1985 report and then in its 1987 decision revoking the doctrine.

On appeal, the Washington, DC Circuit Court affirmed the commission's decision (without dissent). The Supreme Court declined to take *certiorari*, that is to review the decision, and so the decision of the circuit court stands as law. That appellate circuit court upheld in all respects the decision of the FCC, that the Fairness Doctrine suppressed news and chilled speech.

It noted at the outset that the FCC had considered more than one hundred formal comments and reply comments, hundreds of informal submissions, and two days of oral arguments. The circuit court said:

Based upon compelling evidence of record, the Commission, in its 1985 [decision in 1987] Fairness Report, concluded that the Fairness Doctrine disserved the public interest. Evaluating the explosive growth in the number and types of information sources available in the marketplace, the Commission found that the public has "access to a multitude of viewpoints without the need or danger of regulatory intervention."

The court upheld the FCC's finding that the Fairness Doctrine "chills" speech and that "in stark contravention of its purpose, [the Doctrine] operates as a pervasive and significant impediment to the broadcasting of controversial issues of public importance." The FCC concluded, as partly itemized here, that enforcement of the Fairness Doctrine:

Suppressed news and chilled speech;

Inhibited the expression of unpopular opinion;

Placed government in the intrusive role of scrutinizing program content;

Created the opportunity for abuse for partisan political purposes; and

Imposed unnecessary costs upon both broadcasters and the Commission.[2]

The circuit court upheld the FCC finding that the doctrine "chills" speech and deterred broadcast of news and speech because, among other things, the FCC process was vague and unpredictable:

The Commission determined that the Fairness Doctrine, in operation, thwarts the purpose that it is designed to promote. Instead of enhancing the discussion of controversial issues of public importance, the Commission found that the Fairness Doctrine, in operation, "chills" speech.

Each time a broadcaster presents what may be construed as a controversial issue of public importance, it runs the risk of a complaint being filed, resulting in litigation and penalties, including loss of license. This risk still exists even if a broadcaster has met its obligations by airing contrasting viewpoints, because the process necessarily involves a vague standard, the application and meeting of which is hard to predict.[3]

Intimidation and Suppression by FCC Investigations

The circuit court said:

Licensees are intimidated by the FCC from broadcasting even when they believe they are right. More important, however, even if it intends to or believes that it has presented balanced coverage of a controversial issue, it may be inhibited by the expenses of being second-guessed by the government in defending a Fairness Doctrine complaint at the Commission, and if the case is litigated in court, the costs of an appeal.

These various incentives to avoid controversy are not speculative. The record compiled in the fairness inquiry revealed over sixty reported instances in which the Fairness Doctrine inhibited broadcasters' coverage of controversial issues. Those news subjects were denied the public.

The record contained numerous instances in which the broadcasters decided that it was "safer" to avoid broadcasting specific controversial issue programming, such as series prepared for local news programs, than to incur the potentially burdensome administrative, legal, personnel, and reputational costs of either complying with the Doctrine or defending their editorial decisions to governmental authorities. Indeed, in the 1985 Fairness Report, the Commission gave specific examples of instances in which broadcasters declined to air programming on such important controversial issues such as the nuclear arms race, religious cults, municipal salaries, and other significant matters of public concern. In each instance, the broadcaster identified the Fairness Doctrine as the cause for its decision.[4]

The Lessons of the Fairness Doctrine

The overall impact of the Fairness Doctrine on the broadcast press was to restrict reporting on controversial issues. The most telling finding of the commission was that "the fear of governmental sanction resulting from the doctrine creates a climate of timidity and fear, which deters the coverage of controversial issue programming." Stations were intimidated and could not report the news when they believed they were right and the FCC wrong.[5]

This described a result the Supreme Court had not even considered when upholding the Fairness Doctrine and investing in its attractive promise of great benefit to the public. The impact of government enforcement investigations, and even more, the impact of an ever-present threat of such government investigation are inherent in any such state regulation. The state must see what its regulations are doing and enforce them. This requires investigation. This would necessarily be true of any other, similar government regulation of television news and speech enforced by a central government agency.

This lesson of the Fairness Doctrine bears directly on the use of other regulations of news content now being proposed at the FCC. The First Amendment aside, the experience of the Fairness Doctrine is that a theory of benign government regulation to provide contrasting views and opinions on issues will result, in practice, in the suppression of news and speech. That same theory, when used to support government objectives of balance, localism, diversity, and other goals through regulation or control of news and speech, will also necessarily result, in practice, in the suppression of news and speech.

The reviewing circuit court, in striking down the Fairness Doctrine, ended on the concern expressed by the commission in repealing the regulation. It spoke to the ability of the public to determine its own future.

Foremost in suppression and silencing opposing views, the Fairness Doctrine provided a dangerous weapon that government officials could use against the broadcast press when it criticized governmental policy: "The Commission expressed concern that the Fairness Doctrine provides a dangerous vehicle—which had been exercised in the past by unscrupulous officials—for the intimidation of broadcasters who criticize governmental policy."[6]

This is, of course, the most likely and dangerous result of granting or legitimizing any use by the government of state power to affect the substance of news or speech content.

As to the basic theory of government regulation and control of the television press for information and political and social goals, the circuit court concluded from its review of the FCC experience and from its own independent review that the following critical lesson can be taken from the Fairness Doctrine:

> The Fairness Doctrine in operation disserves both the public's right to diverse sources of information and the broadcaster's interest in free expression. Its chilling effect thwarts its intended purpose ...[7]

The circuit court explicitly upheld the conclusion of the commission, stating, "We hold, therefore, that under the constitutional standard established by *Red Lion* and its progeny, the Fairness Doctrine contravenes the First Amendment and its enforcement is no longer in the public interest."[8]

Bias

The circuit court spoke to claims of bias in news coverage and press error, which are a recurring contention and sometimes the fact. It is a frequent reason asserted as warranting government review and censorship of all the press:

> Of course, the press is not always accurate, or even responsible, and may not present full and fair debate on important public issues. But the balance struck by the First Amendment with respect to the press is that society must take the risk that occasional debate on vital matters will not be comprehensive and that all viewpoints may not be expressed ... Any other accommodation—any other system that would supplant private control of the press with the heavy hand of government intrusion—would make the government the censor of what the people may read and know.[9]

The court firmly outlawed government intervention. "Consequently, a cardinal tenet of the First Amendment is that governmental intervention in the marketplace of ideas of the sort involved in the enforcement of the Fairness Doctrine is not acceptable and should not be tolerated."[10]

Indispensable Speech

Why protect news and speech on matters of public concern from government oversight when the government claims that it can best make decisions for the public about free speech and a free press? The circuit court invoked a Supreme Court ruling. The Supreme Court held that under the Constitution, the expression of opinion on matters of public concern is "entitled to the most exacting degree of First Amendment protection." This type of speech is "indispensable to decision making in a democracy." It goes to the heart of our democracy since "speech concerning public affairs is more than a self-expression; it is the essence of self-government." There is a further reason, even more significant. The people in a democratic system "are entrusted with the responsibility for judging and evaluating the relative merits of conflicting arguments." The government is "forbidden to assume the task of ultimate judgment, lest the people lose their ability to govern themselves."[11]

The circuit court repeated the FCC conclusion that the effect of the Fairness Doctrine was to "overall lessen the flow of diverse viewpoints to the public."[12] Proposals to regulate broadcast news with similar doctrines and regulations to provide localism and diversity, now pending before the FCC, will also lessen the flow of diverse viewpoints.

The court also spoke to the self-censorship in the broadcast industry when such regulations were imposed. It said that a "company policy" against presenting certain kinds of programming or material to the public, which had been found in a number of instances, revealed the success of censorship, not journalism inadequacy.

Importantly for the regulatory proposals now pending at the commission, the court said the commission evaluated not only "viewpoints" and "issues" covered by the broadcasters, but the "manner and balance of coverage."[13] Future proposals to regulate "manner and balance" on the theory that such a regulation is valid because it is different from the Fairness Doctrine would have to confront this warning as well.

Moreover, when the court and the commission held that the doctrine indisputably represented "an intrusion into a broadcaster's editorial judgment," they found this came not only from the doctrine's enforcement but also from the threat of enforcement. This is in real life, as opposed to the often-paper world of government proceedings, a major vice of news and speech control regulations. The circuit court identified the overpowering threat of any government power to review speech and news as pervasively harmful to a free press, democracy, and self-government. It is not just the actual review by government of news and speech in a democracy that is out of place. It is the threat of that review and the consequence of that threat to the broadcast of news, speech, thought, and ideas, and their freedom from government intrusion and control that is so dispiriting and so destructive.

The Broadcast Press Should Be a Free Press

Finally, the circuit court pointed out:

In this regard, we note that sound journalistic practice already encourages broadcasters to cover contrasting viewpoints on a topic of controversy. The problem is not with the goal of the Fairness Doctrine, it is with the use of government intrusion as the means to achieve that goal ... We believe that, in the absence of the Doctrine, broadcasters will more readily cover controversial issues.

We believe that the role of the electronic press in our society is the same as that of the printed press ... There is no doubt that the electronic media is powerful and that broadcasters can abuse their freedom of speech. But ... the potential for abuse of private freedoms pose far less a threat to democracy than the potential for abuse by a government given the power to control the press. We concur. We therefore believe that full First Amendment protections against content regulation should apply equally to the electronic and the printed press.[14]

The judgment of the FCC, backed by years of experience trying to manage the television press, was that television news should also be fully protected against government interference. The circuit court, reviewing its conclusion, agreed.[15] The FCC revocation of the Fairness Doctrine was upheld.[16]

The impact of the Fairness Doctrine varied depending on the standing, resources, and strength of the licensee. It was directed at local television stations, many of which were in small markets and had no resources, financial or otherwise, with which to fight the FCC even if they wished to. The three major networks were in a different position. They were not regulated directly, but their programs had to be acceptable to the television stations that would receive them, at the time usually over telephone landlines, and broadcast them over the air to the viewing public. The networks had the responsibility of providing lawful programming and seeing that their programs did not violate the FCC rules. The networks at the time each owned five local stations and their programming had to comply with the FCC rules applicable to programs originated by the local stations. When it came to news coverage, if the Fairness Doctrine required additional programming, the networks had to provide it as a practical matter. The networks had the resources to contest FCC rulings, but any contest with the licensing agency had considerable risk quite apart from the cost in legal fees and the time of personnel required. Stations had no such resources.

The difference can be seen from statements of two news figures at CBS—one a news manager and director, and the other a local station reporter who ultimately became network news anchor.

William Small is a thirty-year veteran of broadcast news. At CBS, he was Washington Bureau chief (1962–1974), senior vice president, and then corporate vice president, Washington, DC (1974–1978). At NBC, he was president of NBC News (1979–1982). He was also president of United Press International (1983–1985). He joined Fordham University as Felix Larkin Professor of Communications (1986–1998) and was appointed dean of Fordham University Graduate School of Business (1993–1994). He was chair of the National Television Academy, News and Documentary Emmys (2000–2010). This is his assessment:

It has always been my assumption that broadcast news is protected by the First Amendment. Though the founding fathers didn't have the foresight to know that radio and television were coming, they did know that open discussion by the press was an essential safeguard against abuses from and mistakes by the three branches of government.

Though aware of the fact that stations are licensed by our government, I operated under the assumption that when it went to court, broadcast news reporting would prevail. I encouraged all who reported to me to do their jobs and let their bosses worry about the consequences. With those who were my bosses, that attitude was never questioned. Some other network executives might get nervous that their owned-and-operated stations could be in jeopardy, but with great supporters of unhampered journalism like Frank Stanton of CBS and, before him, Robert Kintner of NBC, news operations were given great freedom. With it came great public trust.

But by the start of the second decade of the twenty-first century, however, all journalism faced unprecedented challenges. A fading advertising support has pushed many newspapers to the edge of extinction. Similarly, television news faced difficult days and staff and budget cuts abounded at the three original networks. The result inevitably hurt news gathering, especially overseas reporting except in covering news of momentous events like wars and natural disasters.

Can newspapers and over-the-air television news survive? Probably. Their greatest competition comes from the landslide of alternative information delivery systems. But the Internet, the digital age while grabbing the eyes and ears of huge numbers of former readers and viewers, has one major problem—editing. Clearly most of the material lacks the kind of journalistic oversight needed for quality reporting. Anyone, anywhere can be a "journalist" today if he has a computer, a blackberry, or any other digital device. He can blog, he can tweet. And as we know, he may be "visited" by thousands or even millions of fellow human beings with similar digital age equipment. But where is the hand of the professional editor?

And as this happens, professional journalism is diminished by disappearing audiences, declining budgets, and a largely distracted audience. Many young people feel the Internet is their news source and "who needs television or newspapers?" Some newspapers and television networks are trying to grapple with providing services to digital distribution as a source of advertising income to overcome the losses of their traditional income. The opportunity is there but yet to be fully realized.

Meanwhile, hard news coverage is becoming an endangered species. It costs money and while television news and newspapers toy with experimenting with different things to present to the public, the public good still resides with their original mission: covering the news. When that is set aside, we all lose the ability—so valued by the First Amendment—to grasp what our leaders are doing and to question their actions. The only thing at stake is a healthy democracy.[17]

Dan Rather testified about where the Fairness Doctrine fits in all this for the hometown journalist:

When I was a young reporter, I worked briefly for wire services, small radio stations, and newspapers, and I finally settled into a job at a large radio station owned by the *Houston Chronicle*. Almost immediately on starting work in that station's newsroom, I became aware of a concern, which I had previously barely known existed—the FCC. The journalists at the *Chronicle* did not worry about it; those at the radio station did. Not only the station manager but the newspeople as well were very much aware of this government presence looking over their shoulders. I can recall newsroom conversations about what the

FCC implications of broadcasting a particular report would be. Once a newsperson has to stop and consider what a government agency will think of something he or she wants to put on the air, an invaluable element of freedom has been lost.[18]

CHAPTER 7

✐

New Government Threats

It should be said at the outset that over a number of years, many government officials as well as citizens and lawyers in the private sector have fought for and maintained the freedoms of speech and press set out in the First Amendment. But FCC history shows that those freedoms and their values are suppressed by government regulations that may sound fine but in practice are inevitably destructive and suppress the news.

In 1987, when Congress saw that the FCC might terminate the Fairness Doctrine, it hurriedly passed a preemptive statute to make the Fairness Doctrine into an Act of Congress that the FCC could not then revoke. President Reagan vetoed that legislation. His veto letter to Congress said the doctrine was "antagonistic to the freedom of expression guaranteed by the First Amendment":

In any other medium besides broadcasting, such Federal policing of the editorial judgment of journalists would be unthinkable. The framers of the First Amendment, confident that public debate would be freer and healthier without the kind of interference represented by the "fairness doctrine," chose to forbid such regulations in the clearest terms: "Congress shall make no law ... abridging the freedom of speech, or of the press ..."

We must not ignore the obvious intent of the First Amendment, which is to promote vigorous public debate and a diversity of viewpoints in the public forum as a whole, not in any particular medium, let alone in any particular journalistic outlet. History has shown that the dangers of an overly timid or biased press cannot be averted through bureaucratic regulation, but only through the freedom and competition that the First Amendment sought to guarantee.[1]

An effort to override Reagan's veto failed.[2] A bill was introduced later to reinstitute the Fairness Doctrine, but it failed to pass when President George H.W. Bush threatened a veto.[3] Other bills have been introduced since then. None have passed.

In 2009, a number of legislative leaders, senators, and representatives called publicly for reenactment of the Fairness Doctrine.[4] Senators calling for such an action included Senate Majority Leader Harry Reid and Senators Feinstein, Schumer, Stabenow, Durbin, Bingaman, Harkin, and Kerry.[5] On February 4, 2009, Senator Debbie Stabenow said when asked whether it was time to bring back the Doctrine:

I think it's absolutely time to pass a standard. Now, *whether it's called the Fairness Standard, whether it's called something else* [emphasis added]—I absolutely think it's time to be bringing accountability to the airwaves.[6]

Speaker of the House of Representatives Nancy Pelosi "aggressively" pursued reenactment of the Fairness Doctrine. A reporter interviewing her in 2008 asked, "Do you personally support revival of the Fairness Doctrine?"..."Yes," the Speaker replied without hesitation.[7] Others in the House also called for it. Representative Anna Eshoo told the *Daily*

Post in Palo Alto, California on December 15, 2008 that she thought it should also apply to cable and satellite broadcasters.[8]

When Henry Waxman, Chairman of the House Energy and Commerce Committee, gained control of the committee in January 2009, it was reported that his staff immediately went to work to revive the Fairness Doctrine and its regulation of news and speech. It was also reported that FCC senior staff met with advisors to Waxman to discuss "ways the committee can create openings for the FCC to put in place a form of the 'Fairness Doctrine' without actually calling it such."[9] Committee and FCC spokespersons subsequently denied that this meeting had taken place. The reporting news organization stood by its news report.[10]

Former President Clinton supported it in February 2009.[11] President Obama disclaimed an intent to bring back the Fairness Doctrine when campaigning for president. His spokesperson said Obama did not want that to distract from other important issues.[12] After the election, Chris Wallace of ABC News asked David Axelrod, Obama's chief of staff and advisor:

Wallace: Will you rule out reimposing the Fairness Doctrine?

Axelrod: I'm going to leave that issue to Julius Genachowski, our new head of the FCC, to, and the president, to discuss … So I don't have an answer for you now.

In February 2009, a White House spokesperson said that President Obama continued to oppose the revival of the Fairness Doctrine.[13]

Localism, Balance, and Diversity—the New Fairness Doctrine

President Obama appointed Julius Genachowski as FCC chairman on June 29, 2009. The new FCC staff considered regulating television news content. A number of their comments and writings before their appointments to the FCC and their comments and plans at the FCC as well were reported in the online media, which closely followed FCC staff appointments, views, and proposals. One reporter concluded, "Localism is the new Fairness Doctrine."[14]

On August 6, 2009, the chairman appointed Mark Lloyd as FCC Associate General Counsel and Chief Diversity Officer. Lloyd was formerly a senior fellow at the Center for American Progress. He is reported to favor a new "Localism Doctrine" and has written that since the FCC could revoke stations' licenses under this localism doctrine, this would take the place of the "misnamed Fairness Doctrine."[15]

In his essay, "Forget the Fairness Doctrine," Lloyd urged that complaints to the FCC based on new localism requirements should be used to harass conservative radio stations. This would stop some conservative speech and lead to fines that could be levied against those stations that did not fall into line. The money collected would go to public radio to enlarge its role in broadcasting. Lloyd co-wrote a report, "The Structural Imbalance of Political Talk Radio," urging changes in radio broadcasting to provide increased localism and diversity of radio station ownership."[16] This would go well beyond balance in points of view on controversial issues imposed by the Fairness Doctrine regulation.

Lloyd says he does not see freedom of speech or press as his objective. In his 2006 book, *Prologue to a Farce: Communication and Democracy in America,* he wrote, "My focus here is not freedom of speech or the press … the purpose of free speech is warped to protect global corporations and block rules that would promote democratic governance." He would require stations to fund public broadcasting and, as well, focus their broadcast coverage on diverse views and government activities and to cover all local, state, and federal government meetings.[17] Obviously the audience would be relatively small for the reports on some of these events. They would be broadcast in addition to regular daily news and public issues programming. At a Congressional oversight hearing, the chair of the committee, Representative Gregory Walden (D–OR), asked Chairman Genachowski about his appointment of Lloyd as his diversity chief. A report of this reads in part:

Walden: There is a lot of talk about czars. I hope we don't have a government speech czar that is going to drive a whole different mechanism through rulemakings and challenging licensees …

[Genachowski said that the agency needed] a broad range of people with different backgrounds [and a] vibrant exchange of ideas internally … To the extent that there is a concern the commission would engage in any censorship of anyone in the media on the basis of political views and opinions, the answer is, we won't … (adding) It won't happen.[18]

Critics of new Fairness Doctrine proposals have said, for example, "[H]ere's the reality: a new Fairness Doctrine … wouldn't achieve more balance. Rather, it would obliterate political talk radio. If a station ran a popular conservative show … it would face pressure to run a liberal alternative, even though almost all left-leaning efforts to date have failed to capture either listeners or advertising revenue."[19] Both could disappear.

Genachowski appointed Stuart Benjamin, a Duke University law professor, as a Scholar in Residence to advise on spectrum policy and strategic issues. Benjamin had earlier written of his views in a 2009 paper, "Roasting the Pig to Burn Down the House: A Modest Proposal." He wrote that broadcast television is a "powerful source of homogenization and pabulum." He recommended using burdensome FCC regulations to "hasten the demise of broadcasting":

.... some regulations that would be undesirable standing on their own will be desirable once we factor in the degree to which regulations will impose costs on broadcasters and not only have no benefits but also impose additional costs in their effects (e.g., make programming worse). [This would] reduce the viewership of broadcasting and thus hasten the demise of broadcasting, what I [Benjamin] would regard as a win-win.[20]

Benjamin apparently would use the Localism, Balance, and Diversity Doctrine, in effect, and indirectly, to end broadcasting's use of the spectrum. He reportedly sees the new doctrine as a way of doing this by levying expensive regulatory burdens that, he writes, could originate from the Report on Localism issued by the FCC in 2008.[21] (See Appendix 4, FCC Report on Localism and Notice of Proposed Rulemaking.) He adds that the FCC could also rely on the efforts of Lloyd, in charge of diversity at the FCC, to create those burdens. Benjamin points to the added expense of the FCC's new local advisory boards (discussed below as an additional news content control mechanism) as such a burdensome cost.[22]

Benjamin later insisted his comments were misunderstood when he said he was pleased at the "hastening of the demise of broadcasting …" Benjamin says his job "includes advising the chairman on what proceedings to launch," but a larger part of his job is to raise both sides of issues and combat a kind of "groupthink" in Washington with the "clash of ideas" that he says Chairman Genachowski wanted when he reached out to him. In further explanation, Benjamin says that what he "really meant" in his article was that "we are best off moving toward spectrum flexibility … [a]nd we are not going to force any broadcasters off the air, it is going to be a voluntary program. …"[23]

One commentator said, "The FCC is chipping away at the First Amendment not with a scalpel but with a sharp chisel." He sees using local content and diversity rules against talk radio as the FCC's "hidden agenda." He adds that much of Mr. Benjamin's academic research has been devoted to spectrum issues, but it appears that the "FCC is using it for the FCC agenda to end free broadcast television."[24]

Benjamin reportedly welcomed the new court-ordered and FCC-enforced tape delay systems now required for local live broadcasts. Many local stations cannot afford to buy the expensive equipment necessary for this and so will no longer cover live local events. Benjamin commented that now local television has a disincentive to broadcast local events live so "local viewers are less likely to watch the local broadcasters."[25]

Chairman Genachowski appointed Steve Waldman, former news correspondent and communications entrepreneur, as his senior advisor for spectrum and the First Amendment. Waldman examined broadcast news and its future as part of a special FCC study of the future of news in all media—print, cable and electronic—for a report on "The Future of Media." Waldman says that he has been charged by Genachowski with "helping traditional journalism as now practiced by newspapers and TV stations find its place in the digital age" and will study

> the very worrisome and deep contraction of journalism … [and come up with] some ideas for revitalizing it … it's just not newspapers which have suffered most from the relentless assault of the Internet. The health of local TV news and the quality of local TV news is a very important part of the picture …

> The future of news and the future of journalism and information cuts across all these different platforms—local broadcast news, cable, mobile, the Internet, newspapers and radio. They are all interconnected now …[26]

There has been discussion of government subsidies, incentivizing regulation, and private charitable efforts. Some newspaper publishers and broadcasters believe that getting rid of the general FCC prohibition against the ownership of a television station and a newspaper in the same market could be a straightforward, practical step that could strengthen local journalism. It would enable a combination of the talent and skills of broadcast stations and newspapers and reduce costs. This has not found favor at the FCC in the past.

The print media struggles with increasing economic problems and can no longer afford to do as much news gathering and news coverage as before. Broadcasters have their own economic problems after the success of cable and also have financial shortfalls that could be seen as limiting broadcast news. A still further reduction in news coverage would result from official and ongoing government regulation imposing the

Localism, Balance, and Diversity Doctrine to manage broadcast news, like the decline that took place under the Fairness Doctrine. This would mean that the public would be much less informed. In fact, it could be deliberately misinformed. Television would, as a result, prove incapable of acting as the public's watchdog against government abuse.

At the same time, the spectrum requirements of a new national broadband system, the Internet, have become an overriding part of the present administration's plans for the media and news coverage. Waldman spoke of the importance of this to the news media on December 2, 2009 at a Roundtable Conference at the Federal Trade Commission on FCC broadband plans. He said that by February [2010] the FCC would produce a national broadband strategy that would be important for the future of the news media. But he added that "Internet-based innovations to provide better news and information cannot be available only to the affluent or well wired..."[27]

The Future of Media

Steven Waldman, as senior advisor to the chairman of the FCC, officially asked for comments for its study, "The Future of Media," under a FCC Public Notice posted January 20, 2010, "FCC Launches Examination of the Future of the Media and the Information Needs of Communities in a Digital Age." Waldman addressed the critical question of government regulation of news content in these terms:

In the face of proposals to reclaim some of the broadcast spectrum for broadband application, perhaps the best way to ensure that broadcasters keep their spectrum is for them to have and fulfill some kind of public interest obligation that might at the same time "save" journalism ...[28]

Broadcast stations have always had public interest obligations, enforced by the FCC, including the broadcast of news, public affairs programming, and community programming. The suggestion of Waldman to let broadcasters use some spectrum in the future and "save" journalism appears to be expressly conditioned on their acceptance of some new government regulation of news and speech content. The pending FCC proceeding on localism, balance, and diversity has now been folded into the FCC's the Future of Media proceeding. None of the final details of this have been made public, but apparently this new condition for broadcasting Waldman refers to will include the localism, balance, and diversity regulations or their equivalent now pending before the FCC. The Future of Media project has also been proceeding with a broad scope, including management of news.

The Nieman Journalism Laboratory, a press organization, is cautious about such government recommendations and obviously apprehensive that news may be regulated:

> The Future of Media project starts with the assumption that many of the challenges encountered in today's media environment will be addressed by the private for-profit and non-profit sectors, without government intervention. We will remain mindful of the Hippocratic Oath of physicians, "First, do no harm."[29]

Waldman, who has a background in media, spoke about the global state of news and his work on April 16, 2010 and the concept of "accountability journalism"; that is, using news reporting to hold government and institutions accountable to the public:

> The press is one of the only private institutions that the Founding Fathers specifically believed was important to the functioning of democracy. They believed that a vigorous, independent press was a crucial part of holding leaders accountable and making sure citizens have the information they need …

Now consider these statistics. Newspaper ad revenue (including online) has dropped 41 percent in three years. Newspaper spending on reporting and editing is down 30 percent since 2000. The number of reporters covering statehouses is down by a third since 2003. Staffing at news magazines is down by almost half since I worked there in the mid-1980s. Network news division resources are likely down by more than half.

While there is tremendous innovation going on online, it is not yet clear that it will be enough to fill the gap. The Poynter Institute [a private-sector broadcast press research and advisory group] estimated that the drop in reporting capacity was $1.6 billion. They estimated that to help fill that gap, foundations—a major source of funding for local news start-ups—have put in about $140 million during that period. $1.6 billion out. $140 million in.

Obviously, it's not the dollars that matter—it's whether they lead to less accountability journalism and less civically valuable information getting to citizens.

And if there are problems, are there public policies that are making it worse? Are there public policies that could make it better?[30]

Some commentators look to motivation as well as the announced purpose as do some reviewing courts in determining the constitutionality of speech and news restraints. Reported comments may be significant to those questions.

Current Government Threats to Television News Content

The FCC policy reflected in the proposed Localism, Balance, and Diversity Doctrine issued by the FCC in 2008 for comment has many of the same characteristics of the old Fairness Doctrine and can be expected to have similar results. A central government agency substituting its regulatory judgment for the news judgments of thousands of local television station reporters and managers in small and large markets across the country and revising individual station news coverage to meet a government regulatory formula for "localism" in news coverage would necessarily in practice distort local news coverage and deter news reports. Also, in practice, commission quantitative assessments of local news by categories of subject matter could indirectly favor or disfavor some news coverage. The government standard would not be truth but a government-directed localism, balance, or diversity objective the FCC would be required to enforce. In addition, an atmosphere of fear and intimidation created by such enforcement could again suppress news and chill speech. People in the local community would be less informed or misinformed.

The most protected speech in a democracy, political speech and opinion, would again be abridged and curtailed by the government. The installation of an official local board at each local broadcast station, as now proposed, to review program content and enforce more closely and continuously the new Localism, Balance, and Diversity Doctrine would make the new doctrine even more suppressive over time than the old Fairness Doctrine. This also creates the likelihood of board members' political objectives becoming the focus of local programming and news.

The commission reported that in 2008 it had already received a great deal of information during its hearings and from filings on its proposed Localism, Balance, and Diversity Doctrine. (See Appendix 4, FCC Report on Broadcast Localism and Notice of Proposed Rulemaking.) The official report states that it "focuses in particular on broadcaster efforts to provide community-responsive programming such as news and public affairs, and programming targeted to the particular needs or interests of certain segments of the public...." The hearings "included 86 formal presentations and remarks from community interest groups and broadcaster representatives, as well as elected and appointed officials from state and federal governments. The proceedings also included testimony from 421 additional participants." The report issued in January 2008 refers to the FCC process used in the past for ascertaining community needs and interests:

> Many broadcast entities submitted information with their comments outlining the process that each follows to determine the needs and interests of people within their respective communities of license. Licensee commenters also provided detailed data.

The commission report does not assess directly the responsiveness of local station programming to local needs and interest. Rather, it looks at what it describes as the station dialogue: "The record here suggests that the dialogue between broadcasters and their audiences concerning stations' localism efforts is not ideal." (See Appendix 4, FCC Report on Broadcast Localism and Notice of Proposed Rulemaking.)

The commission sets out questions about its concept of a local advisory board for each station, the board's role, and its management of programming, including news coverage. The FCC does not state what procedures a station should follow in consultations with the board. Comments were sought on this, including how often the consultations should be held and on what issues. (See Appendix 4, paragraphs 25 and 26 of the FCC Report on Broadcast Localism and Notice of Proposed Rulemaking.) These arrangements could be of substantial significance in practice and in implementing the regulations under administrative law principles.[31] It would also be important in determining their constitutionality if those consultations are seen as informal negotiations by the local board, restricting press and speech without effective judicial review, which seems likely.

The Localism report of 2008 was in the making for some years. The commission also sought information about localism and diversity in other proceedings, such as those directed to the multiple ownership rule and The Future of Media study. For example, other questions asked by the FCC in those proceedings included: What tests should be applied to measure localism other than programming and its responsiveness to local needs and interests? Should Internet material be assessed as to localism needs? Do the interests of advertisers and producers matter? Are minorities being served? What tests should be applied to measure diversity? Are independent voices being heard? How best to assess various diverse kinds of programming, diverse service to the local community as well as diversity in sources?

Government intervention for diversity must dictate selection and that is an open avenue for suppression. "[L]iberty of the press is in peril as soon as the government tries to compel what is to go into a newspaper. A journal does not merely print observed facts the way a cow is photographed through a plate-glass window. As soon as the facts are set in their context, you have interpretation and you have selection, and editorial selection opens the way to editorial suppression. Then how can the state force abstention from discrimination in the news without dictating selection?"[32]

The FCC and the reviewing circuit court both concluded that the Fairness Doctrine "disserved" the public's right to diverse sources of information. (See Chapter 6, The FCC Revokes the Fairness Doctrine.)

The Future of Media

The FCC's The Future of Media study was released in June 2011. It discusses the state of local news coverage and related issues for the commissioners' information. It is not binding. The study says there are many new local facilities but, for example, little local reporting by radio on the "accountability" of local government and schools. It does not suggest how to provide the substantial financial support needed for more local broadcast reporting on these and other subjects but suggests government use local radio for its advertising that currently appears on national media. It reports that television stations are the number one source of local news and that many television stations are providing excellent local news programs over the air and online. It goes on to say that the impact of cost cutting, however, is reducing the depth of news coverage and that while there are many sources of news online, the great bulk of local reporting is still initiated by local newspapers.[33]

The study recommends against reinstituting the Fairness Doctrine. Waldman, the FCC official in charge of the study, said there was "no case" for its reinstatement. "In fact, it would be a bad idea." Chairman Genachowski associated himself with this position. On August 20, 2011, he removed any vestige of the old Fairness Doctrine from the National Register, marking the technical end of that doctrine. He said, "The Fairness Doctrine holds the *potential* [emphasis added] to chill free speech and the free flow of ideas and was properly abandoned over two decades ago."[34] He did not appear to accept the FCC's findings of fact about the actual harm caused by that Doctrine which the FCC itself found in 1987. He speaks only of its "potential."

The Future of Media study also recommended termination of the pending localism proceeding, since, it said, the doctrine of Localism, Balance, and Diversity contains unworkable and burdensome rules.[35] Genachowski has not commented on this. The current FCC appears divided about a number of the study's conclusions, including ending the localism proceeding, and Chairman Genachowski has not acted to close it. The threats of FCC investigations and Localism, Balance, and Diversity Doctrine decisions that would control news and speech continue. Commissioner McDowell cautioned that even if the Fairness Doctrine were permanently dismantled, "[t]here are many ways to try to accomplish the same goals." Another observer commented that local boards would "keep tabs" on what stations air.[36]

Any further action by the FCC would require a majority vote. The title of The Future of Media study has been changed to "The Information Needs of Communities: The Changing Media Landscape in a Broadband Age."

The impact of the officially named "Localism, Balance and Diversity Doctrine," if adopted, will depend on, in part, its final scope and penalties. The suggestions by official government figures in favor of government imposing localism, balance, and diversity controls on television speech and news, and their threats, are expected to continue.

Local Boards

The FCC has proposed a local advisory board be appointed for each broadcast station to review the station's localism, balance, and diversity programming. It would report to the FCC whether station programming is correctly responding to the community's needs as members of the local board see those needs and programs. The FCC stated, "We believe that these boards will promote both localism and diversity and, as such, should be an integral component of the Commission's localism efforts." The FCC proposal does not shed light on the procedures to be followed or the scope and powers of the local boards over news coverage. Henry Waxman, when he was chairman of the House Energy and Commerce Committee, apparently wanted such local boards to oversee broadcast stations' news and other programs. "One idea Waxman's committee staff is looking at is a congressionally mandated policy that would require all TV and radio stations to have in place 'advisory boards' that would act as watchdogs to ensure 'community needs and opinions' are given fair treatment."[37] This devolution of elements of broadcast management to the members selected to serve on the local advisory boards is unprecedented as a broadcast regulatory structure. It could have critically disruptive impact and even become *in terrorem*.

At license renewal time, the local board would advise the FCC on whether or not in the views of the members of the board the station's programs had been adequate and had appropriately served the local community's interests, and then recommend whether the station license should or should not be renewed. A local board recommendation that a license not be renewed would have to be addressed by the station and ruled on by the FCC. It could be difficult for the FCC to overrule a local board's view that a license not be renewed. The process itself could be intimidating.

Members of the boards across the country could not help being motivated on some issues by political considerations. Station managers could find their licenses held hostage to this as well as to the members' own political preferences. Stations could not rationally run the risk of an adverse recommendation when the board or its members made demands or even suggestions about programming and talent. Most important, whatever First Amendment cautions might be expressed in the regulations, members would inevitably help station management decide, in practice, what to present in local news, political news, and public affairs programming.

Board members' advice on localism, balance, and diversity programming can also be expected to prevail over that of others in the community in light of their unique authority. Board members could favor certain views or oppose them, advance or hinder political agendas, and prefer or oppose certain public or political figures in public affairs programming or in news coverage. These selections could easily be framed by board members as directed to "localism," "community," "diversity," "local interest," "balance," or other social objectives when communicating or negotiating with the management about broadcast licensees. This process could, through its informal influence on local broadcast stations, skirt FCC and appellate courts and their role in protecting the public and the press under the Constitution.

Advisory boards have a particular history when they are part of a regulatory process. They are seen as able to do what an official commission might not be able to do. They can act informally and with what can amount to threats, without the procedures usually required to provide protection and due process. The Supreme Court has rejected this approach in the past when used to censor or restrict print material.[38] There are no FCC regulations or guidelines established for local board action or for reviewable procedures at this point. The FCC leaves that to some future FCC action, presumably after the proposals are adopted.

When recommending against renewal of a broadcast license, in particular, the members of the local advisory board would purport to speak for the community. Their views would likely prevail over individual, group, or other local views because the board would have been established under governmental mandate to represent the local community and to report officially on license renewals to the FCC.

This is a new approach to community ascertainment. Station management has looked, in the past, to impartial and independent program and talent audience measurements, the "ratings," as well as direct, ongoing communication with local community officials and members about community needs and interests. The FCC and stations saw this a reliable way of deciding on responsive local community program service. As a matter of broadcast service and finances, a station usually presents programming that has the greatest audience appeal and provides the greatest revenue, along with public service programming of appeal.

In addition, for many years FCC regulations required broadcast stations to meet with a number of local community leaders who could speak for the various interests of the community to discuss community needs and responsive programming. Now members of the local boards would be quasi-official, not local viewers and local community leaders speaking as such, but officially appointed members of government-mandated local oversight boards. Comments at any time by members of these official boards to station management about coverage of news and opinions could easily morph into informal negotiations, and in turn, informal censorship. Members of the board speaking with the implicit threat of unfavorable license renewal recommendations with the possible loss of the license to broadcast would understandably be given great deference. Many off-the-record promises of help or of threats to recommend against renewal would likely go unreported but nonetheless be quite effective.

The potential for government and board abuse is obvious. The result could easily be a board-pressured change in a station's independent editorial judgment or a restriction or distortion of news coverage and political and other speech. Given the history of regulating television news, it must also be expected that at least some of the decisions of the local board members will increase censorship. Members of the boards can be expected to claim they are just informally "suggesting" or "urging" station managers to delete, add, or revise programs. Some may. But when they are granted the power to affect license renewals, it seems likely that board members' comments or recommendations would result in the broadcast of material that members of the board favored. If not immediately, over time programming that members of the board considered unacceptable would disappear.

Examples from the history of the Fairness Doctrine already discussed illustrate how this might work in practice. A local advisory board might vote on whether the station should broadcast a program on airport congestion as framed by the station journalists and news management or decide that the program should be expanded to include presentations on some contributing factors or sub-issues. Local political leaders might want to speak for their constituents on related issues during the program. Or, for that matter, the board could decide that in the interest of the local community and its businesses the program should not be broadcast at all because of the possible harm to local businesses. (See Chapter 3, How FCC Regulations Suppressed News and Speech: Airport Congestion Case.)

A local board could decide against the broadcast of something like the failed pension plans program if local corporations objected to such a program about their pensions, or the board could insist upon some disclaimer that "the pension system is working." The board members might also want or have to consider some of the many other issues as illustrated by the appellate court opinion in the failed Pension Plans case. (See Appendix 2, Excerpts from The Failed Pension Plans Case.) They also might consider possible loss of revenues or increased costs to a station that would result from their decisions. Whether or not local boards are seen as something burdensome, and adding to broadcast costs for no good reason, as one FCC staff member has suggested, board members would have great power over programming and news coverage. The politics in their selection or approval by the Congress, the incumbent president, the FCC, or in other ways, have not been addressed since that issue of political influence awaits the drafting of the regulations. Yet such politics could have the greatest significance for the freedom of local speech and news, in practice.

Programming and scheduling decisions are part of the station owner and manager's licensee obligation under the Communications Act of 1934, as amended. Now, however, it is proposed that a critical part of that statutory and regulatory obligation be performed or determined in part by members of a local outside board. It must be recognized that it is unlikely that station management would charge its local board with impropriety or illegal conduct since they would have to face the board at license renewal time.

Court appeals might not offer timely protection. Legally non-binding advisory suggestions, comments, etc., may not be appealable; it might only be FCC decisions that would be appealable. Putting aside the difficulty of demonstrating reversible error on appeal from an FCC affirming decision, station acceptance of the decision of the local board might well be prudent out of concern about antagonizing the local board, the licensing agency, and others with the possibility of making things worse. Station management would most likely tend to comply with its local board's suggestions. The board members could thus have final power over station news and other programming, subject only to the centralized FCC review for doctrinal violations.

There must always be concern over the transmission of repeated antisocial statements or a campaign to subvert the values of the community. Although there are some legal steps that can be taken, responsibility for broadcast content rests with the broadcasters. Cable and other transmitters may present different approaches but the institution of broadcasting has demonstrated its responsibility over many years. This has been the case since the revocation of the Fairness Doctrine's oversight, and can be expected to continue without government interference. In addition, as with newspapers, there is continuing community pressure on broadcast news media to reflect community tastes and values as well as the pressure of advertisers who do not want a broadcast vehicle for their commercials that is offensive to the audience they seek.

The Sunstein Theory for Government Control of News

The exercise of government power under the new Localism, Balance, and Diversity Doctrine would be, and apparently is intended to be, of substantial significance.

Support for government control and management of television news has been repeatedly urged by Professor Cass R. Sunstein over many years. President Obama appointed Sunstein Chief of the White House Office of Information and Regulatory Affairs (OIRA), with responsibility, in effect, for reviewing and participating in the development of all federal regulations. Sunstein was a professor of law at the University of Chicago Law School where Barack Obama also was a law professor. He is a friend of President Obama and participated in his presidential campaign. Sunstein was appointed professor of law at the Harvard Law School in 2008 by the then dean, Elena Kagan, who also earlier taught at the Chicago Law School.

Sunstein has explained his theory for government management of the news in his books, *The Partial Constitution* (1993), *Democracy and the Problem of Free Speech* (1993); a new *Afterword* in *Democracy and the Problem of Free Speech* (1995); *On Rumors, How Falsehoods Spread, Why We Believe Them, What Can Be Done* (2009); *and A Constitution of Many Minds* (2009).[39]

He says that the present First Amendment marketplace approach to free speech should be changed. He wrote in 1993 that there should be a "new Fairness Doctrine" and "New Deal" for speech. He has not apparently abandoned those views. He has urged that government agencies be given more control over speech and press, as they were in the New Deal over property, to effect the social and political changes that those in government conclude are desirable. Legislative fairness doctrines, he argues, would not raise any constitutional doubts. Legislative New Deal efforts to restructure the marketplace might even be seen as a discharge of the legislature's "constitutional duty, a duty that courts are reluctant, for institutional reasons, fully to enforce."[40]

Sunstein also would have Congress play a greater role in deciding the constitutionality of legislation, including that affecting speech and news. Sunstein argues that new government controls could affirmatively promote both political deliberation and political equality.[41]

Professor Sunstein's theories are important and demand careful analysis, not only because of his teaching experience with the law but also because of his important position in the Obama administration. Sunstein writes that things have changed in modern times with new technology, so there are more options than when the First Amendment was adopted. In designing government control of news and speech for civic purposes, he would use the First Amendment's underlying goals that he finds in its philosophy, not to protect speech and news from government abridgement, but rather as authority for the government to impose rules to bring about government-selected localism, diversity, and other government goals.[42]

While Sunstein argues that "government controls on the broadcast media to ensure diversity of view and attention to public affairs would *help* [emphasis added] the system of free expression," he does not take into account that, in practice, a government agency would have to execute and enforce controls as it did under the Fairness Doctrine.[43] His argument is flatly contradicted by the experience of the government and the broadcast industry with the controls and news management imposed by the Fairness Doctrine. Those with actual experience with how the FCC regulations worked in practice have starkly different views from those of Sunstein about the effect of FCC policies like the Fairness Doctrine. So did the FCC in revoking the doctrine in 1987. It found that the doctrine had not helped, but its controls had suppressed news and chilled speech.

Dick Salant, the president of CBS News during many of the years when the Fairness Doctrine was in effect, said at the time that FCC regulations of news content under the Fairness Doctrine created "a brooding omnipresence which limits robust journalism ... They put in the hands of government the coercive power, which history has shown government has sought to use, to manipulate and control."[44]

The Radio and Television News Directors Association said that under the doctrine, broadcasters are "unable to present as forcefully as they should the great issues of our time."[45]

The National Association of Broadcasters said that under the Fairness Doctrine broadcasters are "subject to a subtle, continuous, and strong incentive to avoid the [FCC] investigations ... by sticking with the safe and the bland, depriving the public of the kind of journalism that a truly free press is able to provide."[46]

The circuit court upholding the FCC revocation of its Fairness Doctrine said this about its diversity effect:

> The Fairness Doctrine in operation disserves both the public's right to diverse sources of information and the broadcaster's interest in free expression. Its chilling effect thwarts its intended purpose...[47]

Judge David Bazelon, who served on the Federal Circuit Court in Washington, DC that reviewed many FCC decisions over the years, spoke of the Fairness Doctrine in an address to the UCLA Communications Law Symposium, "The Foreseeable Future of the Television Networks" (1979):

> The Fairness Doctrine has not fostered wide-ranging debate spanning the full spectrum of political and social ideas. Rather, it has contributed to suppressing programming on controversial issues almost entirely ... If past efforts are any indication, government intervention is as likely to suppress diversity as to promote it.[48]

In what was Sunstein's seminal work, he wrote of his belief that "politics lies at the core of the [First] [A]mendment." His proposals rely on "government intervention into free speech processes to improve those processes" in various ways.[49] Yet, having a government agency like the FCC decide the acceptability of speech and news under a government standard places a politically appointed government body in control of the intervention and the process, despite the First Amendment.

What is missing is any recognition of the negative impact of "government intervention" on the freedom of speech and press in practice. It must be apparent that press concern about government editorial oversight of broadcast news reflects what news managers and reporters know—it will necessarily result in the loss of press and speech freedom.

A Cato Institute Policy Analysis dated May 27, 2009 of the new FCC localism proposals reviewed the history of the FCC's experience and concluded:

> The history of the Fairness Doctrine confirms the validity of the concerns of the Framers of the First Amendment, because federal officials and their agents used and sought to use the Fairness Doctrine to silence critics of three presidencies. Broadcasters adapted to the Fairness Doctrine by avoiding controversial speech, thereby chilling public debate on vital matters ... Like the Fairness Doctrine, the FCC's localism initiative poses the risk of restricting speech ...[50]

Judge David Bazelon's statement about the Fairness Doctrine is essentially a finding of fact. He concluded, as previously noted, that the Doctrine "has contributed to suppressing programming on controversial issues almost entirely ... " Sunstein does not address this factual statement when urging government control of speech. When the Supreme Court adopted its *Red Lion* decision, the working press warned the Court of the destructive impact that the Fairness Doctrine would have on the reporting of news, in practice. The Court dismissed this out of hand. It said additional FCC enforcement action would correct any press recalcitrance to obey.

Sunstein does not address in his writings how his proposed regulations of press and speech would work in practice. He says the Fairness Doctrine came under attack and that part of the problem with the old Fairness Doctrine was its "sheer rigidity."[51] But the facts reported in the FCC's 1985 findings and its 1987 decision clearly established that government regulation, government investigation, and government revision of news and speech content under the Fairness Doctrine suppressed the news, chilled speech, and was used to censor dissent. The factual findings of the FCC revocation were based on an extensive record as was the FCC's finding that the doctrine was against the public interest. The findings of the reviewing circuit court strongly endorsed this conclusion and the revocation of the Fairness Doctrine.

FCC negotiations with stations to change their news reports to avoid Fairness Doctrine violations are not examples of a too rigid regulation. When finding nuance and creating new issues, it could be said that the FCC was too creative in its approach to the issues, particularly in creating sub-issues and implied issues, and ordering the broadcast of collateral views about them.

There is presently no coherent official description in the proposed new localism regulations of the terms localism, balance, and diversity, and no explanation of what they might require in the regulation of the content of broadcast news and speech. Threats of sanctions would have to be made by the FCC to enforce the new Localism, Balance, and Diversity regulations for balance as they were to enforce the Fairness Doctrine. No comment is made about the regulatory climate likely to be created once again of intimidation and fear, which the FCC found was caused by the old Fairness Doctrine.

If the new proposals plan to rely on fines as well as refusals to renew broadcast licenses, how will the critical distinction be made in practice of which to use and on what basis? There would always be the threat of license revocation, should the station wish to resist a commission finding or a requirement to correct what the FCC might conclude was a localism, balance, and diversity violation. The station might well face a financially impossible fight against the FCC or at least a long and costly litigation. This alone would deter some stations from reporting on controversy and certain subjects in their local news and other coverage as it did under the Fairness Doctrine. Since there is no description of localism, balance, or diversity or the enforcement procedure proposed in the Notice of Proposed Rulemaking, commentators can only speculate.

The most startling and significant proposal for changing the role of the news media in American society is Sunstein's observation that if the marketplace of speech is "skewed" by too much speech for one point of view and too little for its opposition, then content-based regulation of news may be a "corrective."[52]

A Law Review article in 1996 by then Professor Elena Kagan of the University of Chicago Law School (now Associate Justice of the Supreme Court) would implement the Sunstein view. She writes that the "redistribution of speech is not itself an illegitimate end" for government:

> The First Amendment often would permit—indeed require— the reallocation of speech opportunities. The realm of public expression may have too much of some kinds of speech, too little of others; some speakers may drown out or dominate their opposite numbers. Self-conscious redistribution of expressive opportunities seems the most direct way of correcting these defects and achieving the appropriate range and balance of viewpoint.[53]

This Kagan-authored Law Review article also would impose a doctrinal test, a standard of the "ideal state of public debate":

> If there is an "overabundance" of an idea in the absence of direct governmental action—which there well might be when

compared with some ideal state of public debate—then action disfavoring that idea might "unskew," rather than skew, public discourse.[54]

Ordering the broadcast of particular speech or news coverage to bring the actual state of public debate at a particular point in time to the FCC's "ideal state" would be extremely difficult for a rational majority vote of a few politically appointed FCC commissioners. The issues, points of view, facts, and scope of the debate about ongoing events at particular points of time would be difficult if not impossible to assess objectively. This would be even more difficult when the complaint would be that the debate was not in an ideal state at that point. Sunstein himself suggests this may be beyond the capacity of government. He also notes the "serious risk that judicial or legislative decisions about the relative power of various groups, and who is owed redistribution, will be biased as unreliable."[55]

It seems most unlikely that an agency decision and corrective order could be as clear and timely, much less predictable, as needed for the management of news coverage during a controversy, even if that served a public interest purpose. This exposes one of the major faults in government news control, put aside issues of government motivation and constitutionality. This editing procedure would prove administratively impractical for breaking news stories or for covering dynamic political news and speech during presidential or other political campaigns.

The Localism Concept and *Turner* Must-Carry Rules

Professor Sunstein argues that the Supreme Court *Turner* decision could be constitutional authority for the government to regulate television speech and news content for certain purposes. The recent FCC proposals for a Localism, Balance, and Diversity Doctrine with government control of speech and news content follow this same view. The *Turner* decision has now also been cited by the FCC in its

December 2010 decision for authority to regulate access and content on the Internet. The Sunstein reading of the case therefore would have quite serious consequences for free speech and a free press.

The *Turner* case was brought to the Supreme Court when broadcasters supported regulations requiring cable systems to carry their local broadcast signals and provide them to cable subscribers. Many cable homes no longer had antennas capable of receiving local broadcast signals over the air and relied on cable for reception of broadcast signals. Cable was threatening to stop carrying the signals. Congress enacted relief for broadcast stations and their survival by what were called the must-carry rules, which required cable systems to carry the local broadcast signals.

A majority of the Court held in 1994 that the *Turner* must-carry law was constitutional.[56] The Court majority said that cable operators had physical control of cable channels and were "gatekeepers" of broadcast programming intended to be channeled into subscribers' homes that did not have over-the-air reception. At the time, sixty percent of television receiving sets had cable and no over-the-air reception. The decision recognized the danger to the viability of the broadcast free television system itself if local stations' signals were not carried by cable systems, which had an economic incentive to delete broadcast signals and thus cripple their competition. The Court found that there was a substantial public interest in local free broadcast television signals reaching the public, which the government should protect against unfair cable competition.

The record was not sufficiently developed to everyone's satisfaction to show that broadcasting would be injured, as Congress predicted. The Court sent the case back to the lower court for development of record evidence. On return of the case to the Supreme Court in 1997, the Court found the record sufficient.[57]

Sunstein argues that there is an opening now for the government to regulate speech, news, and other programming to further localism and diversity. He says that the Supreme Court had no difficulty in

Turner in finding localism and diversity to be substantial government interests, and therefore regulations advancing those interests could be constitutional. But this was not what the Court found. The majority in the Supreme Court's decision in the *Turner* case explicitly found that Congress granted must-carry privileges to broadcast stations only because the broadcast television industry was in "economic peril" due to the physical characteristics of cable transmission and that the cable industry had economic incentives to end carriage of broadcast signals and prefer its own distribution and business. It held that regulation was required to enable local broadcast signals to reach their intended audience and to save the broadcast system.[58] The Court did not find that the objective of either localism or diversity, individually or taken together, would justify upholding broadcast content regulation as constitutional.

Justice Sandra Day O'Connor dissented in *Turner*. Three other justices—Ginsburg, Scalia, and Thomas—joined her opinion. Justice O'Connor found that the legislation was directed to protection of local broadcast programming, could be considered content-oriented, and was therefore subject to closer review by the Court which, under the Court's customary test, could result in the Court holding must-carry unconstitutional. She also concluded that the government had not established that cable was a gateway, which could justify government interference with private methods of distribution. "It is for private speakers and listeners, not for the government to decide what fraction of their news and entertainment ought to be of a local character and what fraction ought to be of a national (or international) one."

Justice O'Connor also found inadequate support for a diversity of viewpoint argument made by cable. She said, "While the government may subsidize speakers that it thinks provide novel points of view, it may not restrict other speakers on the theory that what they say is more conventional … Government interest in public affairs and educational programming is somewhat weightier than localism, [but] it is a difficult question whether they are compelling enough to justify restricting other sorts of speech. We have never held that the government could impose educational content requirements on, say, newsstands, bookstores, or movie theaters; and it is not clear that such requirements would in any event appreciably further the goals of public education." Justice Breyer did not join in the majority vote as to unfair competition but did join in the rest of the majority decision.[59]

The FCC does not now regulate news and speech content on cable. The Supreme Court has held that would be unconstitutional, except for certain bans on obscenity and pornography.[60] Cable does not use electronic frequencies and there is no issue of scarcity of frequencies for cable operations. The scarcity issue was what subjected television news content to FCC regulation in 1949 and thereafter until 1987.

In January 2009, FCC Commissioner Robert M. McDowell addressed the Media Institute to trace what the commission had learned from its regulation of news and speech in the past.[61] He said, "History teaches us that the government is a poor arbiter of editorial decisions, all constitutional implications aside." He referred to the appellate circuit court decision in the Failed Pension Plans case, which analyzed government control and use of the Fairness Doctrine. (See Appendix 2, Excerpts from The Failed Pension Plan Case.) He continued:

> In general…the evils of communications controlled by a nerve center of Government loom larger than the evils of editorial abuse by multiple-licensees who are not only governed by the standards of their profession but aware that their interest lies in [the] long-term confidence of their audience … If the Doctrine were to return in some form or another, does anyone think that the Commission is any better equipped today than it was in 1973 to untangle the knotty problems of enforcement by assuming the role of editor-at-large for the entire country? The Pensions Case illustrates the great difficulty with applying that Doctrine and the disputes it created which were centered not on inaccuracies or defamation but, rather, on tone, balance and other aspects of the editorial process.

The commissioner addressed practical, real-world problems.

> Even if the FCC had a large number of people to devote to such reviews, which it doesn't, and even if the prospect of government regulators scrutinizing individual editorial choices were not so constitutionally unsavory, does determining what views to present mean that the broadcaster has discretion to choose? Or, if not, how choose? ...

The commissioner continued,

> These are questions that cannot be answered in anyone's law review article, committee hearing, reply comments, or appellate brief. It would be more constructive if such discourse was left to America's free market of ideas and the decision of whether to respond left to individuals, not to the state.

It was argued in 1969 that scarcity of electronic frequency limited the number of broadcast stations and therefore news and speech required government management. That argument should fail today on that ground as a simple factual matter. Commissioner McDowell points out that by 2008, media included cable and satellite television and their hundreds of channels, satellite radio and its hundreds of channels, and the Internet and its millions of low-cost or free outlets for speech, as well as "271 million wireless handsets for accessing more audio and video content."

Within traditional media and its use of broadcast frequencies, there has been enormous growth. By 2008, there were "4,124 radio stations and 1,758 TV stations." Multicasting technology for these stations enables the simultaneous broadcast of multiple programming channels. "With the addition of 851 Low Power FM radio, 550 Class A TV, and 2,272 Low Power TV stations, broadcast facilities now total 19,555."

FCC Commissioner McDowell also voiced his opposition to proposals for mandatory broadcast station "community advisory boards." While he sees a voluntary use of such boards as one of the ways broadcasters can stay in touch with the communities they serve (and it would be good business to do so), the grant of programming power to such mandatory advisory boards is quite different and a threatening proposition. He reasoned, "All Americans should be troubled by any new rules that might give community board members a legal right to dictate broadcast content decisions."

As for a new effort by some in government to use an FCC rule to silence opposing political and other views and determine local television news content, Commissioner McDowell pointed out that the courts should have trouble approving a rule that could again be used by the government to censor core political speech. He said that a National Council for Civic Responsibility representative from the Lyndon B. Johnson era has admitted that what was done to harass opposition under the Fairness Doctrine was wrong. "The new proposal to subject cable and the Internet to the Fairness Doctrine as well would just increase that wrong."

But proposals to reduce protection for speech and news will continue, as will theories about how to do that. For example, the news coverage online of FCC staff comments about the regulations they hoped to impose on television news and speech described earlier in this study reflect suggestions for overturning that protection They also reflect that political views often dominate the debates about those efforts. (See, e.g., endnotes 5–25.)

Reallocation of Broadcast Spectrum

Among the threats now facing broadcasters is the reallocation to the Internet over the next ten years of 500MHz of spectrum, now available to broadcasters, government, and others, for mobile and other uses. This would include 120MHz currently allocated to and used by broadcasters, which is necessary for broadcasting. It may be too early to gauge the impact on broadcasters and broadcast news of this spectrum reallocation but it is a significant issue and must be of concern now for news broadcasting and the public.

The transfer of spectrum under the National Broadband Plan was authorized in 2010 under an agreement made by President Obama, FCC Chairman Genachowski, the FCC, and Congress. There has not been a definitive public analysis or official report on issues such as the desirability of continuing a national television broadcasting system or the terms and conditions to be imposed on broadcast use of spectrum. The commission has not yet made public what actions it plans after it reallocates this spectrum, although the reallocation reportedly could start in three years.

Television stations without access to necessary spectrum may have to go dark or find other transmission arrangements. Stations could try to arrange some other local program distribution, move to unregulated pay cable, or make other arrangements that do not use spectrum, or share the spectrum of others. At first the FCC explored auctioning off the broadcast spectrum to Internet carriers like AT&T and Verizon for large sums, with financial incentives for those broadcasters who abandoned the use of the spectrum. The auctions, announced by Lawrence Summers, Director of the National Economic Council, were expected to raise many billions for the Treasury. Congress then apparently had trouble with the incentives and in March 2011, the FCC chairman announced there would be a modification of the plan. In April 2011, the Chairman called for voluntary incentive auctions and a quick move on the spectrum transfer to mobile use.[62]

The FCC might authorize some spectrum use by broadcasters who wish to continue broadcasting. Steven Waldman, senior advisor to the chairman of the FCC for anti-trust and the First Amendment, and the FCC official in charge of the FCC's future media studies, earlier suggested that any broadcaster's continued use of the spectrum would require its agreement to comply with FCC content regulations. This apparently would include the new Localism, Balance, and Diversity

Doctrine and local control boards. The result would be substantial and unreviewable government power over news and speech content in the guise of new public interest regulations.

Regulating the Internet

On December 21, 2010, the FCC took control of the Internet to regulate traffic, use and content. Its decision could be overturned or amended by Congress or a reviewing court.[63]

The Internet uses broadband to send and receive bits of information from any point to any other point without any appreciable limit and at almost instantaneous speeds. The FCC says:

> The term "broadband" refers to advanced communications systems capable of providing high-speed transmission of services such as data, voice, and video over the Internet and other networks. Transmission is provided by a wide range of technologies, including digital subscriber line and fiber optic cable, coaxial cable, wireless technology, and satellite. Broadband platforms make possible the convergence of voice, video, and data services onto a single network.

The FCC also says broadband technology is a "key driver of economic growth:"

> The ability to share large amounts of information at ever-greater speeds increases productivity, facilitates commerce, and drives innovation. Broadband is changing how we communicate with each other, how and where we work, how we educate our children, and how we entertain ourselves. Broadband is particularly critical in rural areas, where advanced communications can shrink the distances that isolate remote communities.[64]

The FCC Internet decision imposes a few general rules but leaves to future regulation on a case-by-case basis the large number of market and other dispositive questions that will require FCC investigations and rulings. The three rules that are set out for this vast new national and international enterprise that the FCC says are grounded in broadly accepted Internet norms and the FCC's prior decisions are:

i. Transparency. Fixed and mobile broadband providers must disclose the network management practices, performance characteristics, and terms and conditions of their broadband services;

ii. No blocking. Fixed broadband providers may not block lawful content, applications, services, or non-harmful devices; mobile broadband providers may not block lawful websites, or block applications that compete with their voice or video telephony services; and

iii. No unreasonable discrimination. Fixed broadband providers may not unreasonably discriminate in transmitting lawful network traffic.[65]

Addressing only the First Amendment issues of the FCC decision, the Internet has achieved remarkable success from its openness and has done so with little government interference. Congressman Henry Waxman, who was the chair of the House Energy and Commerce Committee until January 2009, considered ways to control Internet content. Senior staff working for acting FCC Commissioner Michael Copps, Chairman Genochowski's predecessor, reportedly held meetings with advisers to Waxman "to discuss ways the committee could create openings for the FCC to put in place a form of the 'Fairness Doctrine' without actually calling it such." It was also reported that Waxman was interested in looking at how the Internet was being used. The Committee staff was quoted:

Do four stations in one region carry Rush Limbaugh, and nothing else during the same time slot? Does one heavily trafficked Internet site present one side of an issue and not link to sites that present alternative views? . . . we are going to have an FCC that will finally have the people in place to answer.[66]

At one time, Professor Sunstein said he believed Internet content should be regulated by the Fairness Doctrine. When he took on the job as head of OIRA, he was interviewed by the press about his views and expected influence over federal regulations. One interviewer, Adam Thierer, reported that some years before, Sunstein had originally called for "popular or partisan Web sites" to be forced to carry links to opposing viewpoints on the Internet, a Fairness Doctrine on steroids, as it were.[67]

Sunstein may now have dropped his support for this method of speech regulation. In a November 2007 interview, he said, "It's reasonable for government to think about creating the equivalent of linking obligations and pop-ups, so that you'd be on one site—say, a conservative site—and there'd be a pop-up from a liberal site. I now believe that the government should not consider that. [It's] certainly an unconstitutional suggestion." How far this disavowal goes is not yet known, and other methods of content regulation remain. Professor Sunstein, for example, appears to support the Localism, Balance, and Diversity Doctrine. Also, Sunstein's writings claim, as noted earlier, that legislative fairness doctrines would pass constitutional muster and their adoption could even be the legislature's duty.[68]

In its December 2010 Internet decision section on First Amendment issues, the FCC cites the *Turner* decision for its authority to regulate Internet content. Perhaps the FCC and OIRA will argue to a new Supreme Court that it should allow regulation of Internet content under the *Turner* decision for select government purposes as Sunstein appears to read the potential of that decision. This position is a clear threat to constitutional self-government and to free speech and a free press.

If the FCC citation of the *Turner* case is intended only to support some future FCC ruling requiring a broadband provider to carry material from a customer that the FCC has determined the network is blocking for its own commercial purpose, this could be a traffic issue and would be confronted under its December decision. But if the blocking is based on news and speech content, the issue would be quite different.

Ideas for content development for the Internet news could be generated by many sources if left unregulated by government agencies. For example, it has been suggested by observers that some greater participation of citizens in news gathering for news accounts could now be a practical possibility. Professor Jonathan Zittrain, co-founder and co-director of the Harvard Berkman Center for Internet & Society, has urged this. Professor Zittrain was previously the chair in Internet governance and regulation at Oxford University and a principal in the Oxford Internet Institute. At a recent lecture at the Harvard Kennedy Center, Zittrain, now professor of law at the Harvard Law School, identified several possible factors that could contribute to the future of news on the Internet. His view is that the values that make the American press great "are worth sharing with the public at large not just through the product of a well-tuned press but through its process ..." He says, "We should be encouraging more people, certainly our kids ... to take part in the *functions* of the press."

He recognizes that "[t]here is a skill to journalism; a solid story requires more than just someone asking questions of a source." Now with the Internet there is the prospect of adding more vigor, depth, and firsthand knowledge to news coverage. The press has the opportunity to recruit people for "their stories that they can tell, their cell phone tapes, their sharp eyes and minds, especially when they live and know the situation that the typical reporter can only approach as an outsider..." The professional press could provide editorial supervision. Zittrain sees a more productive and possibly symbiotic link between press and citizen in local communities.[69] He does not call for government supervision or oversight for social purposes. As Judge Bazelon found, the participation of government in a news process would likely limit it, as did the Fairness Doctrine in suppressing news. The Harvard Berkman Center is also now developing models for the production of interactive documentaries with public participation. This could lead to a significant broadening and deepening of news coverage unless constrained by the government pursuing objectives other than the free flow of information. In July 2011 Professor Zittrain was appointed a Distinguished Scholar to serve at the FCC in its development of the Internet.

The constitutional philosophy of Professor Sunstein must raise concerns above all because government control and management of political speech, which he finds desirable, are in direct opposition to this country's basic belief in the protection of speech and news freedom from government abridgement. Sunstein describes his vision in putting legislatures or government administrative agencies in charge:

> [I]t will be necessary to abandon or at least to qualify the basic principles that have dominated judicial, academic, and popular thinking about speech in the last generation . . . For the next generation, a shift to administrative bodies, and to democratic arenas, generally is necessary."[70]

This view is focused directly and emphatically at television. Sunstein writes that this would result in "large shifts in current understandings and practices—involving government regulation of broadcasting, including above all television." He says this and greater campaign regulation would counteract the "soundbite" phenomenon that currently threatens democratic deliberation in America.[71]

He has for many years maintained that "the democratic goals of the American constitutional tradition" call for "non-judicial actors—Congress, the president, state officials, ordinary citizens—to engage in deliberation about the meaning of the Constitution's broad guarantees."[72] Deliberation is one thing, but, at present, Congress makes laws and their abridgment of the freedom of speech and press is explicitly prohibited by the First Amendment.

Yet, Sunstein has argued that to meet the needs of the modern state, "Free speech principles would have to be revised in some dramatic ways." Sunstein urges the possibility of what he describes as a more democratic conception of the role of the Constitution in the nation's political life. He insists the Constitution is not identical to the interpretations of the Supreme Court. He argues that:

> ...the relevant law should be enacted and implemented by legislatures and administrators, with courts performing a secondary role. Here I suggest a new allocation of authority between the representative branches even or perhaps especially when their actions are inspired by their understanding of what the Constitution requires.[73]

There is now a growing appreciation in scholarly circles of a "deliberative democracy." Persuasion and debate would reach an informed consensus in Congress on major issues and legislation rather than what is described as the present practice of elected representatives' unyielding advocacy and rigid defense of constituents' interests. For this to work at all, there must be the right and the ability to speak freely and openly not only for members of Congress, but for all people. Proposals for this new approach assume, as well, a free press.[74]

The early Americans came to recognize the need to protect their rights from actions of their Congress. In England the threats had come from the king, not the parliament, which was seen as representing the people. But then in America, when state and national legislators abused their power and injured the people and minorities, the Founders created the Bill of Rights.[75]

Pulitzer Prize–winning author Gordon S. Wood, in *The Idea of America: Reflections on the Birth of the United States*, writes of this and that "The Federalists in the 1780s had a glimpse of what America was to become—a scrambling business society dominated by the pecuniary interests of ordinary people . . . In place of a classical republic led by a disinterested enlightened elite, Americans got a democratic marketplace of equally competing individuals with interests to promote." Wood says, "Such a diverse, rootless, and restless people – what could possibly hold them together? [He quotes Tocqueville:] 'Interest. That is the secret. The private interest that breaks through at each moment, the interest that moreover, appears openly and even proclaims itself as a social theory.'"[76]

Those establishing the American government saw the need to have the judiciary protect the people's rights and interests. By the late 1780s, James Madison addressed the problem of parties in the legislature "becoming judges in their own causes and violating the rights of individuals and minorities." Madison along with many other Americans "came to the conclusion that perhaps the judiciary," not the legislature, was "the only governmental institution that could even come close" to providing impartial and even-handed decisions.[77] The power to interpret the First Amendment of the Bill of Rights devolved upon the Supreme Court, not the legislature. The danger seen is reflected in the language of that Amendment. It was Congress that was explicitly prohibited from making laws abridging the freedom of speech and of the press.

Preserving Free Speech and a Free Press

There have been 235 years of American history sustaining the basic principles of a free press and free speech. Speakers and press have generally been protected against government prosecution and punishment for their views or what they have reported. Some exceptions have been made for national security purposes. In 1798, the Alien and Sedition Acts were passed. There was fear that France was planning to go to war against the U.S. In 1917 during World War I, an Espionage Act was passed for the defense of the U.S. in wartime. During the 1920s the fear of communism and socialism taking over the U.S. led Attorney General Mitchell Palmer to conduct prosecutions of speech "for a disease of evil thinking." Since speech and thought are so interconnected, and restrictions on speech can be restrictions on thought, Palmer's approach seemed to make sense at the time. It might be said that the Fairness Doctrine decision in *Red Lion* in 1949 was a similar kind of exception prompted partly out of fear of television and what a scarcity of frequencies limiting the number of publishers in a market might do to the country. The Supreme Court held that the government could take away the license to speak (and enable others to speak) for violating government rules requiring government-approved balance. But the basic principles for the freedom of speech and press in America have generally held fast.

This study has shown how government regulation of the content of speech and news does inevitably suppress news and chill speech that is needed by the people for self-government in a democracy. The record of the Fairness Doctrine shows that when reporters know that the government may investigate and review their news reports for compliance with a government standard, reporters are deterred from covering the news. (See Chapter 6, The FCC Revokes the Fairness Doctrine.) Chapter 4 of this study has earlier reported some of the testimony by CBS News officials about Congressional investigations of press editorial news judgments (see Chapter 4, Congressional Investigations and Censorship):

1. Walter Cronkite, Managing Editor of CBS Evening News: "If reporters must consider the possibility of being summoned before an investigative arm of the government to justify these [reporting and editing] decisions, I believe that independence and vigor in broadcast journalism will be inevitably sacrificed."

2. Daniel Schorr, CBS Correspondent: "A person interviewed would be inhibited . . . if the government could investigate all a reporter's notes."

3. William Small, CBS News Washington Bureau Chief: "Some [have been] unwilling to come to CBS News with reports because CBS was in hot water with Congress and who knew where their investigation would lead."

4. Mike Wallace, CBS Staff Correspondent: "There would necessarily be the imposition of a government standard of truth."

5. Gordon Manning, Vice President and Director and head of CBS hard news: "The editor's chief allegiance must be to the viewer."

6. Burton Benjamin, CBS Senior Executive Producer, "knew of no country where government supervision and control had improved the vigor and integrity of the news."

The FCC found similar concerns on the part of local station news officials and reporters. It also found that FCC investigations, inquiries, and threats had in practice under the Fairness Doctrine created an atmosphere of timidity and fear, deterring news coverage. The addition of an official local board for each station as part of the nation's broadcast regulation scheme would drastically change news coverage and the flow of information to the public, as would the so-called Localism Doctrine itself, in practice. Members of such local boards with the power and regulatory requirement to recommend license revocation for television station failure to obey or follow suggestions would become easy targets for lobbying by any number of special interests, political parties, and factions. There would be no practical protection for the local board members or the local station against those seeking favored treatment, news coverage, and programming that could advantage them or the use of connections, funds, or improper or even illegal conduct to pressure members of the local boards. The new doctrine thus threatens still further intimidation of the broadcast press.

Station news cannot be independent of the government or free from government control, including FCC regulatory control, if it is accountable to an official local advisory board reporting to the FCC. This is particularly of constitutional concern if the station is covering local news and politics and the local advisory board must recommend non-renewal of the station's broadcast license if it concludes that the station has not satisfactorily complied with FCC regulations of news and speech.

The First Amendment's expression of the freedom of press and speech has proved a substantial contribution to freedom in this country. It has done so because it has been enforced against government interference. It continues to be imperative for the country's future that the singular function of a free press to watch the government and report to the country's citizens, as well as reporting other news, be sustained and not suppressed.

The First Amendment Center conducted a public survey in 2009 on the state of the First Amendment. It reported that "Americans still support the idea of a free press as a watchdog on government, and turn to traditional news sources on major news stories despite skepticism about bias in the news media."[78] In a 2006 survey, 34 percent of high school students thought the First Amendment goes too far but 64 percent said high school newspapers should be allowed to report controversial subjects without approval by authorities.[79] This seems a robust and youthful vision of news and speech.

On World Press Freedom Day in 2011, the U.S. State Department spokesman said all citizens must take time to think about the role of a free press and what it means to society. "Journalists should . . . not be the only ones standing for press freedom 'but each one of us who recognize the value of an informed citizenry must also stand up for this fundamental right.' "[80]

In 2010, on World Press Freedom Day, Secretary of State Hillary Clinton made the point:

A free press is essential to an empowered citizenry, government accountability and responsible economic development. Wherever independent media are under threat, accountable governance and human freedom are undermined.[81]

The historian Gordon S. Wood observes what he sees as important to the nation's future:

> What the future will be is impossible to tell. All we can do with our history is to remember that the United States has always been to ourselves and to the world primarily an idea.[82]

It also should be stressed for America's future that free speech and a free press are a vital part of that idea.[83]

CONCLUSION

⁓

The FCC adoption of regulations to manage news content in the name of localism, balance, and diversity would create new opportunities for government suppression of news and speech, intimidation of the broadcast press, and censorship. It would impose government control over news coverage in practice similar to the Fairness Doctrine, which the FCC itself revoked in 1987 as against the public interest.

The reviewing Court affirmed the revocation of that doctrine, holding that it: "... disserves both the public's right to diverse sources of information and the broadcaster's interest in free expression. Its chilling effect thwarts its intended purpose ..."

It found that television "...[l]icensees are intimidated by the FCC from broadcasting even when they believe they are right."

It warned that "... the Fairness Doctrine provides a dangerous vehicle—which had been exercised in the past by unscrupulous officials—for the intimidation of broadcasters who criticize governmental policy."

Yet, it is now proposed by officials in government that a similar doctrine be imposed on television and perhaps even review Internet news and speech for what the government will decide is appropriate to establish news balance and, as well, localism and diversity.

Implementation of this new doctrine would be carried out by a quasi-official local advisory board appointed for each station. The local boards across the country and the FCC would enforce the new social and political policies and regulations with threats of fines and, as with the Fairness Doctrine, loss of the license to broadcast. Members of the local boards would be required to recommend to the FCC that a station's license be revoked if in their opinion the local station had not complied with FCC regulations.

This would create a powerful new government control apparatus whose interference with broadcast news and political speech might not be publicly known and in all events would be largely unreviewable by the courts. The management of broadcast news by the then incumbent administration and the FCC would be unprecedented. It would represent a clear danger to the independence and freedom of the broadcast press.

Freedom of speech and the press would be sacrificed to serve the government's use of news and information to advance certain selected social and political goals. The head of the White House Office of Information and Regulatory Affairs has urged this for a number of years as have some other government officials and members of congress.

The President, Congress, and the FCC have agreed to take over the broadcast spectrum and allocate it to the Internet for use mobile and other technologies. The FCC is acting under that agreement and its decision of December 2010 to take control of the broadcast spectrum and the Internet. FCC history and its present proposals show regulation of news and speech will likely follow.

The record of government management of broadcasting as well as news reports in the past shows that each branch of government and members of both political parties have sought to control and manage television news content, particularly to prevent criticism or the exposure of wrongdoing. They have sometimes succeeded. They have used, as the record shows, government regulations, official charges of wrongdoing, subpoenas, public government hearings, broadcast license challenges, the threat of broadcast license revocations, and various other threats and acts of intimidation.

Some may seek to use government power over news coverage and speech to further their own political or personal purposes, as was the case under the Fairness Doctrine. They will try to force the press to publish what seems to them to be advantageous and to suppress the news that seems unfavorable. Censorship methods of the past to control television news now proposed for the future would be used again to suppress the news, intimidate press coverage, and silence political speech and dissent. Broadcast experience demonstrates conclusively that the government must be kept at arm's length from control of news and information content.

As the print press continues to suffer economic losses, it will become much weaker in its ability to uncover government wrongdoing. The new press, including the broadcast press, should have both the resources and independence from government necessary to act as the public's watchdog over what the government does. But it is imperative that television and Internet news be free of government control and management, which history shows will be used to censor the news and punish the press.

NOTES

Notes for Chapter 1: Television Journalism Begins

1. Only broadcast programming is regulated by the government with policies such as those expressed in the Fairness Doctrine. The Supreme Court has held that the programs cable produces cannot constitutionally be regulated by the government (with some exceptions like obscenity and pornography) because cable does not use electronic frequencies for their transmissions, and thus does not fall under FCC's jurisdiction granted by Congress. Wikipedia, http://en.wikipedia.org/wiki/1948_Republican_National_Convention [Republican National Convention, Wikipedia]; 1948 Democratic National Convention, Wikipedia, google.com/search?client=gmail&rls=gm&q=democratic%20 1948%20national%20convention [Democratic National Convention, Wikipedia]; Reuven Frank, *Out of Thin Air: The Brief Wonderful Life of Network News* (New York: Simon & Schuster, 1991), 7–8. [Hereafter cited as *Out of Thin Air*]. The Dumont Television Network struggled to continue as a network but a number of adverse factors brought about its end in 1956, http://en.wikipedia.org/wiki/DuMont_Television_Network.
2. *Out of Thin Air*, 8–9.
3. Ibid., 8–27.
4. Ibid., 9.

5. Ibid., 7, 11, 12.
6. Republican National Convention, Wikipedia; *Out of Thin Air*, 14.
7. *Out of Thin Air*, 16.
8. Ibid., 18.
9. Democratic National Convention, Wikipedia; *Out of Thin Air*, 18–21.
10. *Out of Thin Air*, 21, 22.
11. Ibid., 22.
12. Ibid., 25.
13. Ibid., 26–27.

Notes for Chapter 2: Regulation of Television News Content Upheld by the Supreme Court

1. http://en.wikipedia.org/wiki/Fairness_Doctrine.
2. Ibid.; http://www.museum.tv/eotvsection. php?entrycode=fairnessdoct (accessed Mar. 14, 2011). [Hereafter cited as Museum.]
3. Ibid.; See Chapter 3, How FCC Regulations Suppressed News and Speech.
4. http://en.wikipedia.org/wiki/First_Amendment_to_the_ United_States_Constitution#Text.
5. *Red Lion Broadcasting Co. v. FCC*, 395 U.S. 367 (1969). [Hereafter cited as *Red Lion*.]
6. Ibid.
7. Ibid.
8. This study does not address restrictions on press and speech for national security, public safety, obscenity, pornography, or issues other than free speech, free press, and protections against government control to manage the content of speech and news for broadcasting, cable, or the Internet.
9. This quantitative rule has been changed but the FCC does still review the station's local news and other local community and public affairs programming. For one example of the ongoing reassessment of such rules, see report of Wiley Rein, www. wileyrein.com/publications.cfm?sp=articles&newsletter=5&id=2 539 [Mr.Wiley, the senior partner of this law firm, was formerly a chairman of the FCC].
10. Excerpts from *Red Lion* decision, Appendix 1, Excerpts.
11. Concurring Opinion in *Columbia Broadcasting System v. Democratic National Committee*, 412 U.S. 94,154, 158,162 (1973), Communications Act of 1934, as amended.

12. *Red Lion*, 448; See Prof. Cass R. Sunstein comments on *Red Lion*, Cass R. Sunstein, *Democracy and the Problem of Free Speech* (New York: Simon & Schuster, 1993, 1995). [Hereafter cited as *Problem of Free Speech*.]

13. http://en.wikipedia.org/wiki/Censorship_in_the_United_States, e.g., "comic books" movies, see Penny Dreadfuls.

14. Professor Archibald Cox, interview by author about the Fairness Doctrine, Harvard Law School, 1979.

15. Communications Act of 1934, as amended, http://en.wikipedia.org/wiki/Communications_Act_of_1934. See Chapter 6, The FCC Revokes the Fairness Doctrine.

16. The 1960s and 1970s were a time of roiling political upset ranging from fear of Communism to losses in the Vietnam War and student demonstrations against the Vietnam War. For example, at one point when President Richard Nixon was addressing the nation on television on his plans to continue prosecution of the war, military troops were secreted in the corridor between the Treasury Building and the White House since no one could safely predict what the public reaction to this speech might be. See also Nixon and Vietnam War, http://en.wikipedia.org/wiki/Richard_Nixon#First_term_.281969-1973.29.

17. Fairness Doctrine station obligation, http://www.bookrags.com/tandf/fairness-doctrine-controversial-issue-tf/.

18. *Time*, http://time.com/time/nation/article/0,8599,1880789.00html.

19. *Miami Herald Post Co. v. Tornillo*, 418 U.S. 241, 258 (1976). [Hereafter cited as *Tornillo*.]

20. *Tornillo*, p. 255, fn. 20: "[L]iberty of the press is in peril as soon as the government tries to compel what is to go into a newspaper. A journal does not merely print observed facts the way a cow is photographed through a plate-glass window. As soon as the facts are set in their context, you have interpretation and you have selection, and editorial selection opens the way to

editorial suppression. Then how can the state force abstention from discrimination in the news without dictating selection?" Z. Chafee, *Government and Mass Communications,* 633 (1947).

21. See Chapter 6, The FCC Revokes the Fairness Doctrine.

22. *CBS, Inc. v. Democratic National Committee*, 412 U.S. 94, 145–46 (1973) (Stewart, J., concurring).

23. The Supreme Court unanimously rejected the legislative requirement of the state of Florida that newspapers provide a right of reply. *Miami Herald Post Co. v. Tornillo*, 418 U.S. 241 (1976).

24. *Tornillo*, 257.

25. *Tornillo*, 258.

Notes for Chapter 3: How FCC Regulations Suppressed News and Speech

1. Communications Act of 1934, as amended by Telecom Act of 1996, http://en.wikipedia.org/wiki/Communications_Act_of_1934.

2. The former general counsel of the FCC, Henry Geller, Esq., explains that commissioners and staff did not have time enough to watch the videos at issue and were forced to rely on print transcripts in many cases. Comment for author, March 3, 2010; Federal Communications Commission, Wikipedia, http://en.wikipedia.org/wiki/Federal_Communications_Commission.

3. Ibid.

4. FCC Commissioner McDowell Address, 2009, Chapter 7, New Government Threats, *infra*.

5. Bill Monroe, the former Washington editor of NBC's *Today* show, interview by author, Washington, DC, 1995. Fairness Doctrine, Enforcement, Wikipedia, http://en.wikipedia.org/wiki/Fairness_Doctrine.

6. This was all accepted practice although some question was raised about it in later years. Professor Archibald Cox, interview by author about the Fairness Doctrine, Harvard Law School, 1979.

7. Fairness Doctrine, Wikipedia, http://en.wikipedia.org/wiki/Fairness_Doctrine; Daniel Schorr, *Clearing the Air* (Boston: Houghton Mifflin, 1997), 34.

8. *DNC v. FCC*, 481 F.2d 543, 156 U.S. App. DC 368 (1973).

9. Broadcast stations were and are directly regulated by the FCC. The networks have not been directly regulated. But to supply their affiliated stations with news, public affairs, entertainment, and children's programming, networks had to comply with the applicable FCC rules so the network programming could be used by the station without danger of violating an FCC rule

or regulation. The FCC, in that way, did oversee much of all broadcast program operations as well as regulate the programming originated by the stations owned by the networks, a maximum of five each at that time. *Broadcasting Magazine,* Network Station Ownership, Wikipedia, http://books.google.com/books?id=Kd_ 1STqyGFcC&pg=PA101&lpg=PA101&dq=broadcasting+magaz ine+network+station+ownership&source=bl&ots=5r2eNzAn0t& sig=9cEdm07VjKzL33jyTWKDIaPK8_4&hl=en&ei=vDCGTc 27Fsz2gAf_3sDSCA&sa=X&oi=book_result&ct=result&resnu m=9&ved=0CEcQ6AEwC A#v=onepage&q=broadcasting%20 magazine%20network%20station%20ownership&f=false.

10. "Our massive strategy was to use the Fairness Doctrine to challenge and harass right-wing broadcasters and hope the challenges would be so costly to them that they would be inhibited and decide it was too expensive to continue." Bill Ruder, Democratic campaign consultant and Assistant Secretary of Commerce, Kennedy Administration, William Ruder, Wikipedia, http://en.wikipedia.org/wiki/William_Ruder.

11. See Chapter 6, The FCC Revokes the Fairness Doctrine.

12. See Chapter 3, How FCC Regulations Suppressed News and Speech: Failed Pension Plans Case; also, Appendix 2, Excerpts, The Failed Pension Plans Case.

13. Ibid., See Chapter 6, The FCC Revokes the Fairness Doctrine.

14. Broadcast License Renewal, Wikipedia, http://en.wikipedia.org/ wiki/Broadcast_license.

15. In the Matter of Inquiry Into WBBM-TV's Broadcast on November 1 and 2, 1967 of a Report on a Marijuana Party, WBBM-TV, 16 RR2d 207 (1969), 18 FCC 2d 124.

16. House, Special Subcommittee on Investigations of the Committee on Interstate and Foreign Commerce, "Report on Deceptive Programming Practices, Staging of Marijuana Broadcast *Pot Party at a University,*" 91st Cong., 1st Sess., 1969, House Report No. 91–108.

17. Broadcast Licensing, Wikipedia, http://en.wikipedia.org/ wiki/Broadcast_licensehttp://en.wikipedia.org/wiki/Federal_ Communications_Commission#Broadcast_licensing.

18. Communications Law, Pike & Fisher, see proposal for change in procedure for Fairness Doctrine violations in the record of the Failed Pension Plans case decision filed by Henry Geller, Esq. (Appendix 2, Excerpts, The Failed Pension Plans Case).

19. Testimony of former Commissioner James Quello, *FCC Fairness Doctrine Hearings*. Federal Communications Commission, (last accessed November 30, 2010). A broadcast license could be denied for a violation of the Fairness Doctrine or for other violations. It is generally said that only one station license was lost because of a program content violation of the Fairness Doctrine. But the threat was ever present and *in terrorem*. The fact is that the FCC investigations and procedures were pursued and broadcasters followed the rules, which is demonstrated by so few FCC findings of violations followed by the assessment of a penalty. For other charges of wrongdoing and license revocation, see, e.g., proceedings before the FCC when RKO General lost a broadcast license in 1987 because of questions raised about the honesty of statements made to the FCC and conduct at a related corporate entity. The Boston station license was revoked without compensation and RKO was required to sell its other broadcast stations at below market value. RKO General, Wikipedia, http:// en.wikipedia.org/wiki/RKO_General.

20. Chapter 6, The FCC Revokes the Fairness Doctrine.

21. *Red Lion v. FCC*, 395 U.S. 367, 396 (1969); See proposal for change in procedure for Fairness Doctrine violations in the record of the *Failed Pension Plans Case* decision filed by Henry Geller, Esq. (Appendix 2).

22. William O. Douglas, BookRags, Quotes, http://www.bookrags. com/quotes. http://www.bookrags.com/quotes; William_O._ Douglas, Wikipedia; Speech and news do not lend themselves to

186

regulation as does, say, canned fish. When the government was regulating speech and news, it was often difficult to persuade regulators of a particular meaning and even the value of thought and speech as well as the importance of audience perception when assessing differences in language, as well as the great differences in individual tastes and understandings of the audience. All this shows how the video, the most persuasive element in many instances, was accepted as described in words chosen by the FCC officials who had seen the video but not the commissioners who voted.

23. Ford Rowan, *Broadcast Fairness, Practice, Prospects*, New York, Longman (1984), 121–123. See Chapter 3, How FCC Regulations Suppressed News and Speech; Chapter 4, Congressional Investigations and Censorship; Chapter 6, The FCC Revokes the Fairness Doctrine; affidavits and statements of CBS News people Walter Cronkite, William Small, and Dan Rather.

24. No precise dollar value is usually placed on a broadcast license standing alone, as such, since it is not an asset owned by the licensee but a grant for a few years, and pretty much everything depends on the broadcast programming, audience, and location and hitting the upside of the audience interest. For a general roundup of FCC licensing and its scope as well as corporate transactions involving stations with licenses, see Answers. com. http://www.answers.com/topic/federal-communications-commission. See also Viacom, Facebook, http://zhhk.facebook. com/note.php?note_id=204650861836, Broadcast License, North America, United States, Wikipedia, http://en.wikipedia. org/wiki/Broadcast_license.

25. Fairness Doctrine, Wikipedia, http://en.wikipedia.org/wiki/ Broadcast_license; Fairness Doctrine, Museum, http://www. museum.tv/eotvsection.php?entrycode=fairnessdoct.

26. Bill Ruder, Democratic campaign consultant and Assistant Secretary of Commerce, Kennedy Administration, http:// en.wikipedia.org/wiki/William_Ruder.

27. *Denver Area Educational Telecommunications Consortium*, 518 U.S. 727 (1996); *Reno v. ACLU*, 521 U.S. 844 (1997); but see FCC Internet Decision of December 21, 2010, FCC 10-201, http://www.fcc.gov/Daily_Releases/Daily_Business/2010/ db1223/FCC-10-201A1.pdf.

28. *In re Committee for the Fair Broadcasting of Controversial Issues v. CBS, Inc.* 25 FCC 2d 283 (1970), *In re Republican National Committee v. CBS, Inc.* 25 FCC 2d 739 (1970), reversed sub nom, *CBS v. FCC*, 454 F2d 1018 (D.C. Cir. 1971); *CBS v. DNC*, 412 U.S. 94 (1973) [including discussion of the Fairness Doctrine and court acceptance of a network refusal to sell political editorial advertising time, relying on its coverage of points of view on controversial issues and regular news coverage of issues as providing news for the viewing public as to these issues].

29. *DNC v. FCC*, 460 F. 2d 891, cert. denied 409 US 843 (1972). See *DNC v. FCC*, 481 F2d 543, 156 U.S. App. D.C. 368 (1973) [including a review by the circuit court of its holdings about political speech]; *CBS v. DNC*, 412 U.S. 94 (1973) [discussion of the Fairness Doctrine and court acceptance of a network refusal to sell political editorial advertising time, relying on its coverage of points of view on controversial issues and regular news coverage issues of providing news for the viewing public as to these issues]; Klein, *Making It Perfectly Clear*; Hebert Klein interview by author, San Diego, CA, 1993.

30. White House Special Files, (WHSF), Charles W. Colson files, Chrono folder, (November 1970).

31. See Chapter 3, How FCC Regulations Suppressed News and Speech: Airport Congestion case; Failed Pension Plans case.

32. Morton I. Hamburg and Stuart N. Brotman, Fairness Doctrine Cases 1960s–1970s *Communications Law and Practice*, books. google.com.

33. Appendix 2, Excerpts, The Failed Pension Plans Case.

34. Ibid.

35. Ibid.
36. Ibid.
37. Ibid.
38. Ibid.
39. Ibid.
40. FCC Failed Pension Plans Decision, 44 F.C.C. 2d 1180, on appeal, *NBC v. FCC*, 516 F 2d 1101 (D.C. Circuit 1974). Excerpts from the appellate court's decision reversing the FCC, Appendix 2.
41. The full appellate court in the Failed Pension Plans case vacated the panel decision of Judge Leventhal.
42. Lucas A. Powe, Jr., *American Broadcasting and the First Amendment* (Berkeley: University of California Press, 1987).

Notes for Chapter 4: Congressional Investigations and Censorship

1. 1968 Democratic National Convention, Wikipedia, http://en.wikipedia.org/wiki/1968_Democratic_National_Convention.
2. Ibid; Reuven Frank, *Out of Thin Air: The Brief Wonderful Life of Network News* (New York: Simon & Schuster, 1991), 270–283 [Hereafter cited as *Out Of Thin Air*].
3. *Out of Thin Air*, 270–283.
4. Ibid., 270–283; 1968 Democratic National Convention, Wikipedia, http://en.wikipedia.org/wiki/1968_Democratic_National_Convention.
5. *Out Of Thin Air*, 271, 270–283.
6. William Small interview by author, New York, N.Y., March 9, 2010.
7. Ibid.; *Out Of Thin Air*, 269–284.
8. *Out Of Thin Air*, 269, 270–289.
9. Ibid., 283, 284. Many thought at the time that broadcast of these demonstrations and the police response as well as the turmoil of the convention itself would hurt the Democrats' election chances. But Bill Small, attending the convention for CBS News, points out that the Democratic candidate for president, Hubert Humphrey, probably lost the election not because of the Chicago convention, but because during his campaign he could not separate himself from President Lyndon Johnson and his unpopular waging of the Vietnam War. William Small interview by author, New York, N.Y.,March 9, 2010.
10. *Out of Thin Air*, 283.
11. Ibid., 270–289.
12. Ibid., 270–289, 284; House, Special Subcommittee on Investigations of the Committee of Interstate and Foreign

Commerce, Staff Report, "Television Coverage of the Democratic National Convention in Chicago, Illinois, 1968," 91st Congress 1st Sess. 1968 (Committee Print, 1969) 1, 3–14, 21.

13. House, Special Subcommittee on Investigations of the Committee of Interstate and Foreign Commerce, Staff Report, "Television Coverage of the Democratic National Convention in Chicago, Illinois, 1968," 91st Congress 1st Sess. 1968 (Committee Print, 1969) 1, 3–14, 21.

14. *Out of Thin Air*, 284.

15. House, Special Subcommittee on Investigations of the Committee of Interstate and Foreign Commerce, Staff Report, "Television Coverage of the Democratic National Convention in Chicago, Illinois, 1968," 91st Congress 1st Sess. 1968 (Committee Print, 1969) 1, 3–14, 21; *Out of Thin Air*, 280.

16. *Out of Thin Air*, 284; Democratic National Convention 1968, Wikipedia, http://en.wikipedia.org/wiki/1968_Democratic_National_Convention.

17. *Out of Thin Air,* 275, 280.

18. Ibid.

19. Ibid., 283, 284.

20. Ibid., 274–286.

21. Daniel Walker, *Rights in Conflict* (New York: Bantam Books, 1968).

22. Ibid., *Out of Thin Air*, 284.

23. Ibid., 285–286.

24. Timothy B. Dyk and Ralph E. Goldberg, "The First Amendment and Congressional Investigations of Broadcasting Programming," *The Journal of Law and Politics* (University of Virginia, 3:4 Spring 1987).

25. In re Press Coverage of Chicago Convention, 15 R R 2d (P &F) 791, 16 F.C.C. 2d 650.

26. Ibid.

27. NBC filing in the FCC Staging proceeding; In re Press Coverage of Chicago Convention, 15 R R 2d (P &F) 791, 16 F.C.C. 2d 650.

28. Ibid.

29. Peter Davis interview by author.

30. *The Selling of the Pentagon* program can be viewed at the Museum of Radio and Television, 25 West Fifty-second Street, New York, NY. The text is set out in the record of the hearings: Subcommittee Hearings (Transcript) 234–245; *The Selling of the Pentagon*, Museum of Radio and Television, New York, NY. See also Corydon B. Dunham, *Fighting for the First Amendment, Stanton of CBS vs. Congress and the Nixon White House, Foreword by Walter Cronkite* (Westport: Praeger Publishing, 1997) 8–16 [hereafter cited as *Fighting for the First Amendment*].

31. U.S. Congress, House Special Subcommittee on Investigations of the Committee on Interstate and Foreign Commerce, Hearings on Subpoenaed Material re Certain TV News Documentary Programs. 92d Cong., 1st Sess., April 20, May 12, and June 24, 1971, Series No. 92–16, 2–3 (hereafter cited as "Subcommittee Hearings"); U.S. Congress, House, Report of the Committee on Interstate and Foreign Commerce, Proceedings against Frank Stanton and Columbia Broadcasting System, Inc., 92d Cong., 1st Sess., 1971, H.Doc. No. 9203491, 138–39 (hereafter cited as "Committee Report").

32. Subcommittee Hearings (Transcript), 234–245; *The Selling of the Pentagon*, Museum of Radio and Television, New York, NY; *Fighting for the First Amendment*, 8–12.

33. Subcommittee Hearings (Transcript), 234–245.

34. Ibid.

35. Ibid.

36. Ibid.

37. Ibid.

38. Peter Davis, telephone interview and letter to author.

39. Ibid.
40. Correspondence, "The Selling of the Pentagon," Gerald R. Ford Library and Museum, 1000 Beale Avenue, Ann Arbor, Michigan.
41. *Barron's*, March 1971; *Washington Post*, March 21, 30, and April 9, 1971; *New York Times*, March 19, 25, 1971.
42. Peter Davis interview and letter to author. Davis wrote an extensive explanation defending the edits against the Pentagon charges in a memo to Salant; March 12, 1971, Salant Files, Salant Reading Room, New Canaan Library, New Canaan, CT.
43. Subcommittee Hearings (Transcript), 245–246.
44. *Perspective, The Selling of the Pentagon*, CBS Library, New York, NY.
45. Subcommittee Hearings, 245–249. Assistant Secretary Daniel Henkin was repeatedly asked to appear on CBS to present his views, but he declined to do so.
46. *Washington Post*, March 24, 1971.
47. CBS program *Postscript*.
48. *New York Times*, March 25, 1971.
49. *Washington Post*, March 24, 1971. Davis said it would have been foolish to mislead the chairman to obtain the film and he had not done so. Cong. Rec. (CBS Staff analysis), 91st Cong., 2nd Sess., E. 13493-99, 13697–700.
50. Cong. Record, 92d Cong., 1st Sess., March 3, 1971, H. 4993-95; March 24, 1971, H. 5875.
51. *New York Times*, March 24, 1971.
52. *Washington Post*, May 19, 1969.
53. Subcommittee Hearings, 10–12; Daniel J, Manelli, Esq., (Acting Chief Counsel of the Committee) and staff interviews by author, Washington, DC, August 17 and December 8, 1994; staff interviews, Michael F. Barrett, Jr. Esq., Washington, DC, March 8, 1994; Mark J. Rabbe, Esq., Washington, DC, March 19, 1994; *Broadcasting* magazine, July 5, 1971.
54. Subcommittee Hearings, 71–75.
55. Ibid.

56. Ibid. The full proceedings appear in the hearings transcript at 71–150.

57. *Broadcasting* magazine, July 5, 1971.

58. See Irving G. Krasnow, Lawrence D. Longley, and Herbert A. Terry, *The Politics of Broadcast Regulation,* 3rd ed. (New York: St. Martin's Press, 1982), 15–25.

59. Daniel Manelli, Esq., Acting Chief Counsel of the Committee, interviews by author.

60. Committee Report, 12–111.

61. Committee Report, 10. Acting Chief Counsel Daniel Manelli, Esq., interviews by author; Subcommittee press release, *New York Times,* June 30, 1971.

62. Committee Report, 11.

63. Frank Stanton letter to House Speaker Carl Albert, *The Selling of the Pentagon,* July 7, 1971, CBS Library, New York, N.Y.

64. Staggers letter to Colleagues, July 8, 1971, CBS Library, New York, NY.

65. Dissenting Members Letter to Colleagues, July 8, 1971, Congressional Record H. 6572.

66. Congressman Broyhill, Letter to Colleagues, July 8, 1971, CBS Library, New York, N.Y.

67. Congressman Lionel Van Deerlin, San Diego, California, interview by author, September 8, 1995.

68. Frank Stanton interview by author.

69. Congressional Record, 92d Cong., 1st Sess., H. 6577–6580.

70. Ibid.

71. Congressional Record, 92d Cong., 1st Sess., H. 6577–6580. Broadcasting history shows congressional and executive investigations have a chilling impact on news coverage, see e.g., Dyk and Goldberg, *The First Amendment and Congressional Investigations of Broadcast Programming,* 3 J. L. & Pol. 625, 636 (1987), 632–40.

72. Frank Stanton interview by author.

73. Acting Chief Counsel, Daniel Manelli, interviews by author.
74. Subcommittee staff, Manelli, Barrett, and Raabe, interviews by author.
75. *Washington Post,* April 11, 1971.
76. *New York Times,* April 19, 1971.
77. *New York Times,* April 19, 1971.
78. *New York Times,* April 18, 1971.
79. Ibid.
80. *New York Times,* April 13, 1971.
81. Frank Stanton interview by author.
82. Gordon Manning interview by author.
83. Acting Chief Counsel, Daniel Manelli said Staggers believed in congressional supremacy and refused to be crossed by someone regulated, Manelli interview by author.
84. *New York Times,* June 30, 1972.
85. *Broadcasting* magazine, April, 1972, 24.
86. Ibid.
87. Ibid.
88. *Face the Nation* transcript, July 1971, 200–215.
89. Ibid.
90. *Broadcasting* magazine, July 5, 1971.
91. Frank Stanton, interview by author.
92. Ibid.
93. President Gerald Ford, telephone interview by author, November 15, 1994; Congressmen Broyhill and Congressman Brown interviews by author; White House Special Files (WHSF), John W. Dean III, Correspondence File, July 1971.
94. Herbert Klein, interview by author, San Diego, California, 1995.
95. Charles W. Colson, letter to author, May 11, 1995.
96. *Clearing the Air*, 48.
97. Charles Crutchfield, CBS affiliated station, Charlotte, North Carolina, interview by author, May 1995; David Hartman,

Counselor to President Gerald Ford, interview by author, Washington, DC, May 31, 1994; President Gerald Ford, telephone interview by author.

98. Congressional Record, 92d Cong., 1st Sess., July 13, 1971, H. 6639-6643.

99. Ibid., 6643–6645.

100. Ibid., 6577–6580.

101. Ibid., July 9, 1971, Extension of Remarks, E. 7501-7508, E. 7513, 175.

102. Ibid., 6630–6670 [running addresses on the House floor].

103. Ibid.

104. Ibid.

105. Ibid.

106. Ibid.

107. Congressional Record, 92d Cong., 1st Sess., July 13, 1971, H 6669.

108. Congressional Record, 92d Cong., 1st Sess., July 13, 1971, H 6669.

109. *Broadcasting* magazine, July 19, 1971.

110. *Television Digest*, July 19, 1971, 1.

111. Frank Stanton, interview by author; Chairman Staggers staff interviews by author.

112. Congressman Van Deerlin, interview by author.

113. Peter Davis, interview by author.

114. Frank Stanton, interview by author.

Notes for Chapter 5: Executive Branch Censorship

1. Thomas W. Hazlett, "Return of the Fairness Doctrine," *The Public Interest* (Summer 1989); William Ruder, Wikipedia, http://en.wikipedia.org/wiki/William_Ruder.
2. President Lyndon Johnson expanded the harassment campaign with increased funds. It was set up more formally with the title National Council for Civic Responsibility. A Nixon staff member, Jeb Magruder, recommended the White House have the FCC do the same for the Republicans, but nothing was done.
3. Thomas W. Hazlett, "The Fairness Doctrine and the First Amendment," *The Public Interest* (Summer 1989), 105.
4. Joseph C. Spear, *Presidents and the Press* (Cambridge, The MIT Press, 1984), 53–56.
5. Ibid., 54–56; Wikipedia, http://en.wikipedia.org/wiki/Nixon's_last_press_conference: "On November 7, 1962 following his loss to Democratic incumbent Pat Brown in the 1962 California gubernatorial election, appearing before 100 reporters at the Beverly Hilton Hotel, Nixon lashed out at the media, proclaiming that 'you don't have Nixon to kick around any more, because, gentlemen, this is my last press conference.'"
6. Richard Nixon, *The Memoirs of Richard Nixon* (New York: Grosset & Dunlap, 1978), 354–355 [hereafter cited as *Memoirs of Richard Nixon*].
7. For example, see Nixon Presidential Materials Project, White House Special Files. (Hereafter WHSF), Staff Member and Office Files, H. R. Haldeman Notes, April 24, 1971. Folders April–June 1971. Also, "just do what we want for the news on TV" (6/30/71).
8. Henry Kissinger, *White House Years* (Boston: Little, Brown and Company, 1979).
9. Alger Hiss, Wikipedia.

10. WHSF, Staff Member and Office Files, H. R. Haldeman Notes, April 24, 1971. Folders April-June 1971; "must realize importance of TV" (8/9/71) (Folder August 1971); National Archives at College Park, MD, [hereafter cited as Folder]; *Presidents and the Press*, 128; see Henry Kissinger, *White House Years* (Boston: Little, Brown and Company, 1979).

11. Herbert Klein interview by author, San Diego, CA.

12. *Memoirs of Richard Nixon*, 410–411.

13. Ibid.

14. Ronald Kessler, *Inside the White House* (New York: Simon & Schuster, 1995), 27; William Safire, *Before the Fall: An Inside View of the Pre-Watergate White House* (New York: Doubleday & Company, 1975), 175–176, 341 [hereafter cited as *Before the Fall*].

15. *New York Times,* October 6, 1972, 6, 43–45.

16. WHSF, Staff Member and Office Files, H. R. Haldeman Notes "putting all we've done together, will hit Stanton" (8/18/71) (Folder August '71). Jeb Magruder recommended establishing "an official monitoring system through the FCC … If the monitoring system proves our point, we have then legitimate and legal rights to … make official complaints from the FCC." Magruder went on to "liken this to the Kennedy Administration in that they had no qualms about using the power available to them to achieve their objectives. On the other hand, we seem to march on tip-toe into the political situation and are unwilling to use the power at hand to achieve our long-term goals …" The FCC's 1985 Fairness Doctrine Report notes that there is no evidence indicating that a Nixon-era Fairness Doctrine "monitoring program" was ever established—even though the Nixon Administration eventually dispensed with the subtleties of "tip-toeing" during its political pursuits.

17. Joseph C. Spear, *Presidents and the Press*: *The Nixon Legacy* (Cambridge: The MIT Press, 1984), 113 [hereafter cited as *Presidents and the Press*].

18. Reuven Frank, *Out Of Thin Air: The Brief Wonderful Life of Network News* (New York: Simon & Schuster, 1991), 297–298 [hereafter cited as *Out Of Thin Air*].

19. Charles W. Colson, Letter to author, May 11, 1995; Charles W. Colson, *Born Again*, (Old Tappan: Chosen Books, 1976), 41 [hereafter cited as *Born Again*].

20. WHSF, Charles W. Colson Files, Chrono Folder, August 1970; WHSF, Staff Member and Office Files, H. R. Haldeman Notes, April 24, 1971. Folders April-June 1971; "must realize importance of TV" (8/9/71) (Folder August 1971, National Archives at College Park, MD, [hereafter cited as Folder]; *Presidents and the Press*, 128.

21. *In re Committee for the Fair Broadcasting of Controversial Issues v. CBS, Inc.* 25 FCC 2d 283 (1970), *In re Republican National Committee v. CBS, Inc.* 25 FCC 2d 739 (1970), reversed sub nom, *CBS v. FCC*, 454 F2d 1018 (D.C. Cir. 1971); Klein, *Making It Perfectly Clear*, 291; See also WHSF, Press and Media No. 1 Part 2, Colson memo to H. R. Haldeman, August 15, 1970.

22. Klein interview by author, San Diego, CA, 1995.

23. *Born Again*, 41–42; WHSF, President's Personal Files, Memoranda from the President, 1969–1974, Folder RN Memo 1968 to Memo December 1969, National Archives, College Park, Md. Re: Haldeman notes on Pres. Meeting, see WHSF, H. R. Haldeman Notes, Folder (July–December 1969 Part 1; William E. Porter, *Assault on the Media: The Nixon Years* (Ann Arbor: University of Michigan Press, 1976), 70, 73 [hereafter cited as *Assault on the Media]*.

24. Nixon Presidential Materials Project, Donated Materials Handwritten Journals and Diaries of Harry Robbins Haldeman, Vol. III, November 1, 1969, National Archives, College Park, MD.

25. *Memoirs of Richard Nixon*, 409–410.

26. Ibid., 410. [David Eisenhower watched the speech with the president and said Nixon commented on the Ho Chi Minh letter, "Kalb could be right"], Daniel Schorr, *Clearing the Air* (Boston: Houghton Mifflin Company, 1977), 38n. [hereafter cited as *Clearing the Air*]; Marvin Kalb, *The Nixon Memo* (Chicago: University of Chicago Press, 1994.) [hereafter cited as Nixon Memo.]

27. *Presidents and the Press*, 114; *Out of Thin Air*, 298.

28. *Memoirs of Richard Nixon*, 410.

29. Ibid., 411.

30. FCC Opinion Letter on Instant Analysis, November 22, 1969; "Concerning Fairness Doctrine Re Networks' Coverage of President's Vietnam Address," FCC 69-1288, November 20, 1969, 20 RR2d 1223.

31. *Washington Post*, March 25, 1970.

32. WHSF, H. R. Haldeman Notes, Folder (July 1970), July 16, 1970.

33. WHSF Charles W. Colson files, Chrono folder (November 1970).

34. Ibid.

35. *Before the Fall,* 175–176.

36. WHSF, H. R. Haldeman Notes, Folder (January–March 1971).

37. WHSF, Charles W. Colson files, Chrono Folder (March 1971). [Nixon met with ABC on January 28, 1971 and with NBC on June 7.]

38. Walter Pincus and George Lardner Jr., "Nixon Hoped Antitrust Threat Would Sway Network Coverage," *Washington Post*, December 1, 1997, A1.

39. *Presidents and the Press*, 81–83.

40. Charles W. Colson telephone interview by author.

41. Herbert Klein interview by author, San Diego, CA (1995).

42. President Gerald Ford telephone interview by author, November 15, 1994; Gerald Ford letter to constituents, July 1971, Gerald Ford Library and Museum; Congressman Broyhill and Congressman Brown interviews by author.

43. Charles Colson letter to author and telephone interview.

44. Chief Counsel Daniel Manelli, interviews by author, said, "The Republicans really got mobilized at the end."

45. *New York Times*, October 6, 1972, 6.

46. WHSF, Charles W. Colson Files, Memo, July 20, 1971, Chrono Folder (July 1971).

47. Walter Pincus and George Lardner Jr., "Nixon Hoped Antitrust Threat Would Sway Network Coverage," Washington Post (December 1, 1997), A1.

48. WHSF, Charles W. Colson Files, Memo, July 20, 1971, Chrono Folder (July 1971).

49. Colson later continued to threaten CBS, and, among other things, complained that CBS had not "played ball." WHSF, Charles W. Colson Files, 1971.

50. Frank Stanton interview by author.

51. *Postcript* transcript.

52. *Postcript* transcript.

53. *New York Times*, March 25, 1971.

54. Klein, *Making It Perfectly Clear*, 291; Klein interview by author, San Diego, CA, 1995. See also WHSF, Press and Media No. 1 Part 2, Colson memo to H. R. Haldeman, August 15, 1970; Joseph Spear, *Presidents and the Press,* 113.

55. Herbert Klein interview by author, San Diego, CA. (1995); Herb Klein, *Making It Perfectly Clear*, (New York: Doubleday & Company, 1984), 214–225, 218–219, 221 [hereafter cited as *Making it Perfectly Clear*]. The antitrust suits were later settled by the government and the networks after they were reinstituted by the Justice Department during the Gerald Ford administration.

56. WHSF, Presidential Office Files, Ehrlichman Memo, September 11, 1971 Folder (September 1971).

57. *Presidents and the Press,* 150n, 152.

58. Henry Kissinger, *White House Years*, (Boston: Little, Brown and Company, 1979) 298–299.

59. Leonard Garment, Counsel to the President, telephone interview by author July 18, 1997.

60. *Washington Post*, June 23, 1972.

61. *Presidents and the Press*, 133.

62. WHSF, Charles W. Colson Files, Chrono Folder (October 1972).

63. *Clearing the Air*, 52–53; *Making It Perfectly Clear*, 212–213; Sally Bedell Smith, *In All His Glory: The Life of William S. Paley* (New York: Simon & Schuster, 1990) [hereafter cited as *In All His Glory*]; Frank Stanton interview by author; "Nixon Hoped Antitrust Threat Would Sway Network Coverage," *Washington Post*, December 1, 1979.

64. *In All His Glory,* 476–478.

65. Ibid., *Presidents and the Press*, 85, 187.

66. *Clearing the Air,* 52–53.

67. Ben Bagdikian, "*The Fruits of Aggression*," Columbia Journalism Review 11:5 (January 1973), 9–20; Cong. Rec., June 1, 1973, H. 1850.

68. *Before the Fall,* 175–176.

69. *Clearing the Air*, 52–53.

70. Stanton interview by author; Powe, *American Broadcasting and the First Amendment*, 134–137, *Presidents and the Press,* 150–152; *Assault on the Media; Out of Thin Air*, 128.

71. Robert Sherrill, *New York Times*, May 16, 1971.

72. Robert Sherrill, *New York Times*, May 16, 1971; Fred Powledge, "The Engineering of Restraint: The Nixon Administration and the Press," a report of the American Civil Liberties Union (Washington, DC Public Affairs Press, 1971) 33–34.

73. Robert Sherrill, *New York Times*, May 16, 1971.

74. Ibid.

75. Ibid.

76. WHSF, H. R. Haldeman Notes, Chrono File, April 30, 1971 (April–June 1971, May 20–June 30, Part II).

77. Herbert Klein interview by author, San Diego, CA, 1995.

Notes for Chapter 6: The FCC Revokes the Fairness Doctrine

Author's Note: The television news reporters and managers I have met over the years did their jobs with integrity and conscientiousness in their search for the truth in their reporting. The broadcast industry experience with the Fairness Doctrine regulation described in this study is what the FCC found to be the case, a situation well known in the industry.

1. H. Geller, "Fairness and the Public Trustee Concept: Time to Move On." *FCJ, Vol. 47, No.1*. See Henry Geller, *Broadcasting*, in 1 *New Directions in Telecommunications Policy Series*, 125 (Paula R. Newberg ed., 1989).
2. Appendix 3, Excerpts, FCC Decision on the Fairness Doctrine and Its Suppression of News and Speech.
3. Ibid.
4. Ibid.
5. Ibid.
6. Ibid.
7. Ibid.
8. Ibid.
9. Ibid.
10. Ibid.
11. Ibid.
12. Ibid.
13. Ibid.
14. Ibid.
15. *Syracuse Peace Council v. FCC*, 867 F.2d 654, Cert. denied, *Syracuse Peace Council v. FCC*, 493 U.S. 1019, 110 S. Ct. 717 (1990). See FCC Decision on the Fairness Doctrine and Suppression of News and Speech, Chapter 7; In re Complaint

of Syracuse Peace Council against Television Station WTVH, Syracuse, NY, 1984 WL 251220, 57 Rad. Reg. 2d (P & F) 519, 99 F.C.C.2d 1389 (FCC December 20, 1984) (NO. FCC 84–518); Vacated, In re Complaint of Syracuse Peace Council against Television Station WTVH Syracuse, NY, 1987 WL 344763, 63 Rad. Reg. 2d (P & F) 541, 2 FCCR 5043, 2 FCC Rcd. 5043 (FCC August 6, 1987) (No. FCC 87–266) Reconsideration Denied, In re Complaint of Syracuse Peace Council against Television Station WTVH Syracuse, NY, 1988 WL 488127, 64 Rad. Reg. 2d (P & F) 1073, 3 FCCR 2035, 3 FCC Rcd. 2035 (FCC April 7, 1988) (NO. FCC 88–131).

16. Remand, In re Complaint of Syracuse Peace Council against Television Station WTVH, Syracuse, NY, 1987 WL 343692, 2 F.C.C.R. 794, 2 FCC Rcd. 794 (FCC January 23, 1987) (NO. FCC 87–133) On appeal, *Syracuse Peace Council v. FCC*, 867 F.2d 654, 57 USLW 2488, 65 Rad. Reg. 2d (P & F) 1759, 276 U.S. App. DC 38, 16 Media L. Rep. 1225 (DC Cir., February 10, 1989) (No. 87–1516, 87–1544); Cert. denied, *Syracuse Peace Council v. FCC*, 493 U.S. 1019, 110 S. Ct. 717, 107 L. Ed. 2d, 737, U.S. Dist. Col. January 8, 1990) (NO. 89–312).

17. William Small, interview by author, March 2010, a requested statement prepared by Mr. Small.

18. Dan Rather, Statement of August 1987 before the FCC Fairness Doctrine Investigation, Thomas W. Haslett, *The Weekly Standard*, Vol. 0010, Issue 25, March 21, 2005.

Notes for Chapter 7: New Government Threats

1. Letter of Ronald Reagan, The White House, June 19, 1987, To the Senate of the United States:

    I am returning herewith without my approval S. 742, the "Fairness in Broadcasting Act of 1987", which would codify the so-called "fairness doctrine." This doctrine, which has evolved through the decisional process of the Federal Communications Commission (FCC), requires Federal officials to supervise the editorial practices of broadcasters in an effort to ensure that they provide coverage of controversial issues and a reasonable opportunity for the airing of contrasting viewpoints on those issues. This type of content-based regulation by the Federal Government is, in my judgment, antagonistic to the freedom of expression guaranteed by the First Amendment.

    In any other medium besides broadcasting, such Federal policing of the editorial judgment of journalists would be unthinkable. The framers of the First Amendment, confident that public debate would be freer and healthier without the kind of interference represented by the "fairness doctrine", chose to forbid such regulations in the clearest terms: "Congress shall make no law... abridging the freedom of speech, or of the press." More recently, the United States Supreme Court, in striking down a right-of-access statute that applied to newspapers, spoke of the statute's intrusion into the function of the editorial process and concluded that "[i]t has yet to be demonstrated how governmental regulation of this crucial process can be exercised consistent with First Amendment guarantees of a free press as they have evolved to this time." *Miami Herald Publishing Co. v. Tornillo*, 418 U.S. 241, 258 (1974)....

Quite apart from these technological advances, we must not ignore the obvious intent of the First Amendment, which is to promote vigorous public debate and a diversity of viewpoints in the public forum as a whole, not in any particular medium, let alone in any particular journalistic outlet. History has shown that the dangers of an overly timid or biased press cannot be averted through bureaucratic regulation, but only through the freedom and competition that the First Amendment sought to guarantee…

… Well-intentioned as S. 742 may be, it would be inconsistent with the First Amendment and with the American tradition of independent journalism. Accordingly, I am compelled to disapprove this measure."

Veto of Fairness Doctrine by President Ronald Reagan, The Heartland Institute 11/03/2010. http://www.heartland.org/ policybot/results/28706/Veto_of_Fairness_Doctrine.html; see also Fairness Doctrine, Wikipedia, http://en.wikipedia.org/ wiki/Fairness_Doctrine#Revocation.

2.	Fairness Doctrine, Wikipedia, http://en.wikipedia.org/wiki/ Fairness_Doctrine#Revocation.
3.	Enver Masud, Broadcasting Fairness Doctrine Promised Balanced Coverage, The Wisdom Fund, http://www.twf.org/ News/Y1997/Fairness.html.
4.	http://en.wikipedia.org/wiki/Fairness_Doctrine#Support; See http://www.factcheck.org/2009/03/the-fairness-doctrine/.
5.	http://www.politico.com/blogs/michaelcalderone/0209/Sen_ Harkin_We_need_the_Fairness_Doctrine_back_.html.

	BILL PRESS [radio show host]: … All we want is, you know, some balance on the airwaves, that's all. You know, we're not going to take any of the conservative voices off the airwaves, but just make sure that there are a few progressives and liberals out there, right?

SENATOR TOM HARKIN (D-IA): Exactly, and that's why we need the fair—that's why we need the Fairness Doctrine back. http://en.wikipedia.org/wiki/Fairness_Doctrine

6. www.factcheck.org/2009/03/the-fairness-doctrine/.

7. http://newsbusters.org/blogs/ken-shepherd/2008/06/25/pelosi-i-want-bring-back-fairness-doctrine.

8. www.democraticunderground.com ›Rep.Eshoo to push for Fairness Doctrine, http://www.democraticunderground.com/discuss/duboard.php?az=view_all&address=102x3646985.

9. "FCC staff meeting with Waxman about bringing back Fairness?" http://spectator.org/archives/2009/02/16/in-all-fairness.

10. Washington Prowler, "In All Fairness," *The American Spectator*, February 16, 2009, spectator.org/archives/2009/02/16/in-all-fairness; John Eggerton, *Broadcasting & Cable*, February 18, 2009.

11. www.infowars.com/more-democrats-call-for-censoring-talk-radio.

12. Ibid.; hotair.com/.../2008/.../spokesman-obama-opposes-the-fairness-doctrine/; See also, http://en.wikipedia.org/wiki/Fairness_Doctrine#Revocation.

13. http://www.politico.com/blogs/michael calderone/0209/Axelrod Punts_on_fairness_doctrine.html. In February 2009, a White House spokesperson said that President Obama continues to oppose the revival of the Doctrine. http://en.wikipedia.org/wiki/Fairness_Doctrine#Opposition; the Doctrine also has an appeal that resonates for those concerned about inflammatory speech. One example of this can be seen from a comment following the attempted killing of Rep. Gabrielle Gifford and the murder of a number of innocent bystanders in Arizona on January 10, 2011. Among the suggestions for dealing with the problem in

this instance of a deranged killer came in a statement reportedly made by one of the House leaders, Representative Clyburn, saying the Fairness Doctrine should be brought back. It was later reported that it was Rep. Clyburn's daughter, an FCC Commissioner, who wanted to bring back the Doctrine. http://www.usmessageboard.com/politics/151220-rep-clyburn-bring-back-fairness-doctrine-4.html; http://www.politico.com/blogs/onmedia/0111/Rep_Clyburn_Bring_back_Fairness_Doctrine.html?showall.

14. Cord Blomquist, *The Technology Liberation Front,* April 23, 2008, techliberation.com/2008/.../23/localism-is-the-new-fairness-doctrine/.

15. http://www.americanprogress.org/issues/2007/07/lloyd_fairness.html; in an essay called *Forget the Fairness Doctrine,* Mark Lloyd said people should use the new localism requirement (to be imposed on stations) to "harass conservative stations with complaints to the FCC." Lloyd pointed out that this would stop some conservative speech and lead to fines to benefit public radio ... and that since the FCC could also revoke stations' licenses under the new localism doctrine, there was no longer need (for what Lloyd described as) the "misnamed Fairness Doctrine"; Mark Hyman, "Media Matters," *The American Spectator,* January 26, 2010, http://spectator.org/archives/2010/01/26/the-fccs-war-on-broadcasting.

16. http://www.americanprogress.org/issues/2007/07/lloyd_fairness.html; Mark Hyman, "Media Matters," *The American Spectator,* January 26, 2010, http://spectator.org/archives/2010/01/26/the-fccs-war-on-broadcasting; John Halpin, Mark Lloyd, "The Structural Imbalance of Political Talk Radio," *Center for American Progress,* June 2, 2007, http://www.americanprogress.org/issues/2007/06/pdf/talk_radio.pdf: FCC's New Hire Targeted Conservative Radio Stations in Writings," *FOXNews.com,* August 10, 2009, firefoxnewsonline.net/?p=3042 : "Mark

Lloyd, the FCC's new Chief Diversity Officer, formerly a Senior Fellow at the Center for American Progress, laid out a 'battle plan' in 2007 for liberal activists to target conservative talk radio stations with the new localism doctrine." This would replace the Fairness Doctrine; See also Brian C. Anderson, "Unfairness of the Fairness Doctrine," *LA Times Article Collection*, March 4, 2009, Fairness Doctrine," http://articles. latimes.com/2009/mar/03/opinion/oe-anderson3; Mark Lloyd, *Prologue to a Farce: Communication and Democracy in America* (Urbana: University of Illinois Press, 2006), www.cnsnews.com/ node/52435.

17. Mark Lloyd, *Prologue to a Farce: Communication and Democracy in America;* Matt Cover, "FCC's Chief Diversity Officer Wants Private Broadcasters to Pay a Sum Equal to Their Total Operating Costs to Fund Public Broadcasting;" CNSNews, August 13, 2009, www.cnsnews.com/node/52435.

18. Testimony reported in John Eggerton, FCC Diversity Exec. Won't Be Working On License Issues, Multichannel News, September 12, 2009, http://www.multichannel.com/ article/354469-FCC_Diversity_Exec_Won_t_Be_Working_ On_License_Issues.php.

19. Brian Anderson, "Unfairness of the Fairness Doctrine," *LA Times* Article Collection, March 3, 2009, http://articles.latimes. com/2009/mar/03/opinion/oe-anderson3; Mark Hyman, "The FCC's War on Broadcasting," *The American Spectator*, January 26, 2010, http://spectator.org/archives/2010/01/26/the-fccs-war-on-broadcasting.

20. Stuart Benjamin, "Roasting the Pig To Burn Down the House: A Modest Proposal," [PDF] January 27, 2009, http://lsr.nellco.org/ cgi/viewcontent.cgi?article=1155&context=duke_fs&sei-redir=1#s earch=%22Stuart+Benjamin,+â%C2%80%C2%9CRoasting+Th e+Pig+To+Burn+Down+The+House:+A+modest+Proposal,â%C2 %80%C2%9D+%5BPDF%5D+January+27,+2009,%22; Patrick

Maines, "Stuart Benjamin, The FCC's Spectrum Reformer," *Media and Communications Policy*, December 17, 2009, http://www.mediacompolicy.org/2009/12/articles/broadcasting/stuart-benjamin-the-fccs-spectrum-reformer/; Joesph Smith, FCC's war against over-the-air TV, *American Thinker*, June 13, 2011; Mark Hyman, "The FCC's War on Broadcasting, Media Matters," *American Spectator*, January 26, 2010.

21. Mark Hyman, "Stuart Benjamin: FCC Isn't Forcing Broadcasters Off Spectrum," spectator.org/archives/2009/02/16/in-all-fairness/1.

22. Mark Hyman, "The FCC's War on Broadcasting, Media Matters," *American Spectator*, January 26, 2010; Joesph Smith, "FCC's War against over-the-air TV," *American Thinker,* January 28, 2010, [posted April, 4, 2011], http://www.americanthinker.com/blog/2010/01/fccs_war_against_overtheair_tv.html; Stuart Benjamin, "Roasting the Pig To Burn Down the House: A Modest Proposal," [PDF] January 27, 2009, http://lsr.nellco.org/cgi/viewcontent.cgi?article=1155&context=duke_fs&sei-redir=1#search=%22Stuart+Benjamin,+â%C2%80%C2%9CRoasting+The+Pig+To+Burn+Down+The+House:+A+modest+Proposal,â%C2%80%C2%9D+%5BPDF%5D+January+27,+2009,%22; "Stuart Benjamin: 'The FCC's Spectrum Reformer,' " *Media and Communications Policy*, December 17, 2009; Stuart Benjamin, "A Stacked Deck," *Broadcast Engineering*, February 1, 2010, Stuart Benjamin, *Broadcast Engineering*, February 1, 2010, broadcastengineering.com/News/; Anthony Kang, Obama Care for the Internet, [Blog], http://www.americanthinker.com08/6/2010/obamacare_for_the_internet.html.

23. John Eggerton, Stuart Benjamin: FCC Isn't Forcing Broadcasters Off Spectrum: Distinguished Scholar draws distinction between his views and commission's, Broadcasting & Cable, January 28, 2010; Stuart Benjamin, "Roasting the Pig

To Burn Down the House: A Modest Proposal," [PDF] January 27, 2009; The Prowler, "In All Fairness," Washington Prowler, The American Spectator, February 16, 2009, http://spectator. org/archives/2009/02/16/in-all-fairness.

24. Patrick Maines, "Stuart Benjamin: The FCC's Spectrum Reformer," *Media and Communications Policy*, December 17, 2009, www.mediacompolicy.org/2009/.../stuart-benjamin-the-fccs-spectrum- reformer/; See also Travis, "Shutting Down Free Speech," *Political Forum*, May 6, 2010, http://www.mail-archive.com/politicalforum@googlegroups.com/msg54724. html. This online reporting at the time included "Team Obama and the 'localism' weapon, Obama needs only three votes from the five-member FCC to define localism in such a way that no radio station would dare air any syndicated conservative programming."

One political aspect of the regulatory debate is the dispute about regulation of radio talk shows. For example, confining talk shows to locally produced programs could prevent broadcast of syndicated programming (not locally produced) like the Rush Limbaugh talk show.

Joesph Smith, "FCC's War against over-the-air TV," *American Thinker,* September 3, 2009, ttp://www. americanthinker.com/2008/11/obama_declares_war_on_ conserva.html , [Benjamin's argument to move broadcasters off the broadcast spectrum], Joesph believes, "feeds into the FCC's agenda of controlling 'free' speech." He continues, "Lloyd's advocacy of using local content and diversity rules against talk radio appears to be echoed in the Benjamin tactic of using spectrum regulations against broadcast television. http://spectator.org/archives/2010/01/26/the-fccs-war-on-broadcast. The Spectator article claims that "the FCC has opened a new front in their attack on broadcast television, which President Obama's FCC views as a medium the government does not yet control, along with talk radio and the internet ..." The article concludes that "Obama's political appointees are systematically attacking free communications, and are well underway in undermining our First Amendment protections," http://spectator.org/archives/2010/01/26/the-fccs-war-on-broadcasting. For contrasting views favoring the Fairness Doctrine, see for example: http://en.wikipedia.org/wiki/Fairness_Doctrine# Support; Anna Bogado, Right-Wing Witch Hunt Reaches FCC, *Fair* (Fairness and Accuracy in Reporting,) November 2009.

Some commentators look at the motivation of those using government power to regulate speech or news and their news reports and comments online can be significant to this issue.

25. www.mediacompolicy.org/2009/12/articles/broadcasting/stuart-benjamin-the-fccs-spectrum-reformer/; Spectrum BS info, March 15, 2010.

26. Steven Waldman, Senior Advisor to FCC Chairman, Delivered Speech on Future of Media, April 16, 2010 [posted April 19, 2010], http://reboot.fcc.gov/futureofmedia/ blog?entryId=377886; http://benton.org/node/31513.

27. Ibid.

28. Ibid.

29. Nieman Journalism Laboratory, January 20, 2010, http://www.niemanlab.org/2010/01/the-fccs-future-of-media-project/.

30. Steven Waldman, Prepared Remarks by Senior Advisor to the Chairman, FCC, before the Free State Institute at the National Press Club, April 16, 2010; www.google.com/search?client=gm ail&rls=gm&q=Steven%20Waldman%2C%20Prepared%20 Remarks%20by%20Senior%20Advisor%20to%20the%20 Chairman%2C%20FCC%2C%20before%20the%20Free%20 State%20Institute%20at%20the%20National%20Press%20 Club%2C%20April%2016%2C%202010; "In All Fairness," Washington Prowler, *The American Spectator*, February 16, 2009; http://spectator.org/archives/2009/02/16/in-all-fairness.

(See Appendix 4, FCC Report on Broadcast Localism and Notice of Proposed Rulemaking.) http://www.fcc.gov/info-needs-communities#download; www.rtnda.org/pages/.../ fccE28099s-future-of-media-report-to-be-released- soon1316. php; http://reboot.fcc.gov/futureofmedia/blog?entryId=302806; www.knightcomm.org › Civic Engagement.

31. http://transition.fcc.gov/localism; http://www.c3.ucla.edu/ research-reports/media-ownership/fcc-proposal-new-localism-requirement/.

32. Zechariah Chafee, Jr., *Government and Mass Communications* (Chicago, IL, University of Chicago, 1947), 633.

33. http://www.lawwatch.com/2011/06/articles/working-group-releases-future-of-media-report/; http://gerardbest.wordpress.com/2011/06/26/a-collection-of-studies-on-the-future-of-media.

34. FCC Press Release re: Regulatory Reform, August 22, 2011; Benton.org/node/76490; benton report 79939.

35. http://www.rbr.com/media-news/washington-beat/wide-spectrum-of-fcc-commissioner-opinion-on-media-report.html.

36. Ibid.; Commissioner Copp states he will continue to push for the localism proceeding; http://freepress.net/news/2011/6/9/ fcc-report-proposes-closing-localism-proceeding-scrapping-enhanced-disclosure.

37. http://hraunfoss.fcc.gov/edocs_public/attachmatch/FCC-07-218A1.pdf. See http://newsbusters.org/blogs/kerry-picket/2009/02/17/rep-henry-waxman-wants-apply-censorship-doctrine-internet; "Waxman's committee staff is looking at a congressionally mandated policy that would require all TV and radio stations to have in place 'advisory boards' that would act as watchdogs to ensure 'community needs and opinions' are given fair treatment. Reports from those advisory boards would be used for license renewals and summaries would be reviewed at least annually by FCC staff."

38. *Bantam Books Inc. v. Sullivan*, 372 U.S. 58 (1963). The Supreme Court has closely examined this kind of procedure when dealing with efforts of boards or commissions to suppress speech informally and has on one occasion rejected it. The Supreme Court ruled "informal negotiations" conducted by a local or state commission to prevent the sale of certain magazines to young people was constitutionally impermissible. A Rhode Island commission did more than discourage the sale of some magazine publications. Threats were made against what the commission believed was speech harmful to youth. Commission representatives told sellers of publications that copies of the lists of "objectionable" publications would be circulated to local police departments, and that it was the Commission's duty to recommend prosecution of purveyors of obscenity. The Rhode Island commission representatives informally advised the sellers which magazines, in the commission's view, should not be sold to young buyers. The Supreme Court held, "What Rhode Island has done, in fact, has been to subject the distribution (of publications) to a system of prior administrative restraints, since the Commission is not a judicial body and its decisions to list particular publications as objectionable do not follow judicial determinations that such publications may lawfully be banned."

The absence of judicial review of such Commission actions was fatal in the Court's view. "There is no provision whatever for judicial superintendence before notices issue or even for judicial review of the commission's determinations of objectionableness." The court found that the effect of the Commission's notices was to intimidate distributors and retailers and that had resulted in the suppression of the sale of the books listed.

The Court said, "We have tolerated such a system only where it operated under judicial superintendence and assured an almost immediate judicial determination of the validity of the restraint." The Court said, "We are not the first court to look through forms to the substance and recognize that informal censorship may sufficiently inhibit the circulation of publications to warrant injunctive relief." While the subject matter may be different from typical broadcast programming, the underlying principles of the freedom from government control of publication, including that from an official board are similar.

In a concurring opinion, Justice William Douglas said, "the Bill of Rights was designed to fence in the Government and make its intrusions on liberty difficult and its interference with freedom of expression well-nigh impossible. All nations have tried censorship, and only a few have rejected it. Its abuses mount high." 372 U.S. 58, 73, 74.

39. Cass R. Sunstein, *Democracy and the Problem of Free Speech* (New York: Simon & Schuster, 1993, with a new Afterword, 1995); Cass R. Sunstein, *The Partial Constitution*, (Cambridge: Harvard University Press, 1993); Cass Sunstein, *A Constitution of Many Minds: Why the Founding Document Doesn't Mean What It Meant Before* (Princeton: Princeton University Press, 2009); Cass Sunstein, *On Rumors, How Falsehoods Spread, Why We Believe Them, What Can Be Done* (New York: Farrar, Straus and Giroux, 2009); Cass Sunstein, *A Constitution of Many Minds: Why the Founding Document Doesn't Mean What It Meant Before*, (Princeton: Princeton University Press, 2000).

40. *Partial Constitution*, 198, 223, 254–256.

41. Cass R. Sunstein, *Democracy and the Problem of Free Speech*, (New York: Simon & Schuster, 1993), Introduction, xix, Chapter 1, "Contemporary First Amendment." Chapter 2, "A New Deal for Speech" 1–51, *Afterword* (1995). Sunstein writes that he will devote attention to the possibility that "government controls on the broadcast media, designed to ensure diversity of view and attention to public affairs, would help the system

of free expression. Such controls could promote both political deliberation and political equality." *Problem of Free Speech*, xix.

42. *Partial Constitution*, 211.

43. Ibid., 203.

44. Ford Rowan, *Broadcast Fairness, Practice, Prospects*, (New York: Longman, 1984), 121–123.

45. Radio and Television News Directors Association Filing in the Failed Pension Plans case. See Chapter 3, How FCC Regulations Suppressed News and Speech.

46. NAB filing in the Failed Pension Plans case. See Chapter 3, How FCC Regulations Suppressed News and Speech.

47. See Chapter 6, The FCC Revokes the Fairness Doctrine.

48. Judge David Bazelon of the Washington, DC Circuit Court of Appeals. Address to the UCLA Communications Law Symposium—1979 on "The Foreseeable Future of Television Networks," Los Angeles, February 1, 1979; Article, "The First Amendment and the New Media—New Directions in Regulating Telecommunications," 201, 205, 212. The judge had extensive experience with FCC decisions and said, "The Fairness Doctrine has not fostered wide-ranging debate spanning the full spectrum of political and social ideas. Rather, it has contributed to suppressing programming on controversial issues almost entirely ..."

49. *Partial Constitution*, 254–256.

50. John Samples, "Broadcast Localism and the Lessons of the Fairness Doctrine," *Policy Analysis*, 637, Cato Institute, May 27, 2009, ttp://www.scribd.com/doc/15480679/Broadcast-Localism-and-the-Lessons-of-the-Fairness-Doctrine-Cato-Policy-Analysis-No-639; ibid.: http://www.cato.org/pubs/pas/pa639.pdf.

51. Cass R. Sunstein, *The Partial Constitution* (Cambridge, MA: Harvard University Press, 1993), 228; *Problem of Free Speech*, 270.

52. *Problem of Free Speech*, 178–179. "Suppose that the marketplace is already skewed; suppose that some people already have disproportionate access to the media … — even viewpoint-based regulation may actually be a corrective." Sunstein says, "It would be exceptionally surprising, moreover, if there were no skewing in the current process." All such skewing could apparently require "correction," or virtually unlimited government management of news and speech.
53. http://www.cnsnews.com/node/65720.
54. http://www.law.uchicago.edu/files/private_speech_public_purpose.pdf.
55. *Problem of Free Speech*, 179.
56. *Turner v. FCC*, 512 U.S. 622 (1994).
57. *Turner v. FCC*, 520 U.S. 180 (1997).
58. Sunstein's view is that the decision may open the door to enforcement of a Localism Doctrine because localism can be considered one of the basic goals of the First Amendment. But the Syllabus shows the usual reading is not as Sunstein may view the case. The Syllabus states that Congress found that the physical characteristics of cable transmission, compounded by the increasing concentration of economic power in the cable industry, were endangering the ability of over-the-air broadcast television stations to compete for a viewing audience and for necessary operating revenues. Congress determined that regulation of the market for video programming was necessary to correct this competitive imbalance and granted must-carry relief. See, e.g. Washington Prowler, "In All Fairness," *The American Spectator*, February 16, 2009, http://spectator.org/archives/2009/02/16/in-all-fairness.
59. *Turner vs. FCC*, 512 U.S. 622 (1994). Sunstein does not claim that all the issues addressed here have been settled by the Court. But he appears prepared to argue that regulation for localism or diversity as a stand-alone proposition even without the

unfair competition context could be constitutional. See Cass R. Sunstein, *Democracy and the Problem of Free Speech* (New York: Simon & Schuster, 1995), Chapter 1, Contemporary First Amendment, and Chapter 2, A New Deal for Speech, 1–51.

60. *Denver Area Educational Telecommunications Consortium, Inc. v. FCC, 518 U.S. 727(1996)*. The Supreme Court upheld a federal law permitting cable system operators to ban "indecent" or "patently offensive" speech on leased access cable channels. Protecting children from certain speech was held to be a compelling state interest. Also, see *Problem of Free Speech*, 260, in which Sunstein emphasizes that in the Court's view scarcity was the basis for the decisions on broadcasting and there is no such scarcity for cable.

61. FCC Commissioner McDowell Address to the Media Institute, January 2009. http://www.mediainstitute.org/Speeches/mcdowell_20090128.pdf.

In his speech Commissioner McDowell referred to the Failed Pension Plans case. NBC News reported on an important problem: in the case of some pension plans, employees discovered there were no funds to pay their pensions when they retired. The program showed a number of pensions that failed and the consequences for the employees. It also included others to show there were many that did not fail. Congress was addressing this problem.

The FCC decided the program was focused not on failed pension plans but on the entire pension system and that NBC had portrayed that as failing. The FCC ruled that NBC should broadcast the contrasting view, in essence that the pension system was all right. NBC refused and appealed. In an exhaustive opinion, the reviewing court examined a number of the issues involved, including the FCC's refusal to accept NBC News' exercise of its discretion that broadcasters had, under the Fairness Doctrine, in selecting the issues and how to present them, as it had done in its news report. The FCC was therefore incorrect in ruling that NBC had violated the Fairness Doctrine. The reviewing court reversed the FCC. (See Appendix 2, Excerpts from the Failed Pension Plans decision.)

The FCC appealed to the full court to review the first court's panel decision. The full court declared it would review the case. This automatically voided the first court's decision. But before the full court could act and decide the case, the FCC withdrew its ruling as moot since Congress had passed corrective legislation in the meantime. This left the Fairness Doctrine intact without court reversal of the FCC. While that decision now has no legal force, it illustrates the kind of detailed analysis that was required in determining FCC doctrinal violations and that would be required now for the new Localism, Balance and Diversity Doctrine decisions. Moreover, as the Commissioner and others have pointed out, when all is said and done, it appears the FCC finding of a violation in the Failed Pension Plans case was based on the "tone" of the news program, which must raise still other concerns for press freedom.

62. genachowski-addresses-economic-club-of- washington/; www.fcc.gov/Daily_Releases/Daily_Business/2011/db0406/DOC-305593A1.pdf; www.nationaljournal.com/tech/genachowski-holds-firm-on-need-for-incentive-auctions-20110412.

63. www.fcc./gov/Daily_Business/2010/.../FCC-10-201A1pdf.

64. http://benton.org/node/31513.

65. See e.g. Reuters report for a summary analysis. http://www.reuters.com/article/2010/12/22/us-fcc-internet-rules-idUSTRE6BJ5DF20101222; http://www.fcc.gov/broadband/ For further comment, see http://abcnews.go.com/Politics/fcc-adopts-net-neutrality-rules-broadband-wireless-internet/story?id=12450657. A more technical broadband definition is: "Broadband or high-speed Internet access allows users to access

the Internet and Internet-related services at significantly higher speeds than those available through "dial-up" Internet access services. Broadband speeds vary significantly depending on the particular type and level of service ordered and may range from as low as 200 kilobits per second (kbps), or 200,000 bits per second, to six megabits per second (Mbps), or 6,000,000 bits per second. Some recent offerings even include 50 to 100 Mbps." FCC.gov/owd/strategicplan/.

66. spectator.org/archives/2009/02/16/in-all-fairness-wax; http://techdailydose.nationaljournal.com/2010lc2/waxman-still-mulling-fccs-openphp.

67. Techliberation.com/2009/.../what-impact-will-cass-sunstein-have-on-obamas- internet-policy/.

68. *Partial Constitution*, 223.

69. Jonathon Zittrain, *The Richard S. Salant Lecture on Freedom of the Press*, Joan Shorenstein Center, on the Press, Politics and Public Policy, John F. Kennedy School of Government, Harvard University (2009). Professor Zittrain was previously the chair in Internet Governance and Regulation at Oxford University and a principal in the Oxford Internet Institute. He was also a visiting professor at the New York University School of Law and Stanford Law School. In June 2011 he accepted an appointment as Distinguished Scholar at the FCC. He has taken a particular interest in the efforts of governments and others to thwart the Internet's great capacity of making information widely available.

70. Professor Sunstein wrote in 1993 in *The Partial Constitution* of the major shift he sought for the American government and for speech and news regulation (at pages 9, 10, 12, and 13):

> I claim that the First Amendment should be understood as a guarantee of a deliberative democracy among political equals. This view argues in favor of large shifts in current understandings and practices—involving government regulation of broadcasting, including above all television

... to counteract the "soundbite" phenomenon that currently threatens democratic deliberation in America. ... I also argue that the relevant law should be enacted and implemented by legislatures and administrators, with courts performing a secondary role. Here I suggest a new allocation of authority between the representative branches of government on the one hand and the judiciary on the other. In particular, I argue for a greater role for the representative branches, even or perhaps especially when their actions are inspired by their understanding of what the Constitution requires.

71. *Partial Constitution*, 12.
72. Ibid., 350.
73. Ibid., 9–12, 349, 350.
74. *The Federalist* No. 10; *Problem of Free Speech*, Introduction, fn.10; James T. Kloppenberg, "A Nation Arguing with Its Conscience: Deliberative democracy, philosophical pragmatism, and Barack Obama's conception of American governance." Forum, *Harvard Magazine*, November–December 2010.
75. Gordon S. Wood, *The Idea of America: Reflections on the Birth of the United States*, New York, NY, The Penguin Press, 2011, 131–139.
76. Ibid., 162.
77. Ibid., 162, 139–169.
78. News release by the First Amendment Center:

Traditional news media still 1st source on big stories, September 16, 2009

WASHINGTON – Americans still support the idea of a free press as a watchdog on government, and turn to traditional news sources on major news stories despite skepticism about bias in the news media, according to findings in the first segment of the 2009 State of the First Amendment national survey conducted by the First Amendment Center.

While new innovations such as Twitter have attracted users and headlines, television and other traditional news media remain the dominant source for Americans on major new stories, the survey found.

Television was the first source for major news stories for about half of all responding (49%), followed by the Internet at 15%, radio at 13% and newspapers at 10% — which places traditional news media (TV, radio and newspapers) as the first source for 72% of Americans. Twitter, e-mails and social-networking sites each were named by 1% of those responding.

Similarly, for 48% of Americans TV is the primary source for follow-up reports on those news stories, followed by the Internet at 29% and newspapers at 9%...

Other results: 71% still see a free press as a necessary "watchdog on government," though nearly half of those responding (49%) strongly disagreed with the statement that the news media reports the news without bias...

79. First Amendment Center, 2006: "Knight Survey finds mixed bag for First Amendment, September 18, 2006."

First Amendment Center Online: "Future of the First Amendment," a new Knight Foundation survey, finds that American high school students "know more about the First Amendment than they did two years ago," yet are "increasingly polarized in how they feel about it," according to the foundation's Web site . . .

But the survey of 34 high schools also found that 45% of surveyed students said "the First Amendment goes too far in the rights it guarantees," *USA Today* said. The 45% figure is an increase from the 35% who expressed a skeptical view in an original 2004 study by the John S. and James L. Knight Foundation. However, student backing for some press freedoms did increase: 30% said the press has too much freedom (previously 32%). 54% said newspapers should be allowed to publish freely without government approval (previously 51%). 64% said high school student newspapers should be allowed to report controversial subjects without approval by authorities (previously 58%).

80. http://www.misa.org/mediarelease/pressfreedom.html.

81. http://www.state.gov/secretary/rm/2010/05/141395.htm.

82. Wood, 334.

83. Among those who have fought for a free press are Frank Stanton, president of CBS, as described in *Fighting for the First Amendment: Stanton of CBS vs. Congress and the Nixon White House, with an Introduction by Walter Cronkite*, by Corydon B. Dunham, and Reuven Frank, producer of news programs and president of NBC News for many years. Both Stanton and Frank were interviewed by the author many times. The author is grateful for the use of Frank's book, *Out of Thin Air: The Brief Wonderful Life of Network News*.

Appendix 1

*◦

Excerpts

RED LION BROADCASTING CO., INC. v. FEDERAL
COMMUNICATIONS COMMISSION 395 U.S. 367 (1969)

MR. JUSTICE WHITE delivered the opinion of the Court:

The Federal Communications Commission has for many years imposed on radio and television broadcasters the requirement that discussion of public issues be presented on broadcast stations, and that each side of those issues must be given fair coverage. This is known as the fairness doctrine, which originated very early in the history of broadcasting and has maintained its present outlines for some time. It is an obligation whose content has been defined in a long series of FCC rulings in particular cases, and which is distinct from the statutory [370] requirement of 315 of the Communications Act [note 1] that equal time be allotted all qualified candidates for public office. Two aspects of the fairness doctrine, relating to personal attacks in the context of controversial public issues and to political editorializing, were codified more precisely in the form of FCC regulations in 1967. The two cases before us now, which were decided separately below, challenge the constitutional and statutory bases of the doctrine and component rules. Red Lion [371] involves the application of the fairness doctrine to a particular broadcast, and RTNDA arises as an action to review the FCC's 1967 promulgation of the personal attack and political editorializing regulations, which were laid down after the Red Lion litigation had begun.

I

A

The Red Lion Broadcasting Company is licensed to operate a Pennsylvania radio station, WGCB. On November 27, 1964, WGCB carried a 15-minute broadcast by the Reverend Billy James Hargis as part of a "Christian Crusade" series. A book by Fred J. Cook entitled "Goldwater - Extremist on the Right" was discussed by Hargis, who said that Cook had been fired by a newspaper for making false charges against city officials; that Cook had then worked for a Communist-affiliated publication; that he had defended Alger Hiss and attacked J. Edgar Hoover and the Central Intelligence Agency; and that he had now written a "book to smear and destroy Barry Goldwater."[note 2] When Cook heard of the broadcast he [372] concluded that he had been personally attacked and demanded free reply time, which the station refused. After an exchange of letters among Cook, Red Lion, and the FCC, the FCC declared that the Hargis broadcast constituted a personal attack on Cook; that Red Lion had failed to meet its obligation under the fairness doctrine as expressed in Times-Mirror Broadcasting Co., 24 P & F Radio Reg. 404 (1962), to send a tape, transcript, or summary of the broadcast to Cook and offer him reply time; and that the station must provide reply time whether or not Cook would pay for it. On review in the Court of Appeals for the District of Columbia Circuit, [note 3] the [373] FCC's position was upheld as constitutional and otherwise proper. 127 U.S. App. D.C. 129, 381 F.2d 908 (1967)....

C

Believing that the specific application of the fairness doctrine in Red Lion, and the promulgation of the regulations in RTNDA, are both authorized by Congress and enhance rather than abridge the freedoms of speech and press protected by the First Amendment, we hold them valid and constitutional, reversing the judgment below in RTNDA and affirming the judgment below in Red Lion.

II

The history of the emergence of the fairness doctrine and of the related legislation shows that the Commission's action in the Red Lion case did not exceed its authority, and that in adopting the new regulations the Commission was implementing congressional policy rather than embarking on a frolic of its own.

A

Before 1927, the allocation of frequencies was left entirely to the private sector, and the result was chaos. [note 4] [376] It quickly became apparent that broadcast frequencies constituted a scarce resource whose use could be regulated and rationalized only by the Government. Without government control, the medium would be of little use because of the cacophony of competing voices, none of which could be clearly and predictably heard. [note 5] Consequently, the Federal Radio Commission was established [377] to allocate frequencies among competing applicants in a manner responsive to the public "convenience, interest, or necessity." [note 6] Very shortly thereafter the Commission expressed its view that the "public interest requires ample play for the free and fair competition of opposing views, and the commission believes that the principle applies ... to all discussions of issues of importance to the public." ... This doctrine was applied through denial of license renewals or construction permits ... After an extended period during which the licensee was obliged not only to cover and to cover fairly the views of others, but also to refrain from expressing his own personal views, Mayflower Broadcasting Corp., 8 F. C. C. 333 (1940), the latter limitation on the licensee was abandoned and the doctrine developed into its present form.

There is a twofold duty laid down by the FCC's decisions and described by the 1949 Report on Editorializing by Broadcast Licensees, 13 F. C. C. 1246 (1949). The broadcaster must give adequate coverage to public issues, United Broadcasting Co., 10 F. C. C. 515 (1945), and coverage must be fair in that it accurately reflects the opposing views. New Broadcasting Co., 6 P & F Radio Reg. 258 (1950). This must be done at the broadcaster's own expense if sponsorship is unavailable.... Moreover, the duty must be met by programming obtained at the licensee's own initiative if available from no other source.... The Federal Radio Commission had imposed these two basic duties on broadcasters since the outset ... and in particular respects the personal attack rules and regulations at issue here have spelled them out in greater detail ...

B

The statutory authority of the FCC to promulgate these regulations derives from the mandate to the "Commission from time to time, as public convenience, interest, or necessity requires" to promulgate "such rules and regulations and prescribe such restrictions and conditions . . . as may be necessary to carry out the provisions of this chapter ...." ... This mandate to the FCC to assure that broadcasters operate in the public interest is a broad one, a power "not niggardly but expansive," ... whose validity we have long upheld .... It is broad enough to encompass these regulations.

The fairness doctrine finds specific recognition in statutory form, is in part modeled on explicit statutory provisions relating to political candidates, and is approvingly reflected in legislative history.

In 1959 the Congress amended the statutory requirement of 315 that equal time be accorded each political candidate to except certain appearances on news programs, but added that this constituted no exception "from the obligation imposed upon them under this Act to operate in the public interest and to afford reasonable opportunity for the discussion of conflicting views on issues of public importance." ... The objectives of 315 themselves could readily be circumvented but for the complementary fairness doctrine ratified by 315. The section applies only to campaign appearances by candidates, and not by family, friends, campaign managers, or other supporters. Without the fairness doctrine, then, a licensee could ban all campaign appearances by candidates themselves from the air [note 13] and [383] proceed to deliver over his station entirely to the supporters of one slate of candidates, to the exclusion of all others. In this way the broadcaster could have a far greater impact on the favored candidacy than he could by simply allowing a spot appearance by the candidate himself. It is the fairness doctrine as an aspect of the obligation to operate in the public interest, rather than 315, which prohibits the broadcaster from taking such a step ... The Communications Act is not notable for the precision of its substantive standards and in this respect the explicit provisions of 315, and the doctrine and rules at issue here which are closely modeled upon that section, are far more explicit than the generalized "public interest" standard in which the Commission ordinarily finds its [386] sole guidance, and which we have held a broad but adequate standard before. FCC v. RCA Communications, Inc., 346 U.S. 86, 90 (1953); National Broadcasting Co. v. United States, 319 U.S. 190, 216–217 (1943); FCC v. Pottsville Broadcasting Co., 309 U.S. 134, 138 (1940); FRC v. Nelson Bros. Bond & Mortgage Co., 289 U.S. 266, 285 (1933). We cannot say that the FCC's declaratory ruling in Red Lion, or the regulations at issue in RTNDA, are beyond the scope of the congressionally conferred power to assure that stations are operated by those whose possession of a license serves "the public interest."

III

The broadcasters challenge the fairness doctrine and its specific manifestations in the personal attack and political editorial rules on conventional First Amendment grounds, alleging that the rules abridge their freedom of speech and press. Their contention is that the First Amendment protects their desire to use their allotted frequencies continuously to broadcast whatever they choose, and to exclude whomever they choose from ever using that frequency. No man may be prevented from saying or publishing what he thinks, or from refusing in his speech or other utterances to give equal weight to the views of his opponents. This right, they say, applies equally to broadcasters.

A

Although broadcasting is clearly a medium affected by a First Amendment interest ... differences in the characteristics of new media justify differences in the First Amendment standards applied to them.... For example, the ability of new technology to produce sounds more raucous than those of the human voice justifies restrictions on the sound level, and on the hours and places of use, of sound trucks so long as the restrictions are reasonable and applied without discrimination....

Just as the Government may limit the use of sound-amplifying equipment potentially so noisy that it drowns out civilized private speech, so may the Government limit the use of broadcast equipment. The right of free speech of a broadcaster, the user of a sound truck, or any other individual does not embrace a right to snuff out the free speech of others. ...

Where there are substantially more individuals who want to broadcast than there are frequencies to allocate, it is idle to posit an unabridgeable First Amendment right to broadcast comparable to the right of every individual to speak, write, or publish. If 100 persons want broadcast [389] licenses but there are only 10 frequencies to allocate, all of them may have the same "right" to a license; but if there is to be any effective communication by radio, only a few can be licensed and the rest must be barred from the airwaves. It would be strange if the First Amendment, aimed at protecting and furthering communications, prevented the Government from making radio communication possible by requiring licenses to broadcast and by limiting the number of licenses so as not to overcrowd the spectrum.

This has been the consistent view of the Court. Congress unquestionably has the power to grant and deny licenses and to eliminate existing stations.... No one has a First Amendment right to a license or to monopolize a radio frequency; to deny a station license because "the public interest" requires it "is not a denial of free speech." ... By the same token, as far as the First Amendment is concerned those who are licensed stand no better than those to whom licenses are refused. A license permits broadcasting, but the licensee has no constitutional right to be the one who holds the license or to monopolize a radio frequency to the exclusion of his fellow citizens. There is nothing in the First Amendment which prevents the Government from requiring a licensee to share his frequency with others and to conduct himself as a proxy or fiduciary with obligations to present those views and voices which are representative of his community and which would otherwise, by necessity, be barred from the airwaves.

This is not to say that the First Amendment is irrelevant to public broadcasting. On the contrary, it has a major role to play as the Congress itself recognized in 326, which forbids FCC interference with "the right [390] of free speech by means of radio communication." Because of the scarcity of radio frequencies, the Government is permitted to put restraints on licensees in favor of others whose views should be expressed on this unique medium. But the people as a whole retain their interest in free speech by radio and their collective right to have the medium function consistently with the ends and purposes of the

First Amendment. It is the right of the viewers and listeners, not the right of the broadcasters, which is paramount. … It is the purpose of the First Amendment to preserve an uninhibited market-place of ideas in which truth will ultimately prevail, rather than to countenance monopolization of that market, whether it be by the Government itself or a private licensee. "[S]peech concerning public affairs is more than self-expression; it is the essence of self-government." It is the right of the public to receive suitable access to social, political, esthetic, moral, and other ideas and experiences which is crucial here. That right may not constitutionally be abridged either by Congress or by the FCC.

B

In terms of constitutional principle, and as enforced sharing of a scarce resource, the personal attack and political editorial rules are indistinguishable from the equal-time provision of 315, a specific enactment of Congress requiring stations to set aside reply time under specified circumstances and to which the fairness doctrine and these constituent regulations are important complements. That provision, which has been part of the law since 1927, Radio Act of 1927, 18, 44 Stat. 1170, has been held valid by this Court as an obligation of the licensee relieving him of any power in any way to prevent or censor the broadcast, and thus insulating him from liability for defamation. The constitutionality of the statute under the First Amendment was unquestioned. [note 17] Farmers Educ. & Coop. Union v. WDAY, 360 U.S. 525 (1959). [392]

Nor can we say that it is inconsistent with the First Amendment goal of producing an informed public capable of conducting its own affairs to require a broadcaster to permit answers to personal attacks occurring in the course of discussing controversial issues, or to require that the political opponents of those endorsed by the station be given a chance to communicate with the public.[note 18] Otherwise, station owners and a few networks would have unfettered power to make time available only to the highest bidders, to communicate only their own views on public issues, people and candidates, and to permit on the air only those with whom they agreed. There is no sanctuary in the First Amendment for unlimited private censorship operating in a medium not open to all. "Freedom of the press from governmental interference under the First Amendment does not sanction repression of that freedom by private interests." Associated Press v. United States, 326 U.S. 1, 20 (1945).

C

It is strenuously argued, however, that if political editorials or personal attacks will trigger an obligation in broadcasters to afford the opportunity for expression [393] to speakers who need not pay for time and whose views are unpalatable to the licensees, then broadcasters will be irresistibly forced to self-censorship and their coverage of controversial public issues will be eliminated or at least rendered wholly ineffective. Such a result would indeed be a serious matter, for should licensees actually eliminate their coverage of controversial issues, the purposes of the doctrine would be stifled.

At this point, however, as the Federal Communications Commission has indicated, that possibility is at best speculative. The communications industry, and in particular the networks, have taken pains to present controversial issues in the past, and even now they do not assert that they intend to abandon their efforts in this regard.[note 19] It would be better if the FCC's encouragement were never necessary to induce the broadcasters to meet their responsibility. And if experience with the administration of these doctrines indicates that they have the net effect of reducing rather than enhancing the volume and quality of coverage, there will be time enough to reconsider the constitutional implications. The fairness doctrine in the past has had no such overall effect.

That this will occur now seems unlikely, however, since if present licensees should suddenly prove timorous, the Commission is not powerless to insist that they give adequate and fair attention to public issues. [394] It does not violate the First Amendment to treat licensees given the privilege of using scarce radio frequencies as proxies for the entire community, obligated to give suitable time and attention to matters of great public concern. To condition the granting or renewal of licenses on a willingness to present representative community views on controversial issues is consistent with the ends and purposes of those constitutional provisions forbidding the abridgment of freedom of speech and freedom of the press. Congress need not stand idly by and permit those with licenses to ignore the problems which beset the people or to exclude from the airways anything but their own views of fundamental questions. The statute, long administrative practice, and cases are to this effect.

...In FRC v. Nelson Bros. Bond & Mortgage Co., 289 U.S. 266, 279 (1933), the Court noted that in "view of the limited number of available broadcasting frequencies, the Congress has authorized allocation and licenses." In determining how best to allocate frequencies, the Federal Radio Commission considered the needs of competing communities and the programs offered by competing stations to meet those needs; moreover, if needs or programs shifted, the Commission could alter its allocations to reflect those shifts. Id., at 285. In the same vein, in FCC v. Pottsville Broadcasting Co., 309 U.S. 134, 137–138 (1940), the Court noted that [395] the statutory standard was a supple instrument to effect congressional desires "to maintain ... a grip on the dynamic aspects of radio transmission" and to allay fears that "in the absence of governmental control the public interest might be subordinated to monopolistic domination in the broadcasting field." Three years later the Court considered the validity of the Commission's chain broadcasting regulations, which among other things forbade stations from devoting too much time to network programs in order that there be suitable opportunity for local programs serving local needs. The Court upheld the regulations, unequivocally recognizing that the Commission was more than a traffic policeman concerned with the technical aspects of broadcasting and that it neither exceeded its powers under the statute nor transgressed the First Amendment in interesting itself in general program format and the kinds of programs broadcast by licensees. National Broadcasting Co. v. United States, 319 U.S. 190 (1943).

D

The litigants embellish their First Amendment arguments with the contention that the regulations are so vague that their duties are impossible to discern. Of this point it is enough to say that, judging the validity of the regulations on their face as they are presented here, we cannot conclude that the FCC has been left a free hand to vindicate its own idiosyncratic conception of the public interest or of the requirements of free speech. Past adjudications by the FCC give added precision to the regulations; there was nothing vague about the FCC's specific ruling in Red Lion that Fred Cook should be provided an opportunity to reply. The regulations at issue in RTNDA could be employed in precisely the same way as the fairness doctrine was in Red Lion. Moreover, the FCC itself has recognized that [396] the applicability of its regulations to situations beyond the scope of past cases may be questionable, 32 Fed. Reg. 10303, 10304 and n. 6, and will not impose sanctions in such cases without warning. We need not approve every aspect of the fairness doctrine to decide these cases, and we will not now pass upon the constitutionality of these regulations by envisioning the most extreme applications conceivable, United States v. Sullivan, 332 U.S. 689, 694 (1948), but will deal with those problems if and when they arise.

We need not and do not now ratify every past and future decision by the FCC with regard to programming. … But we do hold that the Congress and the Commission do not violate the First Amendment when they require a radio or television station to give reply time to answer personal attacks and political editorials.

E

It is argued that even if at one time the lack of available frequencies for all who wished to use them justified the Government's choice of those who would best serve the public interest by acting as proxy for those who would present differing views, or by giving the latter access directly to broadcast facilities, this condition no longer prevails so that continuing control is not justified. To this there are several answers.

Scarcity is not entirely a thing of the past. Advances [397] in technology, such as microwave transmission, have led to more efficient utilization of the frequency spectrum, but uses for that spectrum have also grown apace.[note 20] Portions of the spectrum must be reserved for vital uses unconnected with human communication, such as radio-navigational aids used by aircraft and vessels. Conflicts have even emerged between such vital functions as defense preparedness and experimentation in methods of averting midair collisions through radio warning devices. [note 21] "Land mobile services" such as police, ambulance, fire department, public utility, and other communications systems have been occupying an increasingly crowded portion of the frequency spectrum 22 and there are, apart from licensed amateur radio operators' equipment, 5,000,000 transmitters operated on the "citizens' band" which is also increasingly congested.[note 23] Among the various uses for radio frequency space, including marine, [398] aviation, amateur, military, and common carrier users, there are easily enough claimants to permit use of the whole with an even smaller allocation to broadcast radio and television uses than now exists.

Comparative hearings between competing applicants for broadcast spectrum space are by no means a thing of the past. The radio spectrum has become so congested that at times it has been necessary to suspend new applications.[note 24] The very high frequency television spectrum is, in the country's major markets, almost entirely occupied, although space reserved for ultra high frequency television transmission, which is a relatively recent development as a commercially viable alternative, has not yet been completely filled.[note 25] [399]

The rapidity with which technological advances succeed one another to create more efficient use of spectrum space on the one hand, and to create new uses for that space by ever growing numbers of people on the other, makes it unwise to speculate on the future allocation of that space. It is enough to say that the resource is one of considerable and growing importance whose scarcity impelled its regulation by an agency authorized by Congress. Nothing in this record, or in our own researches, convinces us that the resource is no longer one for which there are more immediate and potential uses than can be accommodated, and for which wise planning is essential.[note 26] This does not mean, of course, that every possible wavelength must be occupied at every hour by some vital use in order to sustain the congressional judgment. The [400] substantial capital investment required for many uses, in addition to the potentiality for confusion and interference inherent in any scheme for continuous kaleidoscopic reallocation of all available space may make this unfeasible. The allocation need not be made at such a breakneck pace that the objectives of the allocation are themselves imperiled. [note 27]

Even where there are gaps in spectrum utilization, the fact remains that existing broadcasters have often attained their present position because of their initial government selection in competition with others before new technological advances opened new opportunities for further uses. Long experience in broadcasting, confirmed habits of listeners and viewers, network affiliation, and other advantages in program procurement give existing broadcasters a substantial advantage over new entrants, even where new entry is technologically possible. These advantages are the fruit of a preferred position conferred by the Government. Some present possibility for new entry by competing stations is not enough, in itself, to render unconstitutional the Government's effort to assure that a broadcaster's programming ranges widely enough to serve the public interest.

In view of the scarcity of broadcast frequencies, the Government's role in allocating those frequencies, and the legitimate claims of those unable without governmental assistance to gain access to those frequencies for expression of their views, we hold the regulations and [401] ruling at issue here are both authorized by statute and constitutional. [note 28] The judgment of the Court of Appeals in Red Lion is affirmed and that in RTNDA reversed and the causes remanded for proceedings consistent with this opinion.

It is so ordered.

Not having heard oral argument in these cases, MR. JUSTICE DOUGLAS took no part in the Court's decision.

[Some discussion, notes, and citations have been omitted.]

Appendix 2

~

Excerpts from
The Failed Pension Plans Case

NATIONAL BROADCASTING COMPANY, INC., Petitioner v. FEDERAL COMMUNICATIONS COMMISSION and the United States of America, Respondents, Accuracy in Media, Inc., Intervenor.

No. 73-2256

United States Court of Appeals, District of Columbia Circuit

Argued Feb. 21, 1974. Decided Sept. 27, 1974. Order Vacating Opinion Dec. 13, 1974. Orders March 18 and 19, 1975. Dissenting Opinion June 2, 1975. Judgment Vacated July 11, 1975.

. . .

Before FAHY, Senior Circuit Judge, and TAMM and LEVENTHAL, Circuit Judges.

LEVENTHAL, Circuit Judge:

On September 12, 1972, the television network of the National Broadcasting Company broadcast its documentary entitled *Pensions: The Broken Promise*, narrated by Edwin Newman. On November 27, 1972, Accuracy in Media (AIM) filed a complaint with the Federal Communications Commission charging NBC had presented a one-sided picture of private pension plans. The handling of this case by the Commission will be discussed in more detail subsequently... For introductory purposes it suffices to say that on May 2, 1973—as it happens, the same day NBC received the George Foster Peabody Award for its production—the Commission's Broadcast Bureau advised NBC that the program violated the Commission's Fairness Doctrine. That decision was upheld by the Commission. We reverse.

I. THE PROGRAM

The *Pensions* program is the heart of the case, and for that reason, it is set out in Appendix A to this opinion. For convenience, we will summarize the main outlines of the program—with notation that certain aspects are dealt with more fully subsequently.

The *Pensions* program studied the condition under which a person who had worked in an employment situation that was covered by a private pension plan did not in fact realize on any pension rights. Its particular focus was the tragic cases of aging workers who were left, at the end of a life of labor, without pensions, without time to develop new pension rights, and on occasion without viable income.

The program had no set format, but its most prominent feature was a presentation of tragic case histories, often through personal interviews with the persons affected.

One group of workers lost pension eligibility when their company decided to close the division in which they had worked. The first of these was Steven Duane, who after 17 years with a large supermarket chain, lost his job as foreman of a warehouse when the company closed the warehouse and discharged all its employees, leaving them with no job and no pension rights. Now in his fifties, starting again with another company, he felt ill-used and frightened of the future.

There were a number of other specific examples of employees terminated by closing of plants or divisions. The program also focused on the problems of vesting, the years of service with the company required for a worker to become eligible under its pension plan. NBC interviewed employees with many years of service who were suddenly discharged just prior to the date on which their pension rights were to have become vested. Thus Alan Soresen asserted that he was the victim of a practice—a "very definite pattern"—under which his employer, a large department store chain, fired men just prior to vesting, assigning 'shallow' reasons to men who had served with records beyond reproach.

A similar account was given by Earl Schroeder, an executive fired by Kelly Nut Company, after he more than met his twenty years of service requirement but was six months shy of the age-sixty condition.

The program also set forth abuses in the literature given employees ostensibly explaining their plans—pictures of contented retirees and words comprehensible only to the most sophisticated legal specialist. It took up examples where the company had gone bankrupt prior to their date of retirement, leaving the employees without pension funds.

The documentary gave instances of pensions lost for lack of portability, citing plans that required the employee be a member of the same local for the requisite period. NBC interviewed a number of teamsters who had worked for the same employer for over twenty years, but who later found that certain changes in work assignment entailed changes in union local representation and ultimately loss of pension.

Much of the program was a recount of human suffering, interviews in which aging workers described their plight without comment on cause or remedy. They told of long years of working in the expectation of comfortable retirements, finding out that no pension would come, having to work into old age, of having to survive on pittance incomes. Interspersed with these presentations by workers were comments by persons active in the pension field, public officials, and Mr. Newman.

None of those interviewed—and these included two United States senators, a state official, a labor leader, a representative of the National Association of Manufacturers, a consumer advocate, a bank president, and a social worker—disputed that serious problems, those covered by the documentary, do indeed exist. Some of the comments related to the overall performance of the private pension system. We shall discuss these later ... In addition to comments on the private system generally, there were isolated expressions of views on the related but nonetheless quite distinct issue of the wisdom of reliance on private pensions, regardless of how well they function, to meet the financial needs of retirees.[3] Finally, several speakers gave broad, general views as to what could be done.

There were also comments on legislative reforms that might be taken to cope with problems. These will be discussed separately in part (VI-D) of this opinion.

Concluding Remarks

It may be appropriate to quote in full the concluding remarks of narrator Edwin Newman of NBC News, since the FCC considered them "indicative of the actual scope and substance of the viewpoints broadcast in the 'Pensions' program." He said:

"This has been a depressing program to work on but we don't want to give the impression that there are no good private pension plans. There are many good ones, and there are many people for whom the promise has become reality. That should be said.[27]

There are certain technical questions that we've dealt with only glancingly, portability, which means, being able to take

242

your pension rights with you when you go from one job to another, vesting, the point at which your rights in the pension plan become established and irrevocable.

Then there's funding, the way the plan is financed so that it can meet its obligations. And insurance, making sure that if plans go under, their obligations can still be met.[29]

Finally, there's what is called the fiduciary relationship, meaning, who can be a pension plan trustee? And requiring that those who run pension funds adhere to a code of conduct so that they cannot enrich themselves or make improper loans or engage in funny business with the company management or the union leadership.[30]

These are matters for Congress to consider and, indeed, the Senate Labor Committee is considering them now. They are also matters for those who are in pension plans. If you're in one, you might find it useful to take a close look at it.[31]

Our own conclusion about all of this, is that it is almost inconceivable that this enormous thing has been allowed to grow up with so little understanding of it and with so little protection and such uneven results for those involved.

The situation, as we've seen it, is deplorable."

Success of Program

Like many documentaries, *Pensions* was a critical success (supra, note 1) but not a commercial success. We shall consider the television reviews in more detail subsequently, but it may be observed here that they were generally enthusiastic. Critics called it, "A potent program about pitfalls and failures of some private pension plans ...," "a harrowing and moving inquiry ...," and "a public service."[5] Dissenting notes were also struck.

Accuracy in Media (AIM), a "nonprofit, educational organization acting in the public interest"[7] that seeks to counter, in part by demanding aggressive enforcement of the Fairness Doctrine, what it deems to be biased presentations of news and public affairs. On November 27, 1972, the executive secretary of AIM wrote to the FCC complaining of the following:

> Our investigation reveals that the NBC report gave the viewers a grotesquely distorted picture of the private pension system of the United States. Nearly the entire program was devoted to criticism of private pension plans, giving the impression that failure and fraud are the rule ... The reporter, Mr. Newman, said that NBC did not want to give the impression that there were no good private pension plans, but he did not discuss any good plans or show any satisfied pensioners.

In subsequent correspondence, AIM added the accusations that NBC was attempting "to brainwash the audience with some particular message the NBC is trying to convey" and that the program was "a one-sided, uninformative, emotion-evoking propaganda pitch." Thus AIM not only claimed that the program had presented one side of an issue of public importance, the performance of private pension plans, it also charged that NBC had deliberately distorted its presentation to foist its ideological view of events on the viewing public.

In its reply, NBC rejected the allegations of distortion. It asserted that the *Pensions* broadcast had not concerned a controversial issue of public importance:

> The program constituted a broad overview of some of the problems involved in some private pensions plans. It did not attempt to discuss all private pension plans, nor did it urge the adoption of any specific legislative or other remedies. Rather, it was designed to inform the public about some problems which have come to light in some pension plans and which deserve a closer look.

Since, in the view of NBC, there was no attempt to comment on the overall performance of private pension plans, no controversial issue had been presented, for all agreed that the examples of suffering depicted were not themselves subject to controversy. Even so, NBC pointed out that it had presented the view that the system as a whole was functioning well; consequently, it asserted, even if it had inadvertently raised the issue of the overall performance of private pension plans, the side generally supportive of the system had been heard.

In a letter to NBC,[13] the broadcast bureau of the commission rejected AIM's allegations of distortion as being unsupported by any evidence but upheld the Fairness Doctrine complaint. The staff took issue with "the reasonableness of your [NBC's] judgment that the program did not present one side of a controversial issue of public importance" and concluded that the program's "overall thrust was general criticism of the entire pension system, accompanied by proposals for its regulation."[14] The staff opinion included extensive quotation from the transcript of the documentary, but little explanation as to how the quoted portions sustained the staff's conclusion. Only four brief statements were singled out as containing "general views" on the overall performance of the private pension system. NBC appealed the Broadcast Bureau ruling to the entire commission.

On December 3, 1973, the commission issued a "Memorandum Opinion and Order" affirming the decision of its staff.[16] Although it acknowledged that the broad issue upon review was "whether the Bureau erred in its ruling that NBC's judgment on these matters was unreasonable," it emphasized, "The specific question properly before us here is therefore not whether NBC may reasonably say that the broad, overall 'subject' of the *Pensions* program was 'some problems in some pension plans,' but rather whether the program did in fact present viewpoints on one side of the issue of the overall performance and proposed regulation of the private pension system."

The commission found that *Pensions* had in fact presented views on the overall performance of the private pension system. It took note of the "pro-pensions" views expressed during the documentary, but concluded that the "overwhelming weight" of the "anti-pensions" statements

245

required further presentation of opposing views. The commission commended NBC for a laudable journalistic effort but found that the network had not discharged its fairness obligations and ordered it to do so forthwith. This petition for review followed: "We now set forth the reasons why we have decided that the case should be determined in favor of NBC."

II. THE FAIRNESS DOCTRINE: GENERAL CONSIDERATIONS

...

The salutary intent of the Fairness Doctrine must be reconciled with the tradition against inhibition of journalists' freedom. That tradition, which exerts a powerful countervailing force, is rooted in the constitutional guarantee of freedom of the press, a guarantee that has vitality for broadcast journalists, though not in exactly the same degree as for their brethren of the printed word.[27] And the same statute that provides authority for the FCC to implement the Fairness Doctrine for its licensees contains a clear provision (in section 326) disclaiming and prohibiting censorship as part of the legislative scheme. In construing the Fairness Doctrine, both the commission and the courts have proceeded carefully, mindful of the need for harmonizing these often-conflicting considerations.

In *Red Lion Broadcasting Company v. FCC*, 395 U.S. 367, 89 S. Ct. 1794, 23 L.Ed.2d 371 (1969), the Supreme Court approved the commission's personal attack and political editorializing rules, which were relatively narrow corollaries of the general fairness obligation. A unanimous Supreme Court reminded the broadcaster of the essential difference between the print and broadcast media: the physical limitations of the latter restrict the number of those who would broadcast, whereas expression by publication is, at least in theory, available to all. To posit a First Amendment restriction on government action taken to enhance the variety of opinions available to the viewer is to protect those fortuitous enough to obtain broadcast licenses at the expense of those who were not. In now-famous language, the Court stated:

> Because of the scarcity of radio frequencies, the Government is permitted to put restraints on licensees in favor of others whose views should be expressed on this unique medium. But the people as a whole retain their interest in free speech by radio and their collective right to have the medium function consistently with the ends and purposes of the First Amendment. It is the right of the viewers and listeners, not the right of the broadcasters, which is paramount.

This has become the guiding principle of the Fairness Doctrine: limitations on the freedom of the broadcaster—even those that would be unacceptable when imposed on other media—are lawful in order to enhance the public's right to be informed. The Court's opinion, written by Justice White, reflects the circumspection of this principle of decision. While rejecting as unfounded claims that the personal attack and political editorializing rules would induce self-censorship by licensees in order to avoid the rigors of compliance with their requirements, the Court cautioned that its judgment might be different "if experience with the administration of those doctrines indicates that they have the net effect of reducing rather than enhancing the volume and quality of coverage."[32] The Court expressly stated that in approving the personal attack and political editorializing rules, it did not "approve every aspect of the Fairness Doctrine."

Journalistic discretion, the Court emphasized, is the keynote to the legislative framework of the Communications Act. The limitations of broadcasting both spawned the Fairness Doctrine and establish that it is dependent primarily on licensee discretion. Perfect compliance is impossible. No broadcaster can present all colorations of all available public issues. 412 U.S. at 111, 93 S. Ct. 2080. Choices have to be made and, assuming that the area is one of protected expression, the choices must be made by those whose mission it is to inform, not by those who must rule. In the words of Chief Justice Burger:

> For better or worse, editing is what editors are for; and editing is selection and choice of material. That editors—newspaper or broadcast—can and do abuse this power is beyond doubt, but that is not reason to deny the discretion Congress provided. Calculated risks of abuse are taken in order to preserve higher values. The presence of these risks is nothing new; the authors of the Bill of Rights accepted the reality that these risks were evils for which there was no acceptable remedy other than a spirit of moderation and a sense of responsibility—and civility— on the part of those who exercise the guaranteed freedoms of expression.

There are no other decisions on the Fairness Doctrine from the Supreme Court, but this court has had occasion to consider the Doctrine in several cases and it has endeavored to maintain the balance between broadcaster freedom and the public's right to know.

In *Democratic National Committee v. FCC*, we faced knotty problems in sorting out the fairness obligations generated by a radio and television address by the president and a reply by the opposition political party. In upholding the commission decision that the licensees had not abused their discretion, Judge Tamm, writing for the Court, stressed the importance of reliance on licensee judgment:

> By its very nature the Fairness Doctrine is one which cannot be applied with scientific and mathematical certainty. There is no formula which if followed will assure that the requirements of the Doctrine have been met. Procedurally, the Doctrine can only succeed when the licensee exercises that discretion upon which he is instructed to call upon in dealing with coverage of controversial issues. Finding no abuse of discretion, we affirmed ...

Converting every newsworthy matter into a controversial issue of public importance and requiring editors to balance every presentation creates a danger. Again in the words of Judge Wilkey, "To characterize every dispute of this character as calling for rejoinder under the Fairness Doctrine would so inhibit television and radio as to destroy a good part of their public usefulness. It would make what has already been criticized as a bland product disseminated by an uncourageous media even more innocuous."

The principle of deference to licensee judgments, unless the licensee has simply departed from the underlying assumptions of good faith and reasonable discretion, is an integral part of the Fairness Doctrine, and a fixture that has been reiterated and applied with fidelity by the courts.76 The question is whether NBC has been shown to have exceeded its "wide degree of discretion" in its *Pensions* documentary.

. . .

IV. APPLICATION OF THE FAIRNESS DOCTRINE TO NEWS DOCUMENTARIES

Our assumption of the propriety of the FCC's current practice that it may make rulings whether particular programs violate the Fairness Doctrine does not lessen our concern as to those rulings; it rather enhances the need for careful scrutiny, particularly where, as here, a ruling is challenged on the ground that it displaces the judgment entrusted to the broadcast journalist.

A. The Function of the FCC

The principal controversial issue the commission identified for the *Pensions* program is "the overall performance of the private pension plan system." In NBC's submission, the focus of the program was the existence of abuses, of "some problems in some pension plans." While one understands NBC's point as made, it might be refined as a statement that

NBC was engaged in a study in abuses and did not separately examine how pervasive those abuses were. On what basis did the commission reject NBC's position and accept AIM's view that the point of the program was the performance of the common run of pension plans?

The staff ruling of May 2, 1973, said:

> The *Pensions* program thus did in fact present views which were broadly critical of the performance of the entire private pension system and explicitly advocated and supported proposals to regulate the operation of all pension plans. Your judgments to the contrary, therefore, cannot be accepted as reasonable.

One is struck by the palpable flaw in the staff's reasoning. The staff actually put it that because the staff found as a fact that the program was broadly critical of the entire private pension plan system, NBC's contrary judgment "therefore" cannot be accepted as reasonable. The flaw looms the larger, in that it appears in the ruling of the staff of an agency operating under the Rule of Administrative Law. Under that rule, agencies daily proclaim that their findings of fact must be upheld if reasonable and if supported by substantial evidence, even though there is equal and even preponderant evidence to the contrary, and even though the courts would have found the facts the other way if they had approached the issue independently.

The commission's opinion of December 3, 1973, corrected the staff's error of logic, but it made a mistake of law. It stated:

The specific question properly before us here is therefore not whether NBC may reasonably say that the broad, overall subject of the *Pensions* program was "some problems in some pension plans," but rather whether the program did in fact present viewpoints on one side of the issue of the overall performance and proposed regulation of the private pension system. (Emphasis added.)

Thus the commission ruled that even though NBC was reasonable in saying that the subject of *Pensions* program was "some problems in some pension plans," in determining that this was the essential subject of the program, its dominant force and thrust, nevertheless NBC had violated its obligation as a licensee, because the commission reached a different conclusion, that the program had the effect "in fact" of presenting only on side of a different subject.

The commission's error of law is that if failed adequately to apply the message of applicable decisions that the editorial judgments of the licensee must not be disturbed if reasonable and in good faith. The licensee has both initial responsibility and primary responsibility. It has wide discretion and latitude that must be respected even though, under the same facts, the agency would reach a contrary conclusion.

The pertinent principle that the commission will not disturb the editorial judgment of the licensee, if reasonable and in good faith, is applicable broadly in Fairness Doctrine matters. It has distinctive force and vitality when the crucial question is the kind raised in this case, i.e., in defining the scope of the issue raised by the program, for this inquiry typically turns on the kind of communications judgments that are the stuff of the daily decisions of the licensee. There may be mistakes in the licensee's determination. But the review power of the agency is limited to licensee determinations that are not only different from those the agency would have reached in the first instance but are unreasonable.

In *Columbia Broadcasting System v. Democratic National Committee,* supra, the Court stressed the wide latitude entrusted to the broadcaster … Congress intended to permit private broadcasting to develop with the widest journalistic freedom consistent with its public obligations.

The broadcaster, therefore, is allowed significant journalistic discretion in deciding how best to fulfill the Fairness Doctrine obligations, although that discretion is bounded by rules designed to assure that the public interest in fairness is furthered.

While the government agency has the responsibility of deciding whether the broadcaster has exceeded the bounds of discretion, the Court makes clear that any approach whereby a government agency would undertake to govern "day-to-day editorial decisions of broadcast licensees" endangers the loss of journalistic discretion and First Amendment values.

What is perhaps most striking and apt for present purposes is the figure used by Chief Justice Burger wherein the licensee is identified as a "free agent" who has "initial and primary responsibility for fairness, balance, and objectivity," with the commission serving as an "overseer" and "ultimate arbiter and guardian of the public interest." [Emphasis added.]

. . .

A substantial burden must be overcome before the FCC can say there has been an unreasonable exercise of journalistic discretion in a licensee's determination as to the scope of issues presented in the program. Where, as here, the underlying problem is the thrust of the program and the nature of its message, whether a controversial issue of public importance is involved presents not a question of simple physical fact, like temperature, but rather a composite editorial and communications judgment concerning the nature of the program and its perception by viewers. In the absence of extrinsic evidence that the licensee's characterization to the commission was not made in good faith, the burden of demonstrating that the licensee's judgment was unreasonable to the point of abuse of discretion requires a determination that reasonable men viewing the program would not have concluded that its subject was as described by the licensee.

Here the commission concluded that the program involved a controversial issue, namely the overall performance of the private pension plan system. If the agency had free rein to make the critical finding we might well support this conclusion as a reasonable exercise of agency discretion. But here the primary discretion was not vested in the government agency but in the licensee. And the agency could not premise any order on a conclusion contrary to that of the licensee unless it was willing and able to take the additional step—which it deliberately avoided—of finding the licensee's conclusion to be unreasonable. "A conclusion may be supported by substantial evidence even though a plausible alternative interpretation of the evidence would support a contrary view."

. . .

In the world of news documentaries, there is inherently an area of "judgment as to what was presented." And if its judgment is not unreasonable, the licensee cannot fairly be held faithless to Fairness Doctrine responsibilities.

Investigative reporting has a distinctive role of uncovering and exposing abuses. It would be undermined if a government agency were free to review the editorial judgments involved in selection of theme and materials, to overrule the licensee's editorial "judgment as to what was presented," though not unreasonable, to conclude that in the agency's view the expose had a broader message in fact than that discerned by the licensee and therefore, under the balancing obligation, required an additional and offsetting program.

The field of investigative exposures, as the commission has noted, is one in which "[p]rint journalism has long engaged [and] been commended," and to which broadcast journalism, also part of the press is "no less entitled." Even for print journalism, not subject to the extreme time coverage limitations of broadcasters, a requirement like the commission's would be considered a "millstone" burdening investigative reporting. We refer to the affidavit supplied to the commission by J. Edward Murray, associate editor of the *Detroit Free Press* and immediate past president of the American Society of Newspaper Editors. These are representative excerpts:

The whole process of investigative reporting is a complex and sensitive equation involving editors with high purpose and intuition, reporters with skill and courage, and publishers willing to incur heavy expense and the risk of offending both public opinion and advertisers. This equation, as I said, is powered by the drive to correct evils in the society.

If we weight the equation with the requirement that the press look for, and report, good wherever it finds and reports evil, we might as well forget investigative reporting. We will have overwhelmed it with the deadly commonplace of things as they are ...

. . .

THE PRESENT RECORD SUSTAINS THE LICENSEE'S EDITORIAL JUDGMENT AGAINST A CHARGE OF REQUISITE BAD FAITH OR UNREASONABLENESS

This is the first case in which a broadcaster has been held in violation of the Fairness Doctrine for the broadcasting of an investigative news documentary that presented a serious social problem. We have already stated that the commission used an unsound legal standard in reviewing the licensee's exercise of discretion. What result ensues—on the record before us—from application of the sound legal standard?

The Issue as to the Issue

In law, as in philosophy, the task of ascertaining the sound rule or precept often turns significantly on rigor in the statement of the problem. Nowhere is this more the case than in the application of the Fairness Doctrine, for in regard to the determination that a program raised a "controversial issue of public importance," the first and often most difficult step is to define the issue.

In our view, the present record sustains NBC as having exercised discretion, and not abused discretion, in making the editorial judgment that what was presented, in the dominant thrust of the program, was an expose of abuses that appeared in the private pension industry, and not a general report on the state of the industry. If this judgment of NBC may stand, there is no showing of a controversial issue. The staff's ruling that NBC was unreasonable in this judgment was not sustained by the commission. And in our view, the present record does not establish a basis for the conclusion that the licensee's judgmental conclusion may be set aside as unreasonable and as constituting an abuse rather than a permissible exercise of discretion.

. . .

2. Application of the correct standard.

Had the commission applied the correct standard of review, the consequence clearly would have been an acceptance of NBC's position as a reasonable statement of the subject of the *Pensions* broadcast. There were a few explicit statements of views on the overall performance of private pension plans that are of no consequence in terms of Fairness Doctrine, as will be presently seen. Otherwise, the plain heft of the program was the recitation of case histories that identified shortcomings of private pensions, and various interviews that identified the abuses in more general terms. But effective presentation of problems in a system does not necessarily generate either comment on the performance of the system as a whole, or a duty to engage in a full study. This is plain from our discussion of investigative journalism.

The licensee does not incur a balancing obligation solely because the facts he presents jar the viewer and cause him to think and ask questions as to how widespread the abuses may be.

The licensee's judgment on an issue of investigative journalism is not to be overturned unless the agency sustains a heavy burden and makes a clear showing that the licensee has been unreasonable, that there has been an abuse of journalistic discretion rather than an exercise of that discretion. We have been presented no basis for sustaining the view that there is such unreasonableness on the part of a licensee who presents undisputed facts—and no party has contended that the abuses identified by NBC do not exist—because it has failed to treat them as a general indictment of a system.

255

Comments on the Overall Performance of the Private Pension Plan

In previous sections of this opinion, we have identified the dangers to broadcast journalism, and investigative reporting in particular, if descriptions of abuses in a system are converted inferentially into a broadside commenting adversely on the overall system.173 A separate question is presented, however, by the comments in the program that differs from the description of particular evils.

1. Adverse comments on overall performance

We examine, seriatim, those passages of the *Pensions* program that may be taken as adverse comments on overall performance. We need not refine whether a Fairness Doctrine obligation is generated by this kind of comment, either alone or with some kind of FCC determination. For in this case, as we shall see, NBC provided offsetting material on the overall performance of pension plans. But this discussion will at least identify our concern with some of the problems. As we shall see, some statements are unquestionably to be given a different reading (such statements addressed seriatim in the decision).

The complaint of inadequacy of pensions is also, perhaps, one meaning that might be given to the caption of "broken promise"—if one posits that there was a promise of an "adequate" retirement income. There is plainly no unreasonable abuse of discretion for the licensee to determine that the complaint of "inadequacy," though surfacing in the program, is simply not the main thrust of the program, which basically turns on whether pension plans do pay out the amounts that were held out to the employees when their work was done, and if not, why not. The FCC, disagreeing with its staff, has held the Fairness Doctrine would be both unworkable, and an intolerably deep involvement in broadcast journalism, if every single statement, inference, or sub-issue, could be built up into a requirement of countering presentation.

Following a statement by Mr. Newman that many plans have restrictions and exclusions buried in fine print, Senator Harrison

Williams commented that the plans "suggest the certainty of an assured benefit upon retirement' which gives 'a sense of false security."

> NEWMAN: Senator, the way private pension plans are set up now, are the premises real?
> WILLIAMS: The answer is, they are not.

Senator Williams enlarges that he wants descriptions of the realities of plans that are clear and that do not require a lawyer.

Here again we have a general comment on the plans, that the eligibility requirements are not clearly identified. But we do not see wherein this comment has been identified by AIM, the commission, or its staff, as inaccurate or as presenting a controversial issue.

2. Favorable comments on overall performance

Toward the conclusion of the program, comments were made by Messrs. Hubbard, of the National Association of Manufacturers, and Anderson, of the Bank of America, which the commission recognized as generally favorable to the performance of the private pension plan system:

> HUBBARD: Over a good number of years, the track record is excellent. It's unfortunate that every now and then some of the tragic cases make the newspapers and the headlines. But it's question of perspective and balance. When you consider that there are thirty million people covered by the plans, that there are five million people receiving about seven billion dollars in benefits. I think that's a pretty good record. That's not to say that there aren't a few remaining loopholes that need closing but we ought to make sure that we don't throw out the baby with the wash water.
> ANDERSON: You must remember that the corporation has set this plan up voluntarily. They have not been required by law to set it up.

ANDERSON: These pension plans are a part of a fringe benefit package. Like hospitalization insurance and so forth, but it's still a voluntary thing on the part of the corporation.

NEWMAN: This has been a depressing program to work on but we don't want to give the impression that there are no good private pension plans. There are many good ones, and there are many people for whom the promise has become reality. That should be said.

ANDERSON: Moreover, Mr. Newman, earlier in the program, made specific reference to some generally good pension programs operated by Teamsters Unions

NEWMAN: [I]n most respects, the pension programs run by the Chicago teamsters union locals are among the best. Benefits are generous and a teamster can retire as early as age fifty-seven.

C. Reasonable Balance

As the foregoing shows, there were a handful of comments on overall performance of the private pension plan system. Some were favorable, more were adverse, but there was adequate balance of both sides of that issue and a reasonable opportunity for presentation of both sides of that issue. The Fairness Doctrine "nowhere requires equality but only reasonableness." On this aspect of the program, the FCC did not say, and in our scrutinizing review we do not consider it could rightfully say, that the licensee had failed to provide a reasonable opportunity for the presentation of contrasting approaches.

CONCLUSION

The First Amendment is broadly staked on the view that our country and our people--rich in diversity of strains and viewpoint—is best served by widest latitude to the press, as broadening input and outlook, through a robust and uninhibited debate that is subject only to minimum controls necessary for the vitality of our democratic society.

The Court has sustained the Fairness Doctrine in broadcasting as an instance of a necessary control in the public interest. The broadcaster cannot assert a right of freedom of press that transcends the public's right to know. But application of the Doctrine must still recognize the enduring values of wide latitude of journalistic discretion in the licensee. And when a court is called on to take a "hard look" at whether the commission has gone too far and encroached on journalistic discretion, it must take a hard look to avoid enforcing judicial predilections.

. . .

We have analyzed the various segments of the *Pensions* broadcast, and have not found them to justify the commission's invocation of the Fairness Doctrine. We also take account of the commission's statement that its decision was based upon the "overall impact" of the program. In some fields, the whole may be greater than the sum of its parts— according to the precepts of Gestalt Psychology. In general, however, the evils of communications controlled by a nerve center of Government loom larger than the evils of editorial abuse by multiple licensees who are not only governed by the standards of their profession but aware that their interest lies in long-term confidence. The Fairness Doctrine requires a demonstrated analysis of imbalance on controversial issues. This cannot be avoided by recourse to a subjective and impressionistic recording of overall impact.

This has not been an easy case to decide. But after sorting out all the strands of decision, we conclude that the commission has not presented a justification sufficient to sustain its order under review. The case will be remanded to the commission with instructions to vacate its order adopted November 26, 1973.

[Some discussion, notes, citations, and structural numbers have been omitted. Decision voided by FCC request for review by the full Circuit Court, which agreed to make that review, automatically voiding this panel decision. Before the Court made that review, the FCC withdrew its proceeding as moot. 40 F.C.C. 2d 958, 1973, applic for review denied, 44 F.C.C. 2d 1027, 1974, rev'd sub nom. NBC v FCC 516 F 2.d 1101 reversal vacated 518 F. 2d 1156, second reversal vacated as moot and reversed, with direction to vacate initial order and dismiss complaint, 516 F. 2d 1180 (D.C. Circ. 1974)].

APPENDIX 3

⟡

Excerpts
FCC Decision Revoking the Fairness Doctrine

In re: Complaint of Syracuse Peace Council against Television Station WTVH, Syracuse, New York

MEMORANDUM OPINION AND ORDER

Adopted: August 4, 1987; Released: August 6, 1987

The FCC conducted an exhaustive investigation and proceeding about the impact of its Fairness Doctrine and issued the first of two decisions about it. The first was issued in 1985 and the second in 1987, ending its enforcement of the Doctrine. Appeals were taken to the District of Columbia Circuit Court of Appeals. That court carefully reviewed what the FCC had done and upheld its decision. The Court wrote in pertinent part:

A. Excerpts from the 1985 Fairness Report

…The Commission recently conducted "a comprehensive reexamination of the public policy and constitutional implications of the Fairness Doctrine." During the course of that proceeding, the Commission considered more than one hundred formal comments and reply comments, hundreds of informal submissions, and oral arguments presented in two full days of hearings. The inquiry culminated in the 1985 Fairness Report released by the Commission on August 23, 1985.

4. Based upon compelling evidence of record, the Commission, in its 1985 Fairness Report, concluded that the Fairness Doctrine disserved the public interest. Evaluating the explosive growth in the number and types of information sources available in the marketplace, the Commission found that the public has "access to a multitude of viewpoints without the need or danger of regulatory intervention." The Commission also determined that the Fairness Doctrine "chills" speech, finding that "in stark contravention of its purpose, [the Doctrine] operates as a pervasive and significant impediment to the broadcasting of controversial issues of public importance." In addition, the agency found that its enforcement of the Doctrine acts to inhibit the expression of unpopular opinion; it places the government in the intrusive role of scrutinizing program content; it creates the opportunity for abuse for partisan political purposes; and it imposes unnecessary costs upon both broadcasters and the Commission.

. . .

C. Discussion

First, in an analysis of any Commission regulation, it is well established that First Amendment considerations are an integral component of the public interest standard. For example, in *FCC v. National Citizens Committee for Broadcasting*, the Supreme Court stated that the "'public interest' standard necessarily invites reference to First Amendment principles," *Columbia Broadcasting System, Inc. v. Democratic National*

Committee, 412 U.S. 94, 122 (1973), and in particular, to the First Amendment goal of achieving "the widest possible dissemination of information from diverse and antagonistic sources," *Associated Press v. United States*, 326 U.S. 1, 20 (1945). This Commission was established by Congress as the expert agency in broadcast matters and possesses more than fifty years of experience with the day-to-day implementation of communications regulation. [We] shall examine the record developed in this case and in the 1985 Fairness Report to determine, in accordance with existing Supreme Court precedent, whether the enforcement of the Fairness Doctrine (1) chills speech and results in the net reduction of the presentation of controversial issues of public concern and (2) excessively infringes on the editorial discretion of broadcast journalists and involves unnecessary government intervention to the extent that it is no longer narrowly tailored to meet its objective.

In the 1985 Fairness Report, the Commission determined that the Fairness Doctrine, in operation, thwarts the purpose that it is designed to promote. Instead of enhancing the discussion of controversial issues of public importance, the Commission found that the Fairness Doctrine, in operation, "chills" speech.

The Commission documented that the Fairness Doctrine provides broadcasters with a powerful incentive not to air controversial issue programming above that minimal amount required by the first part of the Doctrine. Each time a broadcaster presents what may be construed as a controversial issue of public importance, it runs the risk of a complaint being filed, resulting in litigation and penalties, including loss of license. This risk still exists even if a broadcaster has met its obligations by airing contrasting viewpoints, because the process necessarily involves a vague standard, the application and meaning of which is hard to predict.

As the Commission demonstrated, the incentives involved in limiting the amount of controversial issue programming are substantial. A broadcaster may seek to lessen the possibility that an opponent may challenge the method in which it provided "balance" in a renewal proceeding. If it provides one side of a controversial issue, it may wish to avoid either a formal Commission determination that it violated agency policy or the financial costs of providing responsive programming. More important, however, even if it intends to or believes that it has presented balanced coverage of a controversial issue, it may be inhibited by the expenses of being second-guessed by the government in defending a Fairness Doctrine complaint at the Commission, and if the case is litigated in court, the costs of an appeal.

Furthermore, the Commission determined that the Doctrine inherently provides incentives that are more favorable to the expression of orthodox and well-established opinion with respect to controversial issues than to less established viewpoints ... The Commission consequently expressed concern that the Doctrine, in operation, may have penalized or impeded the expression of unorthodox or unpopular opinion, depriving the public of debates on issues of public opinion that are "uninhibited, robust, and wide-open." innovative and less popular viewpoints. As noted above, these various incentives are not merely speculative. The record compiled in the fairness inquiry revealed over 60 reported instances in which the Fairness Doctrine inhibited broadcasters' coverage of controversial issues. The Commission demonstrated in the 1985 Fairness Report that broadcasters—from network television anchors to those in the smallest radio stations—recounted that the fear of governmental sanction resulting from the Doctrine creates a climate of timidity and fear, which deters the coverage of controversial issue programming. The record contained numerous instances in which the broadcasters decided that it was "safer" to avoid broadcasting specific controversial issue programming, such as series prepared for local news programs, than to incur the potentially burdensome administrative, legal, personnel, and reputational costs of either complying with the Doctrine or defending their editorial decisions to governmental authorities. Indeed, in the 1985 Fairness Report, the Commission gave specific examples of instances in which broadcasters declined to air programming on such important controversial issues such as the nuclear arms race, religious cults, municipal salaries, and other significant matters of public concern. In each instance, the broadcaster identified the Fairness Doctrine as the cause for its decision. The record in the fairness inquiry demonstrated that this self-censorship is not limited to individual programs. In order to avoid Fairness Doctrine burdens, the Commission found that stations have adopted company "policies" which have the direct effect of diminishing the amount of controversial material that is presented to the public on broadcast stations.

Historically, the Commission has taken the position that the agency is forced to undertake the dangerous task of evaluating particular viewpoints. The Fairness Doctrine thus indisputably represents an intrusion into a broadcaster's editorial discretion, both in its enforcement and in the threat of enforcement. It requires the government to second-guess broadcasters' judgment on the issues they cover as well as on the manner and balance of coverage.

In this regard, the Commission noted that, under the Fairness Doctrine, a broadcaster is only required to air "major viewpoints and shades of opinion" to fulfill its balanced programming obligation under the second part of the Doctrine ... The Doctrine forces the government to make subjective and vague value judgments among various opinions on controversial issues to determine whether a licensee has complied with its regulatory obligations. In addition, the Commission expressed concern that the Fairness Doctrine provides a dangerous vehicle-which had been exercised in the past by unscrupulous officials—for the intimidation of broadcasters who criticize governmental policy. It concluded that the inherently subjective evaluation of program content by the Commission in administering the Doctrine contravenes fundamental First Amendment principles. We reaffirm these determinations and find that enforcement of the Fairness Doctrine necessarily injects the government into the editorial process of broadcast journalists.

D. Conclusion

In the 1985 Fairness Report, [the FCC] found that the Doctrine inhibits broadcasters, on balance, from covering controversial issues of public importance. As a result, instead of promoting access to diverse opinions on controversial issues of public importance, the actual effect of the Doctrine is to "overall lessen the flow of diverse viewpoints to the public." The Doctrine requires the government to second-guess broadcasters' judgment on such sensitive and subjective matters as the "controversiality" and "public importance" of a particular issue, whether a particular viewpoint is "major," and the "balance" of a particular presentation. The resultant over breadth of the government's inquiry into these matters is demonstrated by the chill in speech that we have identified. The Doctrine exacts a penalty, both from broadcasters and, ultimately, from the public, for the expression of opinion in the electronic press. As a result, broadcasters are denied the editorial discretion accorded to other journalists, and the public is deprived of a more vigorous marketplace of ideas, unencumbered by governmental regulation. We hold, therefore, that under the constitutional standard established by *Red Lion* and its progeny, the Fairness Doctrine contravenes the First Amendment and its enforcement is no longer in the public interest.

Of course, the press is not always accurate, or even responsible, and may not present full and fair debate on important public issues. But the balance struck by the First Amendment with respect to the press is that society must take the risk that occasional debate on vital matters will not be comprehensive and that all viewpoints may not be expressed ... Any other accommodation-any other system that would supplant private control of the press with the heavy hand of government intrusion—would make the government the censor of what the people may read and know.

Consequently, a cardinal tenet of the First Amendment is that governmental intervention in the marketplace of ideas of the sort involved in the enforcement of the Fairness Doctrine is not acceptable and should not be tolerated ...

Indeed, the Supreme Court, in the context of broadcast regulation, recently stated that the expression of opinion on matters of public concern is "entitled to the most exacting degree of First Amendment protection." The Court has recognized that this type of speech is "indispensable to decision making in a democracy." As the Court has stated, "speech concerning public affairs is more than self-expression; it is the essence of self-government." Because it is the people in a democratic system who "are entrusted with the responsibility for judging and evaluating the relative merits of conflicting arguments," the "[g]overnment is forbidden to assume the task of ultimate judgment, lest the people lose their ability to govern themselves ..." In this regard, we note that sound journalistic practice already encourages broadcasters to cover contrasting viewpoints on a topic of controversy. The problem is not with the goal of the Fairness Doctrine, it is with the use of government intrusion as the means to achieve that goal. With the existence of a Fairness Doctrine, broadcasters who intend to, and who do in fact, present contrasting viewpoints on controversial issues of public importance are nevertheless exposed to potential entanglement with the government over the exercise of their editorial discretion.

Consequently, these broadcasters may shy away from extensive coverage of these issues. We believe that, in the absence of the Doctrine, broadcasters will more readily cover controversial issues, which, when combines with sound journalistic practices, will result in more coverage and more diversity of viewpoint in the electronic media; that is, the goals of the First Amendment will be enhanced by employing the very means of the First Amendment: government restraint ... We believe that the role of the electronic press in our society is the same as that of the printed press ... There is no doubt that the electronic media is powerful and that broadcasters can abuse their freedom of speech. But the framers of the Constitution believed that the potential for abuse of private freedoms posed far less a threat to democracy than the potential for abuse by a government given the power to control the press. We concur. We therefore believe that full First Amendment protections against content regulation should apply equally to the electronic and the printed press.

Citations:

In re Complaint of Syracuse Peace Council against Television Station WTVH, Syracuse, NY, 1984 WL 251220, 57 Rad. Reg. 2d (P & F)

519, 99 F.C.C.2d 1389 (FCC December 20, 1984) (NO. FCC 84–518); Vacated, In re Complaint of Syracuse Peace Council against Television Station WTVH Syracuse, NY, 1987 WL 344763, 63 Rad. Reg. 2d (P & F) 541, 2 FCCR 5043, 2 FCC Rcd. 5043 (FCC August 6, 1987) (No. FCC 87–266) Reconsideration Denied, In re Complaint of Syracuse Peace Council against Television Station WTVH Syracuse, NY, 1988 WL 488127, 64 Rad. Reg. 2d (P & F) 1073, 3 FCCR 2035, 3 FCC Rcd. 2035 (FCC April 7, 1988) (NO. FCC 88–131).

Remand, In re Complaint of Syracuse Peace Council against Television Station WTVH, Syracuse, NY, 1987 WL 343692, 2 F.C.C.R. 794, 2 FCC Rcd. 794 (FCC January 23, 1987) (NO. FCC 87–133) On appeal, *Syracuse Peace Council v. FCC*, 867 F.2d 654, 57 USLW 2488, 65 Rad. Reg. 2d (P & F) 1759, 276 U.S. App. DC 38, 16 Media L. Rep. 1225 (DC Cir., February 10, 1989) (No. 87–1516, 87–1544); Cert. denied, *Syracuse Peace Council v. FCC*, 493 U.S. 1019, 110 S. Ct. 717, 107 L. Ed. 2d, 737, U.S. Dist. Col. January 8, 1990) (NO. 89–312)

[Some discussion, notes, and citations have been omitted.]

Appendix 4

⌒

FCC Report on Broadcast Localism and Notice of Proposed Rulemakng

Federal Communications Commission
Washington, DC 20554

FCC REPORT ON BROADCAST LOCALISM
AND NOTICE OF PROPOSED RULEMAKING

Adopted December 18, 2007   Released January 24, 2008

By the Commission: Chairman Martin and Commissioner Tate issuing separate statements; Commissioners Copps and Adelstein concurring in part, dissenting in part, and issuing separate statements; Commissioner McDowell approving in part, concurring in part, and issuing a statement.

TABLE OF CONTENTS

INTRODUCTION

1. This Report on Broadcast Localism and Notice of Proposed Rulemaking (the "Report") provides an overview of the record in this docket, and our conclusions as the result of our review of that record. It also describes actions that we have taken or intend to take in this and the other ongoing Commission proceedings that we reference to ensure that broadcasters are appropriately addressing the needs of their local communities. Finally, the Report includes a Notice of Proposed Rulemaking which seeks public comment on certain issues related to several of these actions that we propose to take. As described below, the voluminous record here demonstrates that some broadcasters devote significant amounts of time and resources to airing "programming that is responsive to the needs and interests of their communities of license."[1] At the same time, in written comments and testimony received during six related field hearings, many other commenters have raised serious concerns that broadcasters' efforts, as a general matter, fall far short from what they should be. Specifically, the record indicates that many stations do not engage in the necessary public dialogue as to community needs and interests and that members of the public are not fully aware of the local issue-responsive programming that their local stations have aired.[2] Against this backdrop, the Commission proposes certain changes to its rules and policies that will promote both localism and diversity. We also discuss ways to encourage broadcasters to improve programming targeted to local needs and interests, and to provide more accessible information about those on-air efforts to the people in their communities.

2. The Report focuses in particular on broadcaster efforts to provide community-responsive programming such as news and public affairs, and programming targeted to the particular needs or interests

---

1   *Broadcast Localism*, Notice of Inquiry, 19 FCC Rcd 12425 ¶ 1 (2004) (the "*NOI*").

2   See e.g., Testimony of Martin Kaplan, Associate Dean, Annenberg School for Communication, University of Southern California (delivered by Joseph Salzman, Associate Dean, Annenberg School for Communication) (Monterey Tr. 63–68).

of certain segments of the public.[3] Because the centerpiece of localism is the communication between broadcasters and the members of the public that they are licensed to serve, the Report also addresses current efforts undertaken by both broadcasters and the Commission itself to make relevant information concerning broadcasters' efforts to serve their communities readily available to the public. The record here suggests that the dialogue between broadcasters and their audiences concerning stations' localism efforts is not ideal. Similarly, it is apparent that many listeners and viewers know little about Commission processes, such as the agency's review of license renewal applications and its complaint procedures, which allow the public to effectively raise concerns about broadcasters' performance.

3. Given the record, we conclude that modification of certain of our rules, policies and practices may be necessary to address the deficiencies of many broadcasters in meeting their obligation to serve their local communities. These proposed changes are intended to promote localism by providing viewers and listeners greater access to locally responsive programming including, but not limited to, local news and public affairs matter. The proposed modifications are also designed to promote diversity by increasing and expanding broadcast

---

3   The *NOI* specifically excluded from consideration in this inquiry the subject of the Commission's structural broadcast ownership rules. *NOI,* 19 FCC Rcd at 12427 ¶ 5. These rules are considered in *2006 Quadrennial Regulatory Review-Review of the Commission's Broadcast Ownership Rules and Other Rules Adopted Pursuant to Section 202 of the Telecommunications Act of 1996* (MB Docket No. 06–121); *2002 Quadrennial Regulatory Review-Review of the Commission's Broadcast Ownership Rules and Other Rules Adopted Pursuant to Section 202 of the Telecommunications Act of 1996* (MB Docket No. 02-277); *Cross-Ownership of Broadcast Stations and Newspapers* (MM Docket No. 01-235*); Rules and Policies Concerning Multiple Ownership of Radio Broadcast Stations in Local Markets* (MM Docket No. 01-317); *Definition of Radio Markets* (MM Docket No. 00-244); *Ways to Further Section 257 Mandate and To Build on Earlier Studies* (MB Docket No. 04-228); *Public Interest Obligations of TV Broadcast Licensees* (MM Docket No. 99-360), Report and Order (adopted Dec. 18, 2007).

ownership opportunities for minority- and women-owned businesses and small businesses. As a result, the actions discussed herein will allow greater diversity in what is seen and heard over the airwaves, and ensure that communities have access to valuable, locally responsive programming.

INDEX

16944378R00171

Made in the USA
Lexington, KY
18 August 2012